# Geraldine Chaplin

**International Film Stars**
Series Editors: Homer B. Pettey and R. Barton Palmer

This series is devoted to the artistic and commercial influence of performers who shaped major genres and movements in international film history. Books in the series will:

- Reveal performative features that defined signature cinematic styles
- Demonstrate how the global market relied upon performers' generic contributions
- Analyse specific film productions as case studies that transformed cinema acting
- Construct models for redefining international star studies that emphasise materialist approaches
- Provide accounts of stars' influences in the international cinema marketplace

Titles available:

*Close-Up: Great Cinematic Performances Volume 1: America*
edited by Murray Pomerance and Kyle Stevens

*Close-Up: Great Cinematic Performances Volume 2: International*
edited by Murray Pomerance and Kyle Stevens

*Chinese Stardom in Participatory Cyberculture*
by Dorothy Wai Sim Lau

*Geraldine Chaplin: The Gift of Film Performance*
by Steven Rybin

www.euppublishing.com/series/ifs

# Geraldine Chaplin

## The Gift of Film Performance

Steven Rybin

EDINBURGH
University Press

Edinburgh University Press is one of the leading university presses in the UK. We publish academic books and journals in our selected subject areas across the humanities and social sciences, combining cutting-edge scholarship with high editorial and production values to produce academic works of lasting importance. For more information visit our website: edinburghuniversitypress.com

© Steven Rybin, 2020, 2022

Edinburgh University Press Ltd
The Tun – Holyrood Road
12 (2f) Jackson's Entry
Edinburgh EH8 8PJ

First published in hardback by Edinburgh University Press 2020

Typeset in 12/14 Arno and Myriad by
IDSUK (Dataconnection) Ltd,

A CIP record for this book is available from the British Library

ISBN 978 1 4744 2796 8 (hardback)
ISBN 978 1 4744 2797 5 (paperback)
ISBN 978 1 4744 2798 2 (webready PDF)
ISBN 978 1 4744 2799 9 (epub)

The right of Steven Rybin to be identified as the author of this work has been asserted in accordance with the Copyright, Designs and Patents Act 1988, and the Copyright and Related Rights Regulations 2003 (SI No. 2498).

# Contents

| | |
|---|---|
| List of figures | vi |
| Acknowledgments | x |
| | |
| Introduction: into the limelight | 1 |
| 1 The Kid: Geraldine Chaplin in the sixties | 18 |
| 2 The Great Dictator: Geraldine Chaplin in the films of Carlos Saura | 59 |
| 3 The Circus: Geraldine Chaplin in the cinemas of Robert Altman and Alan Rudolph | 115 |
| 4 A Woman of Paris: Geraldine Chaplin across French cinema | 156 |
| 5 Modern Times: Geraldine Chaplin across contemporary cinema | 202 |
| | |
| References | 241 |
| Index | 246 |

# Figures

| | | |
|---|---|---|
| I.1 | Geraldine Chaplin's screen debut, in her father's *Limelight* | 3 |
| I.2 | Chaplin in the ballet *Cinderella*, 1963 | 7 |
| I.3 | Geraldine's eyes look past Marlon Brando into the abstract and heavenly space her words imagine beyond the frame, in *A Countess from Hong Kong* | 11 |
| I.4–I.5 | Charlie Chaplin directing Geraldine and others on the set of *A Countess from Hong Kong* | 13 |
| 1.1 | Geraldine Chaplin in a screen test for the part of Tonya in David Lean's film adaptation of Boris Pasternak's novel *Doctor Zhivago* | 18 |
| 1.2 | Alongside Ralph Richardson, in *Doctor Zhivago* | 19 |
| 1.3 | Co-starring with Jean-Paul Belmondo in *Crime on a Summer Morning* | 24 |
| 1.4 | Charlie Chaplin and a play with offscreen space in *The Kid* | 28 |
| 1.5 | Chaplin, with Paul Bertoya, in *Stranger in the House* (a.k.a. *Cop-Out*) | 32 |
| 1.6 | Geraldine Chaplin stars in the World War II drama *Andremo in città* | 33 |
| 1.7 | A one-sheet for *Doctor Zhivago*, emphasizing Chaplin's presence in the film | 38 |
| 1.8 | A character one-sheet for *Doctor Zhivago*, depicting Geraldine Chaplin | 39 |
| 1.9 | Chaplin as Tonya and Omar Sharif as Zhivago in *Doctor Zhivago* | 42 |
| 1.10–1.21 | Geraldine Chaplin photographed by Milton H. Greene | 49 |
| 2.1 | Chaplin as Elena, with a mischievous gesture in *Peppermint Frappé* | 60 |

| | | |
|---|---|---|
| 2.2 | The magnified eye of Chaplin-as-Elena in *Peppermint Frappé* | 61 |
| 2.3 | Chaplin reads Antonio Machado in *Peppermint Frappé* | 62 |
| 2.4 | Charlie Chaplin, in a performative riposte to tyranny, in *The Great Dictator* | 65 |
| 2.5 | Geraldine Chaplin in 1968, in the residence she shared with Carlos Saura | 67 |
| 2.6 | Chaplin-as-Elena, a living embodiment of feminine modernity in *Peppermint Frappé* | 69 |
| 2.7 | Chaplin gazes upon a painting of Brigitte Bardot by Antonio Saura in *Peppermint Frappé* | 71 |
| 2.8 | "Geraldine Chaplin en su sillon" ("Geraldine Chaplin in her armchair"), by Antonio Saura, 1967 | 72 |
| 2.9 | Chaplin as Teresa, shedding an identity in *Stress-es tres-tres* | 77 |
| 2.10 | Chaplin as Ana, calling up a memory through gesture in *Ana y los lobos* | 82 |
| 2.11 | Chaplin in *La madriguera*, frozen momentarily in a tableau | 87 |
| 2.12 | Per Oscarsson, offscreen, gesturing toward Chaplin in *La madriguera* | 87 |
| 2.13 | Chaplin posing as María in her days as a young musical ingénue in *Cría cuervos* | 91 |
| 2.14 | Chaplin and Ana Torrent, in a moment of intimacy in *Cría cuervos* | 94 |
| 2.15 | Chaplin, awakening from sleep in *Elisa, vida mía* | 101 |
| 2.16 | Chaplin, facing the camera in a medium close-up shot frontally framed by Saura, pulls off a thin exfoliating mask in *Elisa, vida mía* | 103 |
| 2.17 | Elisa applies eyeliner, transforming her face into another kind of mask in *Elisa, vida mía* | 103 |
| 2.18 | Chaplin as Emilia, recounting a dream in *Los ojos vendados* | 109 |
| 2.19 | Chaplin, in a dress with arm-length sleeves that flow like leaves in the breeze, arms outstretched as if in flight, in *Mamá cumple 100 años* | 112 |
| 3.1 | Chaplin, as wedding planner Rita Billingsley, in *A Wedding* | 115 |
| 3.2 | Chaplin as Opal, spying Elliott Gould offscreen, in *Nashville* | 120 |
| 3.3 | Opal listens to the crooning of Keith Carradine in *Nashville* | 122 |
| 3.4 | Chaplin as Annie Oakley in *Buffalo Bill and the Indians, or Sitting Bull's History Lesson* | 124 |
| 3.5 | Chaplin as Karen, in her first appearance in *Welcome to L.A.* | 127 |
| 3.6 | Keith Carradine and Geraldine Chaplin talk about Garbo in *Welcome to L.A.* | 129 |

| | | |
|---|---|---|
| 3.7 | Chaplin surveying the landscape in *Remember My Name* | 134 |
| 3.8 | Chaplin as Emily, with a saleswoman, in *Remember My Name* | 136 |
| 3.9 | Charlie Chaplin's use of stillness in *One A.M* | 137 |
| 3.10 | Chaplin's Emily privately rehearses her gestures and movements in *Remember My Name* | 138 |
| 3.11 | Chaplin comically ducking below a window frame in *Remember My Name* | 140 |
| 3.12 | Chaplin as Emily kicks off a new stage in her life in *Remember My Name* | 143 |
| 3.13 | A caricature of Geraldine Chaplin, published in the 1960s in the French magazine *La vie Parisienne* | 146 |
| 3.14 | Chaplin and Keith Carradine, flirting in *The Moderns* | 147 |
| 3.15 | A close-up of Chaplin with a portrait by Modigliani looming behind her, in *The Moderns* | 148 |
| 3.16 | Chaplin as Nathalie de Ville, caressing the frames encasing two Matisse works she particularly loves, in *The Moderns* | 149 |
| 3.17 | Chaplin as Lily Bart, creating a *tableau vivant* in *The House of Mirth* | 154 |
| 3.18 | Chaplin's Lily Bart, haunted by ghostly figures in *The House of Mirth* | 154 |
| 4.1 | Chaplin masquerading as Leon Mandrake in *I Want to Go Home* | 157 |
| 4.2 | The *Jeunesse Cinema* cover girl | 162 |
| 4.3 | A 1960s photo spread for French *Vogue* | 163 |
| 4.4 | As Mademoiselle Muller in *Sur un arbre perché (Perched on a Tree)* | 164 |
| 4.5 | Chaplin plays Isabelle in *Mais où et donc Ornicar* | 168 |
| 4.6 | Chaplin raises her hand and mimics pulling back an invisible curtain to an imaginary dressing room, in *Le Voyage en douce* | 170 |
| 4.7 | A striptease that stops short of full revelation in *Le Voyage en douce* | 172 |
| 4.8 | Charlie Chaplin, lingering offscreen in the dispersive mise en scène of *Monsieur Verdoux* | 176 |
| 4.9 | Invoking *Shane* and other intertextual references in *Noroît* | 179 |
| 4.10 | Chaplin's intense, invocative eyes, gazing beyond the edges of the frame in *Noroît* | 180 |
| 4.11 | Chaplin, as a foreshortened Morag in *Noroît* | 186 |
| 4.12 | Blindfolded in *Noroît* | 188 |

| | | |
|---|---|---|
| 4.13 | Chaplin, confidently poised as a performer in *Noroît* | 189 |
| 4.14 | A moment of companionship between Chaplin and Jane Birkin in *L'Amour par terre* | 194 |
| 4.15 | Chaplin encounters Cupid in *L'Amour par terre* | 195 |
| 4.16 | Chaplin as Nora Winkle in *La vie est un roman* | 198 |
| 5.1 | Charlie Chaplin in the final frames of *City Lights* | 203 |
| 5.2 | Geraldine Chaplin as her grandmother Hannah in *Chaplin* | 203 |
| 5.3 | An extreme close-up of Chaplin's eyes in *Z.P.G.: Zero Population Growth* | 210 |
| 5.4 | Chaplin, in close-up in *Z.P.G.: Zero Population Growth* | 211 |
| 5.5 | A striking close-up of Chaplin and her eyes, rhymed to an image of the two jewels stolen from Queen Anne's necklace, from *The Three Musketeers* | 214 |
| 5.6 | Chaplin as Marilyn in *Roseland*, guarding her mouth with her hands | 216 |
| 5.7 | Chaplin's Marilyn in *Roseland*, in mirror reflection | 218 |
| 5.8 | Chaplin's first appearance in *Talk to Her* takes the form of a framed photograph | 219 |
| 5.9 | Chaplin's Katerina describes her vision for a new ballet in *Talk to Her*: "The ethereal, the impalpable, the ghostly" | 220 |
| 5.10 | Michel Piccoli eventually sweeps Chaplin up in his arms in an attempt to carry her to a boat, in *Boxes* | 225 |
| 5.11 | In *Boxes*, Chaplin expresses her character's desire to live in the present moment, rather than in the past | 226 |
| 5.12 | In *Sand Dollars*, Chaplin's eyes register both affection and uncertainty | 229 |
| 5.13 | The play of the nightclub's flashing pink and green neon lights across Chaplin's face, in *Sand Dollars* | 229 |
| 5.14 | Chaplin's expressivity in "The Return" is partially obscured by a hat, large glasses, and the cigarette she repeatedly brings to her lips | 234 |
| 5.15 | A shared moment of tenderness between Chaplin and Kristen Stewart in "Once and Forever" | 235 |
| 5.16 | Chaplin appears in a stylized silent-film intertitle card in *The Forbidden Room*, playing a figure known only to us as "The Master Passion" | 238 |

# Acknowledgments

I am grateful for the enormously supportive, patient, and careful work of the editors and designers at Edinburgh University Press, particularly Gillian Leslie, Richard Strachan, Bekah Dey, Stephanie Pickering, and Eliza Wright, without whom this book would not exist. It would not exist either without the equally encouraging support and input of the series editors of the International Film Stars series, Homer B. Pettey and R. Barton Palmer. I am indebted to them.

I was the grateful recipient of the Andreas Award in the Department of English at Minnesota State University, Mankato, in July 2017, funds which enabled me to travel to perform research at various institutions. I thank all of my colleagues in the department, in particular Donna Casella and Matthew Sewell, for their generous support of this project symbolized by this award. I also thank the institution for the receipt of a Faculty Research Grant which enabled additional research travel. I am also appreciative of the careful attention and labor of the librarians and archivists who helped me locate research materials at the institutions where I performed research. Kate Hutchens, Reader and Reference Services Librarian at the University of Michigan, helped me locate scripts, photographs, and other materials in the Robert Altman collection. At the Charlie Chaplin archives in Cineteca di Bologna, I am especially grateful to Anna Fiaccarini for helping me arrange my visit and giving me access to viewing materials. I thank the entire staff at the Margaret Herrick Library in Los Angeles for helping me locate and photocopy materials pertaining to my research.

Colleagues in the discipline of film studies provide the sort of community that help me find meaning in my work. Their impact on this manuscript was variously direct and indirect; their voices have nevertheless inflected it in ways that have made it better and more thoughtful. Many scholars in the field of film performance, especially, have shaped my own ways of thinking about acting and without their work and their examples I doubt much of what follows would have been written, or at least not very well. I thank especially Cynthia Baron, Andrew Klevan, Murray Pomerance, William Rothman, and George Toles, who remain for me exemplars in how to write about film acting with grace, creativity, and insight. I also thank Donna Kornhaber for her excellent book on Charlie Chaplin, which helped me frame certain key ideas at very crucial junctures in my own project.

I am personally indebted to Jessica Belser who gives me support, encouragement, and love. I appreciate her without measure. Without her my career as an academic would not have been possible.

Thank you to my family, Jerry Rybin, Therese Rybin, and Amanda Rybin Koob, for their good humor which always lifts my spirits and loving support.

I thank Alan Rudolph for the time he spent corresponding with me about Geraldine's performances in his films. I thank the Chaplin Film Office in Paris, and in particular Kate Guyonvarch, for her helpful correspondence. And I thank Geraldine Chaplin herself for these performances, many of which have fascinated me since I was a kid.

| | |
|---|---|
| YEVGRAF: | Tonya! Can you play the balalaika? |
| DAVID: | Can she play? She's an artist! |
| YEVGRAF: | An artist? Who taught you? |
| DAVID: | No one taught her. |
| YEVGRAF: | Ah. Then it's a gift. |

– Final lines of dialogue in *Doctor Zhivago* (1965)

# Introduction
## Into the limelight

> The glamour of limelight, from which age must pass as youth enters.
> – Opening title card to Charlie Chaplin's *Limelight*

The opening sequence of *Limelight* (1952) finds vaudeville clown Calvero, played by Charlie Chaplin, drunkenly ambling up the steps to his apartment building. A nearby organ grinder provides unsolicited musical accompaniment to Calvero's wobbly gait. Prior to Chaplin's arrival on the scene, the street musician's hurdy-gurdy commands the attention of three small children, enchanted by the music. These kids are Chaplin's own, from his marriage to Oona O'Neill: Geraldine, aged seven at the time of making this film, alongside the younger Michael and Josephine.

In his review of *Limelight*, Robert Warshow suggests that Chaplin cast his children in this opening scene in an attempt to win back the sympathy of his audience after the commercial failure of 1947's *Monsieur Verdoux* (2001: 196). In that film, Chaplin sheds his Little Tramp persona to play a fictionalized version of Henri Désiré Landru, bigamist and murderer. Chaplin's children do bring to *Limelight* a momentary, playful innocence, in counterpoint to the otherwise disturbing picture the film paints in its initial moments. Prior to Calvero's appearance, Chaplin's camera tracks inside the apartment to reveal his neighbor, the former ballerina Terry (Claire Bloom), supine on her bed, breathing in gas fumes – a suicide attempt. These three children – in a 1951 draft of the script, there is a role here for only one "small child," but by time of filming they had multiplied into three (see Chaplin 1951, draft) – offer a gleam of joy in this otherwise somber opening passage of the film.

The Chaplin children are not presented in *Limelight* as undifferentiated moppets. Each projects a personality in the few seconds they enjoy onscreen. Josephine, the youngest of the three, initially refuses to follow her siblings to the hurdy-gurdy: she stubbornly remains on the steps, enthralled by something beyond the frame. Michael, by contrast, happily follows older sister Geraldine to the organ grinder, hitting his marks alongside her, indulging in the fun she has found and toward which she is directing him. But while Michael remains fixed on the music, Geraldine turns her head to look at something offscreen. She appears to be anticipating Calvero's appearance: the young Geraldine knows that it is time now to look for her dad.

Chaplin's camera subsequently tracks back inside Terry's apartment, the return to her suicide attempt a stark counterpoint to the atmosphere of fun and music outside; then, cut back to the front of the building as Calvero arrives. As he bounces up the steps, Geraldine and her siblings, preoccupied with the music, are again looking away from him. A closer shot shows the intoxicated Calvero fumbling with his key, defeated by the lock on the front door. Then, back to Chaplin's three children, now positioned at the bottom of the steps, their attention fully fixed on their father. Charlie, still struggling with the key, tries to steady the door with his hands, as if the front porch were a teetering boat. It is a momentary reminder of Chaplin's peerless skills in pantomime (and perhaps also, in the story world of *Limelight*, a residue of similar skills Calvero once possessed). He gives up his efforts with the key and knocks on the door, before the film switches back to the kids.

"Mrs. Alsop's out!" Geraldine cries, an expression of concern passing across her face (Figure I.1). Geraldine's words seem to carry her father's character successfully into the apartment (knowing the dreaded landlord Mrs. Alsop is out motivates Calvero to give the key one more hearty go – and he finally jangles the door open). And, then, once again: "Mrs. Alsop's out!" – this time, Josephine is the one crying out, in charming imitation of her sister.

Calvero, once inside the apartment, will discover Terry's suicide attempt, and save her. As their friendship develops, Calvero will attempt to return to vaudeville and also try to provoke Terry to become the great ballerina she might yet be. Some critics recognized in this story of *Limelight* something quite personal to Chaplin: as its melancholy epigraph reminds us, the film is about old age passing on its secrets – the gift of its artistry – to youth. André Bazin noted that for Chaplin, aging onscreen meant the removal of a mask – the visage of the Little Tramp. "The first film interpreted by the great actor Charles Spencer Chaplin," Bazin writes of the earlier *Monsieur Verdoux*, "is also precisely the first where we do

**Figure I.1** Geraldine Chaplin's screen debut, in her father's *Limelight*

not recognize his face anymore. I mean the first that forces us to give up the reference point of Chaplin's eternal maturity" (Bazin 1985: 52). The removal of the mask, for Bazin, prompts the viewer to grapple with a now older Chaplin – here no longer the familiar figure of the Tramp – who in his late films is gradually becoming a figure of history. The presence in this film of three of his children also suggests something else: the potential for Chaplin's myth not only to survive him but to be renewed, to be performatively transformed by others who carry his name. The spotlight still shines brightly on Charles Spencer Chaplin in *Limelight*, but from this position Chaplin, eventually if only by fact of mortality, must step away, as youth enters in her way.

## Chaplin dances

This book is about one of those children in the opening sequence of that film, the one who steps most remarkably and beautifully into the limelight. Her work in cinema is the subject of the pages to follow. Geraldine Chaplin is the first daughter of the cinematic legend, and the first of Charlie Chaplin's eight children with Oona O'Neill. What follows is an appreciation of some of what she has achieved in films, a study of film performance that takes seriously her work across nearly seven decades of cinema. I locate a certain share of that seriousness in the fact that she inherits – all while creatively reworking – a precious cinematic heritage.

Geraldine Chaplin is a transnational film performer, meaning her work in cinema traverses national boundaries. She makes films in Britain, France, Italy, Spain, the United States, and elsewhere; and her screen achievements circulate around the world. The cosmopolitan dimensions of her career will emerge as this book unfolds, as her performances take her from an imagined Russia (located and shot by the British director David Lean in Spain, in 1965, in *Doctor Zhivago*) to the Spain ruled by the dictatorship of Francisco Franco, where Chaplin pursues a creative partnership with director Carlos Saura in the late sixties and seventies; and from there, to her roles in the ensembles of Robert Altman and Alan Rudolph in New Hollywood cinema; to the cinemas of Jacques Rivette and Alain Resnais, and other French films; and through mainstream film industries across the globe, no more movingly than in a role as her own grandmother in the biopic *Chaplin* (1992). These films, and others, will be taken up for discussion at various points in this book. But my initial point of fascination with Chaplin is her cinematic inheritance and the filmic memory that goes along with it: the inescapable fact that in these films she is a living citation. She creatively embodies, in whatever role she plays, the traces of film history – the memory of her father's creative imagination, as expressed, refigured, and ultimately made her own, through performances onscreen.

In the voluminous reportage that exists on her father's career and life, Geraldine Chaplin is a more than occasional presence. A Scottish nanny named Edith McKenzie, affectionately renamed "Kay-Kay" by the infant Geraldine, remembers how, according to Chaplin biographer David Robinson,

> [Charlie] Chaplin watched and held his first daughter with as much joyful wonder as a twenty-year-old first-time father. In fact his two sons, now grown up, were both in the army. Less than three weeks after Geraldine was born there was a melancholy reminder of his first unhappy marriage: Mildred Harris died at the age of forty-three in the Cedars of Lebanon Hospital. Chaplin sent a spray of orchids, roses and gladioli to the funeral. (1985: 525)

Amidst this biographical and historical flux, on July 31, 1944, Geraldine was born – into a world again at war, in which two half-brothers were already fighting, and to a father whose beaming adoration for his daughter could not, according to Robinson's account, completely assuage painful memories. Yet within all this turmoil of adult history and devastation emerges the trace of a whisper – little Geraldine cooing "Kay-Kay" to her nurse. Her whisper is a reminder that the oldest of Charlie and Oona's children would make her own creative and playful interventions into the world she would inherit. Curiously, this little baby babble is the only trace of Geraldine that finds its way into her father's account of his life: although she is an important supporting figure in Robinson's biography of her dad, Charlie Chaplin does not mention Geraldine by name or her birth at all in his 1964 book *My Autobiography*. Her presence is nevertheless implied, for he does mention the nanny, using the moniker Geraldine bestowed upon her: "Kay-Kay" (Chaplin 1992: 466).

Chaplin's inclusion of his oldest daughter in *Limelight* is more remarkable than any mere mention in an autobiography might be, and in any event the line firmly separating *Limelight* from Charlie Chaplin's personal life is not so clear. The rapt attention Geraldine's character bestows upon her father's drunken Calvero as he finally finds his way up the steps renders her a sympathetic viewer for her father's character in the film, and the involvement of Chaplin's family in its making gives the project a reflexive, autobiographical patina. As Guillermo Cabrera Infante's writings remind us, Chaplin's cinema was always autobiographical:

> *The Kid* is his infancy in the East End of London; *The Circus*, his beginnings in music hall by the hand of Karno, garrulous producer of pantomimes; *City Lights* is the rescue of many of his celebrated actresses, from anonymous obscurity to the hideous clarity of fame ... *Limelight* is an admitted autobiography and a new version of *City Lights* (1991: 126)

– and so on. Yet it is less the explicitly and literally autobiographical elements of these films that interest me: rather, it is how Charlie Chaplin's work functions as a kind of implicit gift to his daughter, moments from his own performances and films potentially functioning, also, as gifts to us, little clues we can use to think through what Geraldine achieves as a performer. In that sense, the very shape the story of *Limelight* takes has interesting resonances with the direction of Geraldine's performative life in the years following its release. Many have noted the physical resemblance between Claire Bloom, cast as Terry in *Limelight*, and Oona O'Neill – underscored further by the fact that O'Neill, herself a former ballerina, doubles in a shot for Bloom in one of the film's sequences (Gehring 2017: 52). Striking from a later vantage point is Bloom's – and, of course, O'Neill's – resemblance to the young woman Geraldine would become – a young woman herself interested, early in her career, in dancing, and whose first flash of publicity would arrive in her casting in a small role in Paris, in a ballet production of *Cinderella*.

It was Geraldine Chaplin's appearance in that ballet in 1963, the indirect product of her studies at the Royal School of Ballet in London in the early sixties, which prompted the first series of publicity materials about her. "In *Cinderella*," an uncredited writer for *Life Magazine* reports, "Geraldine plays one of the luckless princesses, a languorous Persian charmer" – one of the unfortunate women on whose foot the glass slipper does not fit ("New Chaplin in Limelight": 77). This information accompanies an array of photographs of Geraldine and her mother and father, a journalistic orchestration of images and text meant to remind us she is not simply a new face on the stage but the privileged progeny of two celebrated and famous people. The *Life* article paints the picture of Geraldine's performance in *Cinderella* as a "show-stopping" debut, but it was only a minor, supporting role, even if her presence in the play was the main attraction for many in its audience. There can be no doubt Geraldine's interest in ballet was earnest, and the story of *Cinderella* is one that resonated in her childhood: a March 1956 letter from Sydney Chaplin to his niece reminds Geraldine how much she loved his variation of the Cinderella fairy tale which he wrote for her when she was a child; in the letter, Sydney refers to his variation of the tale as "The Modern Cinderella" (Sydney Chaplin, "Letter to Geraldine," 1956).[1]

Her father did not approve of Geraldine's appearance in this ballet; Charles Chaplin feared too many in the audience were attending for her name rather than for her talent. Geraldine, speaking with Rex Reed a year later, agreed:

> When I first left home to become a ballerina, I was terrible, but I ended up on the front pages. Only one of twenty little dancers in the chorus of *Cinderella*, but you'd have thought I was Pavlova. Sure, they were exploiting me. My father was furious! (Reed 1969: 200)

Furious, perhaps, because to attend the ballet only for the name "Chaplin" threatens the possibility that an audience member might imagine seeing Geraldine everywhere, projecting "Chaplin" onto stage figures that own no right to the family name. A fragment of this ballet survives on film (from a British Pathé newsreel); in it there are glimpses of professional dancers, embodying Cinderella, the Wicked Stepmother, and her sisters, leaping and prancing onstage. After a moment, Geraldine emerges, not quite soaring in the air, as a Persian temptress (Figure I.2). Imagine watching all this from the rafters, not knowing whom Geraldine was

**Figure I.2** Chaplin in the ballet *Cinderella*, 1963

playing or at what point she might appear: but she was the reason you were there, owing to all the photos and accompanying chatter about this "Chaplin girl" that were coursing through the French papers at the time; and imagine affectionately projecting her image, glimpsed from those publicity pages, onto every figure that bounded onto the stage – from the balcony, many of them might look a bit like a Chaplin. No wonder Charles Chaplin found distress in this potential loss of distinction, in this terrible idea that the intrinsic merit signaled by the name "Chaplin" might be located in a source other than Chaplin herself.

A dance by a Chaplin should not be mistaken for a dance by any other. And its power should emerge from her own gestures and movements, not solely from a loving projection bestowed upon her by the audience. Charlie Chaplin's performances are themselves testaments to this idea that actors are the source of a performance's thoughtful substance. "Everything I do is a dance," Chaplin said of his movement on the screen; "I think in terms of a dance" (Vance 2003: 361). If dance serves Chaplin as a descriptive metaphor for everything he does and thinks in cinema, this idea could also manifest itself in actual dances onscreen: Chaplin's Little Tramp dancing while babbling his "Nonsense Song" in the jazz club scene in *Modern Times* (1936); varieties of social dancing, usually involving his Tramp character and an onscreen paramour, in *The Gold Rush* (1925), *Shanghaied* (1915), and *The Count* (1916); and dances created through Chaplin's playful appropriation of previously inanimate objects – like the famous bread roll dance in *The Gold Rush*, a routine borrowed from Roscoe "Fatty" Arbuckle (who first made the bread dance in the 1917 film *The Rough House*) and later mimicked by both Robert Downey, Jr., playing Charlie in the biopic *Chaplin*, and by Johnny Depp in *Benny and Joon* (1993), but never more magically performed than by Chaplin in his film.

And it is this distinguished dance, created by a dancer who cannot be mistaken for any other, that Charlie Chaplin takes as his subject in *Limelight*. In that film, Calvero wants to help Terry become the kind of dancer worthy of inheriting what he leaves behind when he dies; this is a film about performance as a kind of gift that might pass from one actor to another. In his novel "Foot Lights," on which he based *Limelight*, Chaplin describes Thereza, the anguished former ballet dancer, as "gracile and madonna-like with moonlight paleness and large sad eyes set far apart. Her selenic beauty complemented her dancing" (Chaplin and Robinson 2014: 33). This description is the image of the young dancer that Thereza used to be, the dancer that Calvero, his own best days as a performer behind him, wants her to become again through his gift of inspiration. As Chaplin describes it in "Foot Lights," at the moment of his death after a fall from the stage during a comic routine, Calvero glimpses Thereza's transcendent rediscovery of herself as a dancer from the foot lights:

> And Calvero was carried gently to the side of the wings where he could see Terry … Calvero gazed at her wistfully with tired dull eyes. "She's so beautiful," he whispered. Then his head sank back and his eyes closed. And from the outer corner of the eyelids, a tear appeared and slid down the side of his cheek. (Chaplin and Robinson 2014: 85)

Calvero shortly thereafter dies, and the moment he dies is joined – on the level of Chaplin's syntax, with a semi-colon – to the beauty of Thereza's dancing:

> And from the ambulance attendant, [the doctor] took a sheet and drew it over Calvero's head; while on the stage, Terry pirouetted and flexed radiant authority. She was light … quicksilver! Efflorescing! A Diana spinning wisps of beauty about her. (Chaplin and Robinson 2014: 85)

On film, Chaplin finds the emotional equivalent of that semi-colon in a camera movement, cinematically tracing a spiritual line between the death of Calvero and the beauty of Thereza's dancing. A sorrowful crane shot (scored to Chaplin's lovely musical score) begins on Calvero backstage before the camera pulls back onstage to reveal Thereza twirling into frame, now in confident possession of her balletic art.

It is no wonder that, having imagined in "Foot Lights" and then in *Limelight* how dance could work so beautifully as an expression of both the death of an artist and another artist's rebirth – dance as a gift of and through performance – that Charlie Chaplin was slightly disappointed that his daughter's name should have been used in *Cinderella*, and in public discourse about the ballet, for the purpose of commercial exploitation, and in ways not so distinguished.

## A gift for performance

Geraldine Chaplin does go on to dance, though, memorably and distinctively and in ways that cannot be mistaken for the movements of anyone else. Her dancing in the Paris production of *Cinderella* was the effort of a young artist still trying to find herself. But soon Geraldine would achieve gracefulness in films – sometimes, even, while dancing (in a different idiom, quite far from ballet): at an aristocratic ball in the arms of Omar Sharif, in *Doctor Zhivago*; ecstatically, to a Spanish pop song in Carlos Saura's *Peppermint Frappé* (1967); with Christopher

Walken, in the ballroom dance film *Roseland* (1977); and even alongside Marlon Brando, under the direction of her father, in *A Countess from Hong Kong* (1967).

But in *A Countess from Hong Kong* Charlie Chaplin's direction of Geraldine in a dance sequence does not quite take the form of the ecstatic final minutes showcasing Thereza in *Limelight*. The earlier film is earnest in its emotion; by contrast, the dancing (and much else) in *A Countess from Hong Kong* is inflected by irony. Donna Kornhaber has shown, in her writing on Chaplin's late style, how *A Countess from Hong Kong* works as a send-up of Charlie Chaplin's earlier tendency to pontificate (in *The Great Dictator*) and emote (such as in *City Lights*). "What Chaplin once presented as heartfelt," Kornhaber suggests, "is now replayed as ridiculous" (2014: 275). In the midst of *A Countess from Hong Kong*'s lengthy ballroom sequence, Marlon Brando's stoic ambassador-designate Ogden Mears finds himself in the arms of several young socialites, one of whom, in the space of a couple of minutes, speaks nearly more than any other supporting character in the entire film. All this flighty talk is about her "daddy," and his ideas: "I think dancing stimulates conversation. Wasn't it Aristotle who used to walk and lecture around the Lyceum and talk of the soul? Daddy says [Aristotle] never had a clear idea of what the soul is. But Daddy has."

Kornhaber notes how this chatty debutante's stream of words functions as ironic self-criticism on Chaplin's part, a gentle parody of his tendency to make much speech in *The Great Dictator*. Kornhaber also discloses that Geraldine Chaplin was originally supposed to have played this role (2014: 275). But to cast Geraldine as that socialite might have made her father's critique of his earlier screen persona a bit *too* personal, with all her talk of "daddy" and his ideas. And so instead she appears, and briefly, as the next socialite Ogden Mears is obliged to dance with in the sequence.[2] In counterpoint to the first girl's loquaciousness, Geraldine says only "I've been wondering about the immortality of the soul" with eyes that look past Marlon Brando into the abstract and heavenly space her words imagine beyond the frame (Figure I.3).

If Charlie Chaplin is poking a bit of fun here at his earlier talking pictures, the spirit of play that pervades *A Countess from Hong Kong* is also something of a gift to his daughter, the first moment in her film career in which her performance is placed in a sequence that emphasizes sharp, thoughtful possibilities of irony. *A Countess from Hong Kong* was released two years after Geraldine's star-making turn in the romantic epic *Doctor Zhivago*, discussed at greater length in the next chapter. At the time of the

**Figure I.3** Geraldine's eyes look past Marlon Brando into the abstract and heavenly space her words imagine beyond the frame, in *A Countess from Hong Kong*

initial release of David Lean's film, and also in the two years preceding it (dating back to 1963, when she first entered the public eye as the supporting star of the production of *Cinderella* in Paris), Geraldine was discussed as something of a socialite herself in magazines and newspapers, and characterized as not unlike these flighty debutantes Brando's Ogden Mears finds in his arms in this dance scene from *A Countess from Hong Kong*. She was, in other words, not yet a respected actor but already quite a celebrity figure.

Rex Reed, in a characteristically catty profile of Geraldine that appears in late 1965, around the time of her debut as an adult in feature films, gets a lot of mileage out of a description of all these public appearances:

> Newspapers and magazines record her every sigh. Geraldine Chaplin gypsy dancing at the Feria de Sevilla. Geraldine Chaplin presented to society in a white Castillo gown by the Aga Khan. Geraldine Chaplin parachute-jumping. Geraldine Chaplin having a bull dedicated by El Cordobés in the bullring. Geraldine Chaplin in Lebanon gowned by Ricci, getting more attention in the slick magazines than Jean Shrimpton. It's Geraldine Chaplin all the way: swimming at Monte Carlo, frugging at the Piper Club in Rome, living it up as the darling of the jet set. And why not? When you're the daughter of Charlie Chaplin and the granddaughter of Eugene O'Neill, a girl has to do *something*! (Reed 1969)

In Reed's snippy account, Geraldine is described as quite like the socialites in the ballroom scene from *A Countess from Hong Kong*. She is photographed and framed in this discourse as a figure of social fascination, an ingénue – an ingénue who is also a Chaplin – doing fabulous things, with cameras drawn to her as she so prettily does them. If it is difficult for us to read performative agency into such descriptions of her public presence during these years, in which Geraldine is taken as the object of unaffectionate discourse rather than described as an active and creative subject, what is interesting about her brief appearance in *A Countess from Hong Kong* is the ironic attitude both the film and her brief performance in it strikes in relation to this kind of public objectification. The socialite Geraldine plays in *A Countess from Hong Kong* is certainly portrayed as vacuous (this vacuity is part of the film's comical project of understanding "elevated" social talk as empty chatter). But she is played by someone who certainly understands, by the time of the film's making in 1966, what it means to be regarded as such a figure. The film is not a perpetuation of the presentation of Geraldine as an overexposed starlet, but rather a performative and comical commentary on the very persona into which she had been cast by so many commentators prior to the making of this film.

Here, then, in *A Countess from Hong Kong*, we have an important early glimpse of a performative intelligence at play, one that will be present throughout Geraldine's remarkable career and a trait this study seeks to appreciate. Geraldine's performance in *Countess* embodies a character at the same time as it works, in relation not only to its own operations but also to extra-filmic discourse, as a kind of commentary about that embodied person. This ironic, reflexive shading in Geraldine's performances will be an important motif of this book, especially in her performances for the art cinema auteurs explored in later chapters. For the purposes of explicating my method, though, I want to understand what is going on here in *A Countess from Hong Kong* as a kind of gift, a secret passed from the older Chaplin to the younger one. This idea of the film, and Chaplin's direction of Geraldine within it, functioning as a gift, resonates also with the photographs of the young actor taken with her father on set. These images (Figures I.4 and I.5) show us Chaplin directing his daughter. Whatever Charlie Chaplin's desire to keep earnest emotion out of the ironic fun of the film itself, these photographs are affecting historical artifacts, presenting the image of a legendary filmmaker creating his final film, all the while showing his daughter how she might thoughtfully inhabit mise en scène.

It is well known that Charlie Chaplin would often act out other roles besides his own for the benefits of the actors he was directing, and that appears to be what is happening here; in the first photograph

**Figure I.4 and I.5** Charlie Chaplin directing Geraldine and others on the set of *A Countess from Hong Kong*

(Figure I.4), Chaplin takes the place of Brando briefly as he shows his daughter how he means for her to dance in front of the camera. This method of performative direction harkens back to Chaplin's early silent career. However, it is notable that the techniques Chaplin uses to film his daughter and Brando in this brief moment in *A Countess from Hong Kong* differ markedly from his early silent work. Donna Kornhaber describes Chaplin's early film style as remarkably anti-classical, a form of direction focused on the movement of the entire body rather than the sequencing of the film actor into an analytical series of master shots, medium shots, and close-ups (2014: 146). Kornhaber also reads Chaplin's refusal to sequence his film through the expected patterns of classical analytical editing as a kind of proto-modernist cinematic technique that, in his later work, takes on subversive undertones. She notes that because techniques of analytical editing "are not fundamentally constitutive of how he communicates his narrative, which is most typically handled within the frame itself ... he is free to repurpose them," in "a kind of subversion of the aesthetic assumptions that these techniques most typically convey" (2014: 154). These photographs of Chaplin directing his daughter and Brando on the set of *A Countess from Hong Kong* are visual documents of Chaplin's orchestration of the anti-classical style Kornhaber describes, production photographs that are themselves like medium shots, in terms of their composition. The finished film presents Geraldine dancing with Brando through a camera view that sways with the two figures as they dance. This close-up of Geraldine in *A Countess from Hong Kong*, however, is in keeping with Chaplin's penchant for anti-classical style, for it does not give us the earnest emotional expressivity often glimpsed in this kind of shot in classical film aesthetics. That is part of the film's playful joke, and of the director Chaplin's subversion of what is routinely expected of such shots in conventional filmmaking practice.

But reading the film alongside production photographs of Chaplin's direction of the actors prompts an understanding of this moment from *A Countess from Hong Kong* as more than just a subversion of classical editing technique. Chaplin would appear to be subverting his *own* directorial style here, a style which places emphasis, in his early comedies, on the entire movement of the performative body, an approach which, in this sequence from the film, is abandoned in the final editing. (We can see more of Geraldine and her fellow dancers in the production photos than we do in the finished film; and photographs of Geraldine pensively watching her father direct the other actors on set, as in Figure I.5, convey more thoughtful interiority than her socialite in *Countess* ever expresses.) Ultimately, what is being passed on here from director to actor (and from father to daughter) is not a certain kind of style or even a particular method of acting but rather a way of thoughtfully inhabiting whatever style in which one is presently framed: not simply a way of moving but a way of knowing how and why to move, a way of thinking through how expectation and convention might be thwarted, redirected, or played with in gesture, movement, and expression.

In her later films for Robert Altman, Geraldine Chaplin will take this kind of sharp, performative knowingness further, inhabiting characters such as daffy BBC reporter Opal in *Nashville* (1975), Annie Oakley in *Buffalo Bill and the Indians, or Sitting Bull's History Lesson* (1976), and her flustered wedding planner in *A Wedding* (1978) in ways that ironically play with certain assumptions about her public image. She will, of course, play more straightforwardly emotional characters, too; the power of her work in films ranging from *Le Voyage en douce* (1980) to *Dólares de arena* (*Sand Dollars*, 2014) comes from an expressivity that, in the context of those films, is earnest and direct (even as she creates characters who remain thoughtful, sharp, and active in the worlds of the films). My main point here is to suggest that Geraldine Chaplin's gift as a performer was not given her by her father through direct or specific instruction in gesture or poise, although some of those ideas, as these production photos documenting his direction of her on the set suggest, were no doubt conveyed in the bargain. This gift is also not something bequeathed through sheer biology. After all, her gift is her own, one that distinguishes itself from her siblings who have tried their hand at film acting. It is rather that she knows beautifully how to convey, through her gestures, movements, and expressions, a kind of thoughtfulness that, although part of her father's playful comic project in *A Countess from Hong Kong* and a gift to her in his instruction on the set of that film, becomes fully hers.

\* \* \*

*Geraldine Chaplin: The Gift of Film Performance* unfolds across five chapters, more or less chronologically exploring Chaplin's career, with occasional leaps across time to explore resonances between different characters and performances. The idea, introduced in the preceding paragraphs, that Charlie Chaplin's films contain kinds of secrets or gifts that bind them intellectually and emotionally with those of his daughter will also become important to each chapter. I will at times cite moments from Charlie Chaplin's films to open up a key idea about acting in film that is refigured and played with creatively by Geraldine in her own performances. In those cases I am not suggesting that Geraldine was consciously channeling or directly influenced by her father's work. These poetic parallels are mainly for the benefit of Geraldine's viewer, to enhance appreciation of what she achieves in particular moments of film acting and how those moments resonate with the cinematic history of which her presence onscreen is a citation, and of which her performances are, in part, a kind of reworking.

The first chapter explores her emergence as a public personality and her first performances in *Doctor Zhivago* and other films in the 1960s. Chapter 2 looks mainly at her invigorating collaboration with Spanish filmmaker Carlos Saura across nine films, from 1967 to 1979, a focus through which the cosmopolitan, transnational aspects of her screen presence saliently emerge (a presence in Spain to which Pedro Almodóvar pays tribute in his casting of Chaplin in the 2002 film *Talk to Her*, a discussion of which appears later in the book). A close look at her work in U.S. cinemas of the 1970s and 1980s is at play in the third chapter, which focuses mainly on Chaplin's performances for directors Robert Altman and Alan Rudolph. The fourth chapter appreciates her important place in French cinema, particularly her striking presence in films by Jacques Rivette and Alain Resnais. The fifth and final chapter examines her work across many different films that fall outside the frameworks of the earlier chapters, which focus mainly on Geraldine's contributions to an eccentric, cerebral art cinema of the 1960s, 1970s, and 1980s. In a departure from that framework, the final chapter uses the close-up as a performative motif to understand a small selection of her expansive body of work that goes beyond the focus of the earlier chapters. Chaplin is an incredibly prolific actor in the second half of her career; by my count, since her role playing her own grandmother in the 1992 biopic *Chaplin*, she has appeared in over seventy films. Because of the prolific nature of her career, this book is necessarily selective in the films it chooses for analysis. To my mind, the performances discussed in the pages to follow represent Chaplin's most striking screen achievements.

To the extent that her presence and her performances remind us of her cinematic heritage, it is also wise to remember that Geraldine does not merely "reproduce" her father or his legacy on film, any more than his direction of her in *Limelight* or *A Countess from Hong Kong* sought to reproduce his star image. If she undoubtedly evokes an important swath of film history through her very presence, she also nevertheless puts her own disruptive, eccentric powers into play, not simply inheriting a lineage or a history but inflecting our understanding of what that history might mean. The poetic encounters I stage between father and daughter at certain points in this book are only rarely literally onscreen ones (those are limited to *Limelight* and to the production photographs of the two of them together on the set of *A Countess from Hong Kong*), and more often imagined ones, such as when, in the next chapter, I suggest how a moment from Charlie Chaplin's *The Kid* (1921) might offer a little clue in understanding one aspect of Geraldine's early work. These are kinds of poetic resonances that, far from stunting our grasp of Geraldine's own creative contribution to cinema – and it is her contribution with which this book is concerned – instead help us imagine what a gift from a father to a daughter, in cinema, might in fact mean. It also means to understand how moments from Charlie Chaplin's films are kinds of gifts to us, as critics and viewers, in understanding the remarkable artistry Geraldine herself achieves in film.

# Chapter 1

# The Kid: Geraldine Chaplin in the sixties

Geraldine Chaplin filmed a screen test in 1964 for the part of Tonya in David Lean's film adaptation of Boris Pasternak's novel *Doctor Zhivago* (Figure 1.1). This audition came at a crucial point in her career, the prospect of starring in a David Lean film an attractive proposition for any young performer. The screen test consists of two takes of Chaplin, framed in close-up, playing Yuri Zhivago's wife Tonya, reading aloud a letter from her husband (Alexander, her father, is played by Ralph Richardson, who listens and occasionally responds offscreen). Chaplin is framed, in both takes, by a stationary camera, from the left side of her face in take one and

**Figure 1.1** Geraldine Chaplin in a screen test for the part of Tonya in David Lean's film adaptation of Boris Pasternak's novel *Doctor Zhivago*

from the right side in take two. In the letter she reads, Zhivago reports of the end of the war, and muses that he may finally have time to write poetry; he mentions Lara (played by Julie Christie in the eventual film), soon to become Zhivago's lover; he asks of family members; and wishes Tonya love. "The rest is for me," Chaplin says shyly, her downcast eyes underscoring that Zhivago's remaining words are for Tonya alone.

Tonya is not yet fully a character here: Chaplin in this test is only edging herself into the part. This scene in the eventual film *Doctor Zhivago*, in which Chaplin now fully incarnates Tonya, is orchestrated more complexly by Lean (being now a fully realized cinematic scene and not a screen test), and performed more exuberantly by Chaplin. In the film, she delivers only a brief stretch of dialogue in close-up, the sequence now punctuated by reaction shots of Richardson and two-shots of Richardson and Chaplin that keep both actors in the same widescreen frame (Figure 1.2). The final line from the screen test, in which Tonya observes that the remainder of the letter is for her eyes only, is excised. The removal of this line gives Chaplin the opportunity to silently underscore her character's desire to read these words privately. As the moment ends, Richardson, on the left side of the frame, becomes distracted with some of Zhivago's words, while Chaplin, on the right, goes on quietly reading. Her ability to economically and touchingly imply Tonya's inner life, as in this moment, is key to her performance in the film.

Lean did not initially want to test Chaplin as Tonya. According to Kevin Brownlow, Lean first imagined Audrey Hepburn in the part, before agreeing to a screen test of Chaplin at the behest of Carlo Ponti, the film's producer (1997: 513). But there is in this test, as Lean discovered, a

**Figure 1.2** Alongside Ralph Richardson, in *Doctor Zhivago*

glimmer already of the character Pasternak creates in the book. In the novel, Tonya grows up alongside Yuri Zhivago; he is adopted by Tonya's aristocratic family after the death of Zhivago's parents. Zhivago is possessed of a poetic consciousness but is bred for a professional life as a doctor; nevertheless, his desire to become an artist, a poet, is salient. As characterized by Pasternak, Tonya is not without poetry herself – early in their courtship, Zhivago describes Tonya and her striking beauty in a line of poetry he might write (Pasternak 2010: 105). Pasternak conveys how Zhivago – the subjective center of the novel – perceives the transformation and maturation of his childhood sweetheart into a complex, alluring adult:

> Tonya, this old comrade, this person so clear that she needed no explanations, turned out to be the most unattainable and complex of all that Yura could imagine, turned out to be a woman. With a certain stretching of fantasy, Yura could picture himself as a hero climbing Ararat, a prophet, a conqueror, anything you like, but not a woman. (2010: 93)

As this paragraph indicates, Tonya – a friend and spiritual mate to Zhivago in childhood and adolescence – is possessed with an "unattainable" and "complex" subjectivity that is only implied through Zhivago's perspective, a perspective much more developed than Tonya's in the novel. If, in the passage above, Tonya moves Zhivago to poetic musing, as he sees now before his eyes not an aristocratic child but an adult woman of warmth, feeling, and thoughtfulness, this is also nevertheless a woman whom Pasternak only sketches in the book. Pasternak's description above of how Zhivago *sees* Tonya as a woman, for the first time, intimates that something of Tonya's inner life escapes from his (and the novel's) purview, remaining "unattainable." It is this inner life that Chaplin, presented to us in the scene with the letter apart from Zhivago's presence, cues us to recognize in both the screen test and the ensuing film. Her Tonya is a real person, rather than a mystery.

What Pasternak's prose does makes clear enough is Tonya's growth from a child to a mature woman. Maturity is precisely what Lean, prior to filming the screen test, feared Chaplin could not yet project onscreen. Lean was initially skeptical of Chaplin's ability to play the part largely because of her age and her inexperience. (Chaplin was only nineteen at the time of casting; in the book, Tonya begins as the adolescent friend of Zhivago and ends, years later, as his wife and mother of two.) The idea that Chaplin herself needed in some way to mature – in order to convincingly present her character's own growth into adulthood – was key to Lean's consideration of Chaplin for the role before filming began in 1964. Brownlow tells us that Chaplin showed up to the screen test "dressed in jeans, and looking about sixteen – and [David Lean's] heart sank" (1997: 513). Lean, however, was convinced by the screen test, as he expressed in a letter to Oona O'Neill in explanation of why her daughter was right for the part:

> I suggested we had a quiet little run-through expecting I'd have to spend quite a time slowing down her movements, changing intonations and explaining this and that facet of mature behavior. Not at all. Did it like a bird! All the technicians madly impressed and a lot of talk between all of us about her Mum and Dad – and that's why I'm writing this. I hope she does play the part – and it's a very good one – and I hope I have your blessings. Please don't trouble to reply. Geraldine does not know I've written this. (Quoted in Brownlow 1997: 513)

Lean's missive to Chaplin's mother – a letter whose sincerity there is no reason to doubt – invokes two key tropes present in public discourse about Geraldine during the sixties, before and after the release of *Doctor Zhivago*. First, there is the idea that Chaplin must, at this stage of her career, win serious consideration as an actor by displaying her mature and natural gifts in front of the camera's lens, without the laborious directorial intervention Lean feared he would have to make with so young and unproven an actor ("Did it like a bird!"). Second, there is in Lean's letter the mention of Chaplin's parents. Chaplin must not only convincingly demonstrate her ability to perform adulthood onscreen, but she also must at the same time remain vibrantly and socially the daughter of two very famous people, the daughter whose mere presence invokes, as Lean puts it, "a lot of talk between all of us about her Mum and Dad."

These paired and contradictory tropes involving, on the one hand, maturity (or her perceived lack thereof) and, on the other, her privileged upbringing and parentage, swirled around Geraldine everywhere she went in the sixties. Journalistic and tabloid writing on Chaplin during this period crafts easily digestible, gossipy reportage of her "rebellion" against her father even as these same accounts almost always eventually resituate her within the Chaplin family fold. Nearly all the English-language profiles on Chaplin I have read from this period (1964–6) begin their narrative with her inheritance of the Chaplin name, and occasionally with her "struggle" with or resistance to that inheritance, before describing Geraldine in ways that reconcile some aspect of her persona or presence with her famous father. In doing so, they emphasize both Chaplin's lack of maturity (often casting her, with varying degrees of approval, as an immature or somewhat spoiled socialite celebrity) and her famous family name. Gerold Frank, in a 1965 article with the melodramatic headline "The Tragedy of Charlie Chaplin and His Children," emphasizes Geraldine's independence, highlighting her refusal to accept money from her parents while she lived a bohemian life in Paris (1965: 128). Frank also puts into play descriptions of Geraldine Chaplin that remind us of her dad's child-like screen character. He remarks that "if the talk shifts away from her, she tends to brood and become silent, or suddenly find an excuse to disappear" (Frank 1965: 128) – a description that evokes Parker Tyler's understanding of Charlie Chaplin as the "adult version of the child aristocrat" (1948: 35) and Robert Warshow's characterization of the Calvero character, in a review of *Limelight*, as narcissistic and self-involved (2001: 204). Nearly every journalistic piece I have found on Chaplin finds genealogical links between Geraldine and her famous father: "There is a hint of her father's joy around her when she laughs," Robert Deardorff writes in a March 1965 magazine profile (Deardorff 1965: 59); "Charlie Chaplin is still around," one uncredited writer tells us in 1967; "and it seems he has a daughter who looks and acts, well, sort of like ... Charlie. But *her* name is Geraldine" ("Charlie's Girl Tries Television" 1967); and so on.

Some of these writers who interview Geraldine during this time period do glimpse something striking and even original about her presence; like David Lean, they eventually see something of a creative spark. But like Lean in his letter to Oona O'Neill, they cannot quite convey it in words free from the tropes of maturity and privilege familiar elsewhere in their writings on Geraldine. Perhaps not surprisingly, their efforts to record what they see as traits belonging to Geraldine herself take the initial form of physical descriptions, although in most of the examples this eventually opens up something more spiritual, intangible, or creatively performative. Frank describes how

> Under her eyes are two tiny black moles which give her a funny, little sad-clown look, as though she had dropped two black tears while everyone else is laughing ... She is full of sudden quick glances ... her moods are chameleon-like, now animated, now depressed, her voice dying away to a whisper. (Frank 1965: 128)

First describing her transformation into Tonya on the set of *Doctor Zhivago*, Harold H. Martin, writing a profile of Chaplin shortly before the release of the film, writes similarly of her ability to shift from one state of being to the next like quicksilver:

> Off camera and out of costume, Miss Chaplin could change with equal swiftness into a gamine again. Shooting *Zhivago* in the little Spanish town of Soria, she held court on the long winter evenings in the lobby of the Florida hotel, chattering in French and English with ease, laughing a shrill, almost cackling laugh, and doing imitations of her father doing imitations of other people. (Martin 1966: 30)

"On another occasion," Robert Deardorff writes in a profile,

> she left a group of friends with whom she had been sitting in a hotel lobby, went over to a piano in the corner and began playing softly to herself. Tiring of that in a little while, she wandered to a big chair, sat down and like a child was sound asleep, oblivious of people around her. (1965: 59)

Of course, these characterizations – with their various connotations of Chaplin as clown, Chaplin as imitator, and Chaplin as child – again echo the figure of her father, recalling specifically Raymond Durgnat's description of Charlie Chaplin's Tramp persona as a figuration of "a child trying to be an adult" (1972: 78). But Deardorff's writing, rather than settling, like the other profiles, with a simple parallel between daughter and father – and rather than again bemoaning Geraldine's lack of maturity – highlights instead her own inimitable way of moving through a room. Her sheer presence in such an account, no matter how much she reminds these writers of her famous parents, conveys the sense of a unique performative personality beginning to break free of the familiar tropes of maturity and privilege that discursively underscore her emergence as a celebrity in the early sixties.

If Geraldine eventually slips away from familiar descriptions in these profiles and interviews, similar tropes of maturity and privilege nevertheless find their way into the films she makes immediately prior to and after the release of *Doctor Zhivago* in 1965. In these early films, Chaplin is sometimes cast in roles that explicitly reflect her own public status, frequently playing the child of privileged men, cast as an immature, spoiled, or pouty daughter who eventually grows up in one way or another as the film unfolds. In Jacques Deray's 1965 French potboiler *Crime on a Summer Morning* – Chaplin's feature-film debut as an adult and her only major role prior to being cast by Lean in *Doctor Zhivago* – Chaplin plays

Zelda, the daughter of a wealthy industrialist. Zelda is kidnapped for ransom by Jean-Paul Belmondo, who represents existential resistance to bourgeois society, as he did for Jean-Luc Godard in *Breathless* (1960) – a film to which *Crime on a Summer Morning* makes playful reference. In *Crime*, the Belmondo character is also quite childish: he is immersed in what appears to be an incestuous relationship with his sister, and his brief courtship with the Chaplin character is bereft of anything resembling adult behavior. Belmondo playfully dunks Chaplin's head under a shower after she tries to run away, a moment which is followed by a scene of flirtation whose eroticism is tempered by the fact that it takes place in a child's room. Nevertheless, it is this very eroticism that signals the "maturation" of the Chaplin character in the film, which in this case also involves the character stepping out of her social and economic class. She begins as an aristocratic, self-absorbed child of privilege, concerned only with her tennis game; she ends as a potential lover of earthy Jean-Paul Belmondo, whose working-class criminal anti-hero is presented as object of desire for Chaplin's Zelda (Figure 1.3).

Chaplin plays a broadly similar character in the later *Stranger in the House* (1967), a British film released in the U.S. market under the title *Cop-Out* (the British version is ten minutes longer than the U.S. release version, which was cut by the distributor). The film is an adaptation of the 1940 Georges Simenon novel *The Strangers in the House*. Here, Chaplin is Angela, the daughter of John Sawyer (James Mason), a once-prominent barrister stung by alcoholism after his wife's death. The film employs familiar generation-gap tropes not present in the original novel (perhaps informed by tabloid reports of Geraldine Chaplin's own late-adolescent

**Figure 1.3** Co-starring with Jean-Paul Belmondo in *Crime on a Summer Morning*

spats with her father, who objected to her early work in the ballet and in films and did not attend the premiere of *Crime on a Summer Morning*), with Mason's character objecting to Angela's indulgence in a late-sixties "swinging" lifestyle. Both of these character traits involve a sort of growth beyond and apart from her father, who remains stodgily detached from the youth culture in which Angela is immersed. Yet by the end of the narrative, once Mason has given up drink and come out of retirement to defend Angela's boyfriend against charges of murder, Chaplin and her onscreen father are reunited in a privileged, upper-class environment set apart from the various urban haunts Angela traverses earlier in the film.

Neither of these early films give the Chaplin character much narrative agency. Both films also frame immaturity as a negative trait, something that somehow needs to be corrected (a protracted childhood is linked to incest in *Crime on a Summer Morning*, while the Chaplin character's "childish" behavior in *Stranger in the House* leads to the death of a friend). The ways in which these narratives frame her characters as somehow lacking maturity is echoed in the idea, circulated in discourse about Chaplin during this time period, that Chaplin herself had not yet fully grown – not as a person, nor as a performer. This attitude is often signaled through repeated reference to her parents, who are still seen as kinds of surrogate figures bestowing presence and authority Geraldine herself does not yet possess. There is, in Lean's appreciative letter to Oona O'Neill, the seemingly inescapable presence of "Mum and Dad" – and with it the implication that whatever talent Chaplin uses here to win this part of Tonya, and no matter how earnest Lean's belief that she is right for it, her achievement is eclipsed by her position as a daughter of celebrity and privilege. Such a framing of Chaplin, which is reflected in the characters she plays in *Crime on a Summer Morning* and *Stranger in the House*, fails to grasp the complexity that is at least implicit in Tonya in Pasternak's novel, a complexity that contains within it the possibility of transformation, and the possession of an inner life that escapes Zhivago's subjectivity. This inner life is not fully explained by the conventional tropes of growth and maturity that Lean admiringly describes in his note to Oona O'Neill, and that many journalists imply Chaplin to be lacking in their words about her.

That these various filmic and journalistic narratives draw parallels between Geraldine and her famous mother and father is not, by itself, a problem. Rather, what is frustrating about these early journalistic accounts of Chaplin – as well as some of the films in which she is cast during this period – is that the narratives they sketch are, for the most part, simple ones, built on an understanding of Geraldine as an essentially spoiled young woman. Even the ways in which she transcends these characterizations, as in Deardorff's comparatively interesting account, are always relative to narratives that initially cast her as a kind of screen-world debutante, not yet in possession of performative maturity. There is no way to escape the fact that Geraldine is a Chaplin, of course, and a viewer fascinated by her screen performances should not want to: her status as the daughter of cinema's most famous clown is a key aspect of her distinction as a figure of study. One of the guiding ideas of this book is that moments from Charlie Chaplin's films have some part to play in helping us understand what Geraldine herself achieves onscreen. But the parallel between Geraldine and her dad – the gift she possesses – should be understood as a catalyst for understanding her performative creativity rather than as a metaphorical straitjacket which she must continually be made to slip away from. Further, the trajectory of her development as an actor cannot be understood only as one that takes her from an "immature" state of being to a "mature" one: whatever Lean's genuine appreciation of what Chaplin reveals in her screen test for *Doctor Zhivago*, my words in this chapter will partially rest on the notion that part of Chaplin's gift is her striking ability to lead us away from worlds of boringly "adult" concerns and into other kinds of fascinating reality. In the next section, before looking at moments of performance from *Doctor Zhivago* and some of her other sixties films, I want to suggest that one of her father's early films offers instruction and a reminder for how we might better understand his daughter's own emergence as a performer possessing her own individual distinction in the 1960s.

## The ambiguous frame

*The Kid* was directed by Charlie Chaplin in 1920 (and released in 1921). As Charles J. Maland points out, at the time of release the film maintained Chaplin's already developed star image as the Little Tramp and also supported his developing reputation as a serious artist through his combination of pathos and comedy (1991: 55–7). Artistically, *The Kid* finesses what was, by 1920, Chaplin's sophisticated sense of framing and staging, employing clever uses of offscreen space and figural movement to tell its story of a relationship between the Tramp (Chaplin) and the orphaned child (played by Jackie Coogan in the scenes in which the child is five years old) who becomes his companion.

Chaplin's filmmaking style is often understood as an importation of theatrical tropes to the art of cinema. Such assertions, however, also rest on the idea that Chaplin was somehow a less sophisticated *director* than, for example, Buster Keaton, whose films began to receive increased appreciation from critics and scholars in the sixties. Nevertheless, as Donna Kornhaber (2014) notes, Chaplin's use of the frame in many of his silent shorts and features is striking in its resistance to then-developing norms of classical film editing. His use of framing, in particular, signals a filmmaker with his own singular philosophy of how to present performance onscreen.

*The Kid* offers vivid examples of Chaplin's framing. Kornhaber explores how Chaplin's use of the frame often creatively obscures important information from the audience, a device used for a range of purposes in the film. In *The Kid*, she writes,

> the first time that we see the Tramp he approaches us from the far background of the frame, snaking his way through a tenement alleyway littered with debris and carefully avoiding the garbage being dumped into the street … By the time he makes it to the foreground of the frame, Chaplin seems to have successfully navigated the terrain … Yet just as he seems to have made it all the way through, a mass of garbage falls on him from a point unseen above the upper reaches of the frame. (Kornhaber 2014: 166–7)

Noting that this sudden downpour of rubbish, through Chaplin's choice to keep its source offscreen (Figure 1.4), surprises both the Tramp and the viewer, Kornhaber finds in this use of the device a larger idea about cinema: "To frame is to exclude," she writes, "and Chaplin asks us always to be aware of these exclusions and to regard the placement of the frame with a kind of skepticism" (167).

Exclusion, of course, is also a narrative trope of Chaplin's films: the Little Tramp lives on the margins of society, excluded from the innerworkings of institutions that do him harm (the police who often chase him through the films, for example) and even from those that seek to give him help (in *The Kid*, Chaplin and Coogan are saved by Edna Purviance, playing a generous actress who uses her success to help the Tramp and the child). The Tramp is distinguished not only by his insistence on retaining certain signifiers of a lost aristocracy (the bowler hat, bamboo cane, and floppy shoes) but also by the fact that he remains excluded from the new

**Figure 1.4** Charlie Chaplin and a play with offscreen space in *The Kid*

form that aristocracy takes in his films, a bourgeois class of professional adults that is often ambivalent toward, and indeed frequently the object of, Charlie's slapstick behavior.

Chaplin's answer to this situation is to underscore the value of immaturity. The film's title signals its interest in childhood, but *The Kid* also exudes a certain ambiguity, since the immaturity at play in the film belongs as much to Chaplin's Tramp as it does to Coogan's kid, given the Tramp's own refusal to become a part of normative, adult society. One of the memorable scenes in *The Kid* links Chaplin's clever framing strategies and their connotations of skepticism to a valorization of those who retain a child-like attitude toward the workings of the "mature" world. Midway through the film, Chaplin and Coogan develop a strategy for earning money that might be used for food and shelter. The two devise a plan whereby Coogan throws rocks through windows that Chaplin's Tramp, conveniently nearby after the crime, will offer to fix for a fee. Here the Tramp finds in the use of the frame, formerly a source of unwelcome surprise, a creative way to inhabit his world. While Coogan devilishly chucks rocks through glass, the Tramp slips offscreen, out of the view of both the owners of the windows in the story world and the viewers of the film itself. The Tramp only reveals himself, and his ready supply of replacement glass, once Coogan has left the frame, their separation and distance key to convincing shop owners and police that this offer to fix the windows is an innocent one. In this sequence, whenever Chaplin and Coogan are glimpsed together, their pairing onscreen is problematic: the Tramp must try to shoo the kid out of frame lest a police officer become wise to their fraud.

We are thoroughly on the side of the Tramp and the kid as they concoct and perform this scheme, situated as viewers by Chaplin as nearly complicit as the two characters co-opt a normative facet of adult life (here, the exchange of money for the service of repairing windows). Chaplin's delightful embrace of childlike behavior as a positive value – a value, as this discussion of his framing strategies implies, that might also be *artistically* expressed in a sophisticated way – was an important theme in the reception of Chaplin's work in intellectual circles. Sergei Eisenstein, for example, in a late essay intriguingly titled "Charlie: The Kid," makes the argument that the source of Chaplin's comedy is the "child's eye view" (1996: 244) that he brings to cinema, a productive form of "infantilism" that is designed to circumvent adult institutions. William Solomon, in his reading of this piece, suggests that

> Eisenstein presumes that the actor utilizes the motif of infantilism as a means of liberating himself from the pressure to conform to the norms of American society ... There is thus a collective purposefulness underlying the fact that [Chaplin's] plots are frequently organized around the conflict between an innocent, childlike attitude toward life and the stern, adult reproofs such an outlook inevitably engenders. (Solomon 2016: 123–4)

If Chaplin's framing of the world provokes us to question and become skeptical of the adult world recorded and framed in the cinematic image (the world the Little Tramp comically traverses), his performance style and creative use of that frame encourages us to recognize the value of immaturity as a potential response to that normative world.

Geraldine Chaplin, in her performances, does not enjoy the same control over the placement of the frame and the use of filmic space as her father does in the direction of his films. She does not have anything like direct creative agency over the form of her films until her collaboration with Carlos Saura begins in the late 1960s. Later, in the seventies, her films with Robert Altman, Alan Rudolph, and Jacques Rivette place her in privileged positions in ensemble casts, giving her room to improvise and invent. However, in most of her sixties films, she is placed in the frame by filmmakers whose understanding of what she might achieve in front of the camera, as I have already suggested, is informed by certain preconceptions regarding her status (or lack thereof) as a "mature" actor and as the daughter of famous people. Chaplin's performances in these films are nevertheless interesting because of her characters' own relatively marginal placement in relation to narrative developments. Sometimes the narratives themselves, which insist on the maturation of her characters, are gently counterpointed by Chaplin's performances, which highlight attractively immature qualities at some distance from the adult social world that eventually resolves the problems presented in the plots of these films. Regardless of such ostensible narrative resolutions, Chaplin's performative control over her characters bestows upon them a vivid inner life that parallels her father's earlier valorization of immature, and often marginalized, figures.

## Three sixties characters: Angela, Lenka, and Tonya

Geraldine Chaplin made seven feature films in the 1960s prior to settling in Spain to begin her nine-film collaboration with auteur Carlos Saura. In addition to those already mentioned – the French crime thriller *Crime on a Summer Morning*, the epic *Doctor Zhivago*, and the British drama *Stranger in the House* – Chaplin appears in a variety of other films across various national cinemas: *Andremo in città* (*We'll Go to the City*, 1966), an Italian neorealist-style drama with a screenplay by Cesare Zavattini, based on an Edith Bruck novel; her father's *A Countess from Hong Kong*; in an uncredited and nearly illegible cameo as a Keystone Kop, in a pair of long shots near the end of *Casino Royale* (1967); and, following her star turn as Tonya in *Doctor Zhivago*, as another aristocratic daughter in the Italian-French historical drama *I Killed Rasputin* (1967). In all of these films, Chaplin's character is either a passive figure or is located at the margins of the narratives. Further, these roles – with the exception of *A Countess from Hong Kong* – do not yet demonstrate Chaplin's development of an ironic performative personality, a sharp trait exhibited in her later work in the self-conscious art cinemas of Saura, Altman, and Rudolph. Nevertheless, certain moments in her early performances bestow upon her characters vivid and playful subjectivities that resist the norms of the narratives as well as the social worlds implied in the fictions.

## Angela in *Stranger in the House*

Chaplin's character of Angela Sawyer in the London-set *Stranger in the House* is thoroughly immersed in "Swinging Sixties" culture. She is the daughter of John Sawyer, played by James Mason. Sawyer is a formerly successful lawyer given to seclusion and drink after the death of his wife, sheltering himself from trends in fashion and popular music in which Angela indulges. *Stranger in the House* is itself the sort of film the reclusive John Sawyer – swathed in the melancholy of his own past – would never go to the cinema to see. Viewed today, the film plays like a forgotten relic of the 1960s, but it is surreal and strange enough to hold interest (the odd casting of Bobby Darin as Barney Teale, a lecherous drifter who becomes involved with Angela and her friends, is perhaps the most unusual touch; Darin was something of a fading pop star in the late 1960s, suggesting that *Stranger in the House* was already a kind of artifact of a bygone era upon its first appearance). The film's plot, which involves John Sawyer eventually giving up drink to soberly defend Angela's boyfriend in court (he is accused of a crime he did not commit), is based only very loosely on the Simenon novel. The book centers on the character of Hector Loursat, an alcoholic lawyer who drowns his past successes in booze. One evening, a dead body (which ends up being that of Teale) is found in the house he shares with his daughter (named Nicole in the novel), a discovery which provokes Loursat to begin paying attention to Nicole and her way of life. Nicole does not have an autonomous subjectivity; just as the reader only understands Tonya through Zhivago in Pasternak's *Doctor Zhivago*, Nicole in Simeon's *The Strangers in the House* is described only through her father's perspective, a point of view distorted by his abuse of drink. In contrast to the book, in the film *Stranger in the House* Angela is presented in scenes in which her father is not present. In these moments, Chaplin is given the opportunity to shape a vivid character whose ways of being are more memorable than the film's narrative machinations.

In an early scene that showcases Angela's personality, Chaplin languidly handles the various objects in her character's bedroom (pop records, a picture of her deceased mother), as Angela's boyfriend Jo (Paul Bertoya), a handsome, working-class Greek immigrant who will be wrongly accused of Barney Theale's murder, watches. Here, in this playful space, the dialogue between the two characters centers on Angela's father's total lack of interest in her life and her friends, further cementing this bedroom as a private space in which Angela can enjoy the popular music and friends her father finds distasteful. Chaplin is dressed and coiffed (Figure 1.5) in the chic look

**Figure 1.5** Chaplin, with Paul Bertoya, in *Stranger in the House* (a.k.a. *Cop-Out*)

of this era in this scene, wearing a short jersey dress and with her hair styled in a short, boyish cut. Angela's image here evokes various aspects of British fashion trends during the late sixties, in particular, the look of fashion magnate Mary Quant, and the style of Ted Lapidus, a designer whose fashions often flirted with androgyny and who tailored Chaplin herself in fashion photographs during the same period in which this film was made. Significantly, this scene is the first in Chaplin's filmography in which her character enjoys and exhibits anything like sexuality (the earlier flirtation between her and the Jean-Paul Belmondo character in *Crime on a Summer Morning* is left mostly undeveloped). While her character admiringly looks at an old picture of her mother ("she's much prettier than me"), Chaplin's presence in the scene strikes a more modern, late 1960s vision of feminine beauty. Key to this is Angela's own desire, made palpable through the way in which Chaplin regards her male co-star: while the striking Paul Bertoya as Jo sits nearly immobile, Chaplin moves freely around the room, laughing and squinting her eyes and nose in playful flirtation at her lover before joining him on the bed.

The narrative of *Stranger in the House* will insist that Angela leave all this Swinging Sixties fun behind, as she is enlisted to become her father's helpmate in his defense of Jo in court and also in her father's eventual victory over his own alcoholism. Tellingly, as Angela performs this maturation, she also leaves behind her trendy styles, appearing as the film comes to its conclusion in bourgeois, buttoned-up attire. The bedroom scene just described, though, sparks the imagining of a much more interesting sort of story. Andrew Klevan, in his writings on performance, has suggested that memorably acted moments in films can inspire in their viewers thoughts of paths not taken, implying potential narratives that might have been told in films. "A fragment of another story," Klevan writes, "has risen to the surface; it is glimpsed but not laid out, and not told by the film" (2004: 89). This brief bedroom scene in *Stranger in the House* is one of those moments: Chaplin's gestures and movements incarnate a playful, modern, spirited young woman, whose potential story the film, so otherwise centered on the James Mason character's ability to effectively practice law again, does not otherwise tell. Where Geraldine's own father, in *The Kid*, encourages viewers to become skeptical about the truth of what the cinema frame presents and excludes, Geraldine Chaplin's appealing moments of performance in her early films often encourage her viewer to be skeptical of the idea that the films in which she is appearing at this point in her career are telling the most potentially interesting story about her character.

## Lenka in *Andremo in città*

Shortly after *Doctor Zhivago* and a year before *Stranger in the House*, Chaplin appeared in Italian filmmaker Nelo Risi's World War II drama *Andremo in città* (Figure 1.6). Chaplin plays Lenka, a young Greek-Jewish woman whose father has likely died in the camps. As her surrounding village becomes suspicious of any citizens with traces of Jewish ancestry,

**Figure 1.6** Geraldine Chaplin stars in the World War II drama *Andremo in città*

Lenka must continue to care for her younger brother, Miscia (Federico Scrobogna), who is blind. The two of them attempt to hide from the eyes of Nazis in rural Yugoslavia (the film itself is mostly shot in Italy). Lenka soon meets Ivan (Nino Castelnuovo), a partisan resistance fighter who adores her. Eventually, the SS discovers both Lenka and Miscia; the film ends when the two of them are taken away to a concentration camp after refusing to divulge Ivan's whereabouts.

*Andremo in città* is the only film to feature Chaplin in its central leading role prior to the beginning of her collaboration with Carlos Saura in 1967. At least one scholar of Italian neorealism has had difficulty accepting the presence of Chaplin's name above the title. Millicent Marcus, in her book *Italian Film in the Shadow of Auschwitz*, argues that Chaplin's star presence distracts from the film's otherwise noble efforts to represent the historical experience of the Holocaust: "Featuring the young and willowy Geraldine Chaplin in the role of the film's protagonist, Lenka, *Andremo in città* functions as a star vehicle for a fledgling actress whose image becomes a visual obsession for Risi's infatuated camerawork" (2007: 45). The suggestion that Chaplin's star presence detracts from neorealist values echoes the earlier reception by some Italian critics of Ingrid Bergman in films by Roberto Rossellini (see Gelley 2012: especially 11–14). Marcus's words here are also striking for the way in which they pointedly attempt to delegitimize Chaplin's performance. She regards her very physical presence in the film, condescendingly described as "young and willowy," as a detriment to the otherwise noble realist project of *Andremo in città*. She underscores Chaplin's status as a "fledgling" actor at that time, a word that once again frames her as an immature and not-yet-fully developed performer (in contrast, indeed, to the fully developed, and at the time of the film's making, even somewhat nostalgic, tradition of Italian neorealism). Finally, she condemns both the film's affectionate attachment to Chaplin as an attractive presence framed by "Risi's infatuated camerawork." For Marcus, all of this loving attention to Chaplin as a beautiful movie star in the center of a very serious historical narrative is "unseemly," only properly balanced by "the unglamorous austerity of its black-and-white photography and the intrinsic interest of its quaint, Middle European village environment" (2007: 45).

The presence of a star performer in a realistically grounded story is not at all unusual to the tradition of Italian neorealism, of course. As Karl Schoonover (2012) points out, Italian neorealist films often mix professional and non-professional performances, rejecting not stars themselves but only the idea of relying upon a pre-established "star persona" to convey important narrative information. Neorealist visions of star performances prefer instead to defamiliarize preconceptions about stars by placing them alongside non-professional actors and within starkly realistic settings that refigure what the star might signify. However, what makes Chaplin's presence in *Andremo in città* somewhat different in comparison to, for example, the already established star Anna Magnani's performance in the neorealist movement's founding film *Open City* (1945) is that *Andremo in città* is a film that is simultaneously trying to present a vision of historical reality and establish Chaplin as a leading star presence. (This also differentiates the films from the Rossellini works with Ingrid Bergman, for Bergman was already an established Hollywood star prior to her involvement in neorealist cinema.) *Andremo in città* is Chaplin's first starring vehicle; so rather than strip away a glamorous persona in a new aesthetic context (as neorealist style plausibly had done in the case of Magnani, and to some extent also Bergman, in earlier films), *Andremo in città* finds itself in the relatively unusual position of presenting a new leading star and attempting to narrate historical reality all at once.

But the film's infatuation with Chaplin, and its efforts to tell a story about human experience in World War II, do not strike me as necessarily counterintuitive or contradictory. Rather than negatively set Chaplin's "young and willowy" presence against the stolid and serious "black-and-white photography", as Marcus does, I suggest that Chaplin's very placement within that cinematography works to ground the narrative in ways that act in contradistinction to the destruction of life occurring offscreen. If we become infatuated with Chaplin, as does Risi's camera, in *Andremo in città*, this nevertheless is a kind of emotion (affection for a filmed human being) that works in counterpoint to the inhumane devastation occurring just beyond the edges of the film's frames. Like many films about World War II and the Holocaust, the narrative of *Andremo in città* inevitably culminates in the grimmest horror of the twentieth century. And like her other characters in this time period, Chaplin's Lenka has very little agency or control over this narrative (which, in *Andremo in città*, is the most devastating of historical narratives). In this context, our attraction to Chaplin's performance in the film, unlike her turn in *Stranger in the House*, does not necessarily serve as the indication of another potential narrative, since the film's obligations to history place a necessary limit on the range of stories a viewer might imagine the film telling. Chaplin's performance does, however, draw our attention to qualities of humanity and inner life that stand in stark opposition to the horrors of the Holocaust that, in the film's presentation of reality, are kept mostly abstract (the film includes no representation of the camps, preferring instead to remain focused on Lenka and Miscia's life in the countryside as they attempt to resist anti-Semitism). In counterpoint to this incomprehensible – and offscreen – devastation, Chaplin's Lenka connects to the world in the frame in a sensual, tactile, and human way, creating a performance that is in tune with the film's neorealist sensibility (for more on the importance of tactility to neorealist performance, see Schoonover 2012: 40–4). The viewer's own sensual connection to the film's star performer supports, rather than contradicts, the film's essential project of reaffirming a grounded, emotional attachment to the world. Chaplin's performance emphasizes Lenka's palpable connection to that world, which in turn characterizes Lenka as one who guides her brother through terrain he cannot see: for example, her caressing of blades of grass in the opening shot of the film and handling of food and other objects as she helps Miscia through his day. Her gestures – and the film camera's undeniable, but hardly unseemly, attraction to them – incarnate an ongoing belief in life, even as the most devastating forms of death remain beyond the frame.

## Tonya in *Doctor Zhivago*

The most widely seen of all of Chaplin's films during the sixties was *Doctor Zhivago*. Her performance as Tonya in this film combines aspects of her work in the aforementioned films, at once implying alternative possibilities of narrative (as in *Stranger in the House*) while also grounding us, in a concrete way, within a sprawling historical narrative (as in *Andremo in città*). The character of Tonya herself represents a kind of alternative narrative for the character of Doctor Zhivago, played by Omar Sharif; as the Russian Revolution unfolds, Zhivago finds himself torn between a life of domestic comfort and loving warmth (represented by his marriage to Chaplin's Tonya) and a potential life of poetry and unbridled passion (signified by Zhivago's ongoing desire for Lara, played by Julie Christie). *Doctor Zhivago*, insofar as it functions as a romantic star vehicle (rather than as an accurate representation of Russian history), uses this love story as its main point of interest for the viewer: where Risi's camera is devoted to Chaplin in *Andremo in città*, in *Doctor Zhivago* it is, like its main character, divided in its affections for both Christie and Chaplin as star presences, even as the narrative trajectory (and desires of its central male character) nudges viewers closer to the former.

A 2015 trailer for the film's anniversary rerelease in Britain credits Julie Christie and Omar Sharif above the title of the film, relegating Chaplin to a list of supporting actors (alongside Ralph Richardson, Rod Steiger, Siobhan McKenna, and others). But when it was originally released, the film's credits and advertising (which employed an alphabetical strategy in their presentation of star names) emphasized the cast as an ensemble rather than singling out Christie and Sharif as the two primary stars. The original posters for the film alternated in their presentation of either Christie or Chaplin as the leading female star in the film, with some figuring Christie's presence in the foreground, while others emphasized Chaplin's (Figure 1.7). The film was also publicized in a series of nine one-sheet posters, each of which was devoted to the illustration of a separate performer from the ensemble (see Figure 1.8). And publicity discourse on the film, rather than signaling out Christie as the main appeal, focused instead on "The Two Loves of Doctor Zhivago" (as the headline of one magazine article put it; see Martin 1966), encouraging viewers to contemplate the various charms of both Chaplin and Christie in preparation for (and also in encouragement of) their viewing of the film.

This strategy, although a reflection of the film industry's star system, also arguably derives from the novel itself, which employs the familiar trope René Girard calls "triangular desire," wherein a literary work makes the desire of a character palpable via reference to a mediator existing between that character and the desired figure (1965: 1–52). While Lean and screenwriter Robert Bolt excised many supporting characters as they adapted the novel into a film, focusing on Zhivago's divided affections for Lara and Tonya as a device to explore the conflict between practicality and desire in post-Revolution Russia, the contrast between Tonya and Lara as romantic interests is already present in Pasternak's prose. The distinctions between the two characters become especially vivid about halfway through the book, after Zhivago and Tonya leave Moscow by train to settle in Varykino, a smaller city where it is thought their former aristocratic status will be less conspicuous. In the passages focused on Zhivago's domestic life in this new home, Pasternak includes long passages which describe his main character's subjective consciousness. In these words are traced visions of a woman whom Zhivago cannot consciously identify, but whom the reader understands is certainly Lara,

**Figure 1.7** A one-sheet for *Doctor Zhivago*, emphasizing Chaplin's presence in the film. Author's collection

**Figure 1.8** A character one-sheet for *Doctor Zhivago*, depicting Geraldine Chaplin. Author's collection

the nurse with whom he tended to the injured near the end of the war. As Zhivago grapples with these poetic visions, he weighs them against his life with Tonya:

> The dream left my head, in my consciousness there remained only the cause of my waking up. I was wakened by a woman's voice, which I heard in my sleep, which in my sleep resounded in the air. I remembered its sound and, reproducing it in my memory, mentally went through all the women I know, searching for which of them might be the owner of that chesty, moist voice, soft from heaviness. It did not belong to any. I thought that my excessive habituation to Tonya might stand between us and dull my hearing in relation to her. I tried to forget she was my wife and moved her image further off, to a distance sufficient for clarifying the truth. No, it was not her voice either. So it remained unclarified. (Pasternak 2010: 336)

This voice, that "resounded in the air," is clearly Lara's, whose romantic aura will be contrasted by the reader with more grounded descriptions of Tonya elsewhere in the book. Tonya is described as a woman whose vision of life, rather than imagining a world beyond her limits as Zhivago does in his expansive subjectivity, remains happily domesticated, with a desire for a private life which she preserves, even after the Revolution insists on the development of a collective purpose and consciousness. Zhivago, too, is resistant to what is depicted in the book as the purely instrumental and rational post-Revolution way of Soviet life, but his resistance comes in the form of a desire for poetry (and ultimately for Lara), while Tonya's is expressed quietly, through her maintenance of the family's daily activities.

Pasternak scholar Edith W. Clowes understands Tonya, in contrast to the more rebellious Lara, as a "relatively flat character... because of her role as conformist epic heroine. She experiences few conflicts or crises which would provide opportunities for her character to unfold" (1990: 325). Given this, the characterization of Tonya is one area in which Robert Bolt's screenplay improves upon the Pasternak text, as Lean himself recognized ("better than Pasternak" in its characterization of Tonya, the director opined; see Brownlow 1997: 504). What makes Tonya more interesting in the film is, however, also very much to Chaplin's credit, in concert with Lean's filmmaking strategies and the film's publicity discourse (which underscored Chaplin as a star of equal, if different, appeal, in contrast to Julie Christie). Rather than present a narrative in which the rebellious romance of Zhivago and Lara is set against an unchanging domestic life symbolized by Tonya, *Doctor Zhivago* achieves instead an interesting narrative balance in which Zhivago's doomed love for Lara is balanced alongside Chaplin's no less appealing (but qualitatively distinct) creation of a character who offers Zhivago a quieter, everyday kind of affection. This narrative balance is fully in keeping with *Doctor Zhivago*'s status as a product of the international film industry's star system, which depends upon the charms of both Chaplin and Christie to function.

Chaplin's first appearance in the film comes midway through the first hour, in which she meets her childhood friend Yuri Zhivago as she disembarks from a train just arriving home in Moscow from Paris. In this scene, Chaplin is costumed in a pink fur coat and hat, studded with black trim and buttons, a largesse from Tonya's visit to Paris and the most memorable fashion display in the film. Tonya, however, is not characterized as a selfish or shallowly materialistic socialite just waiting for come-uppance after the workers' revolt in the Russian Revolution. The film insists on the wealthy Tonya as a person of friendly affection, qualities conveyed by Chaplin's expression of warm regard for Sharif's Zhivago – and for the poetry he writes (she brings back a newspaper from Paris in which, as she lovingly tells Zhivago, he is described as one of the most important of the new Russian poets). Christie's Lara, later, will be characterized as a proletarian woman who, after Zhivago meets and falls in love with her, inspires the writing of poetry (rather than being a person who appreciates it). But this characterization does not prevent the film from making clear what is appealing about Zhivago's other love: Tonya's adoration of Zhivago also involves both an admiration for poetry and for this man who writes it.

Tonya, in some respects, interestingly parallels the public persona of the star playing her in 1965: just as Chaplin left her father's home to embark on an artistic and social life in Paris in the early 1960s, so too is Tonya introduced as having just returned from Paris, which makes her *Doctor Zhivago*'s most cosmopolitan character, despite the fact that she is a woman perfectly comfortable remaining in her bourgeois environment. This pleasure in comfort and in a kind of centripetal private life (in contrast to the centrifugal desire that draws Zhivago out in search of Lara in the second half of the film), *Doctor Zhivago* does not condemn; nor does it simplify Tonya's desires or her appeal, even as it makes clear the title character's growing passion for Lara. The poetry of Tonya as a character is perhaps most acutely felt in the middle section of the film, which dramatizes the Zhivago family's settlement in Varykino. In these sequences, Zhivago's desire to find Lara becomes palpable, but at the same time the scenes narrate the birth of Tonya's second child and her maintenance of this family. In these moments, Chaplin's domesticity is portrayed as not at all at odds with a certain idea of poetic beauty. In one sequence, as Zhivago, after a sleepless night, pines for Lara while watching dawn break outside a frozen window, the film cuts to a shot of Tonya waking up and wondering what her husband is doing. She walks over to join Zhivago near the window, the stream of light it admits working in happy collaboration with Chaplin's expressivity to frame a face full of moving affection for her husband (Figure 1.9). These scenes of quiet domestic life are clearly set into counterpoint with Zhivago's tortured pining for Lara. But the point, and the reason why the romantic conflict in *Zhivago* is never simple, is that these moments with Tonya are also beautiful.

In this way, *Doctor Zhivago* underscores the fact that Chaplin, and her character Tonya, are meant to be understood, in comparison to Christie and her character Lara, as equal, if different, in appeal to both Zhivago and an implied viewer. Tonya, in both book and film, is a supporting character (even if the film takes the development of the character slightly further), with Chaplin given relatively limited screen time in which to create her. Further, the film, like the book, is told mainly from Zhivago's point of view, and while Chaplin is able to offer glimpses and suggestions of Tonya's inner life, her turn in *Doctor Zhivago* is ultimately a supporting role, one that is meant finally to offer the viewer a very clear image of what it is Zhivago has decided to give up when he sets out for Lara. That Chaplin nevertheless creates a memorable character in Tonya, alive with an inner life, is precisely why the narrative of *Doctor Zhivago* works as effectively as it does.

**Figure 1.9** Chaplin as Tonya and Omar Sharif as Zhivago in *Doctor Zhivago*

## Chaplin photographed by Milton H. Greene

This structure of "triangular desire," in which Zhivago's desire for Lara is mediated through the presence of Tonya, is key to the way *Doctor Zhivago* functions narratively. And these kinds of comparisons are embedded in the star system itself. The appeal of any given star often emerges through comparisons with other stars, qualities of distinction and attractiveness thrown into relief against the traits of other performers. Geraldine's eccentric persona, as subsequent chapters in this book show, will eventually take her beyond conventional Hollywood logic, and into the alternative formations of cinema practiced by directors such as Carlos Saura, Robert Altman, and Jacques Rivette. But during her emergence in the sixties, the star system is still attempting to situate Chaplin within its discourse and in its films, making an effort to place her within an international celebrity culture and alongside other transnational stars whose appeal, like Chaplin's, traverses cultural and national borders.

The way the film industry of the 1960s viewed Geraldine Chaplin's potential as a star performer can be understood through a look at industry discourse that compares her talents and attributes to other female performers of the period. Industry correspondence about one leading part Chaplin was considered for but did not win offers some indication of her placement within the structure of the star system during her early career. For nearly three years, Chaplin was considered by producers and casting agents for the part of Anne Boleyn in the American-British costume film *Anne of the Thousand Days*, a historical epic that, when eventually released in 1969, starred Geneviève Bujold as Anne, opposite Richard Burton as Henry VIII. In inter-office communication between producer Hal Wallis, various employees of the studio, and casting agents, conversations which begin in 1965 and continue into early 1968, a number of American and British actresses of the period are discussed as possibilities for the part of Anne. These include major figures such as Faye Dunaway, Jane Fonda, and Elizabeth Taylor. But certain names recur in the correspondence more than others: in addition to Chaplin, Wallis also repeatedly mentions Julie Christie, Judy Geeson, Audrey Hepburn, Olivia Hussey, Romina Power, and Claire Bloom, who had played Thereza in Charlie Chaplin's *Limelight*. Strikingly, even pop singer Marianne Faithfull is considered for the role early in Wallis's correspondence, singled out to Wallis by casting agent Joy Jameson because "She is only eighteen and although she has this kind of quality Geraldine Chaplin has, she is physically very much more like

Julie Christie" (Jameson 1965).³ Offering a window into how casting directors think about female actors (in this agent's missive to Wallis, Marianne Faithfull is imagined as an impossible synthesis of the "two loves" from *Doctor Zhivago*!), such discourse reminds us that Chaplin's talents, like that of any potential film star, were often understood through her perceived difference from or similarities to other actors of the period. This idea of stars defined through their comparative qualities is mirrored in journalistic writings of the period, too. In an early profile of Geraldine, American journalist Radie Harris draws parallels familiar from industry discourse:

> When she smiles, her whole face lights up with Audrey's same inner radiance, but actually she bears a more striking resemblance to that other Hepburn – Katharine. She has the same coltish quality that Kate had when she first flashed on the screen in *Morning Glory*. I predict that Geraldine will have the impact of both Hepburns. (Harris, "Writings 1944–1953," Radie Harris Papers, pp. 2–3)

Comparisons to Marianne Faithfull, Audrey Hepburn, and Katharine Hepburn now seem somewhat irrelevant, given the trajectory of Chaplin's career beyond Hollywood in the decades to follow and her place near the edges (rather than the center occupied for decades by each Hepburn) of mainstream American filmmaking. But such discourse is a reminder that in the sixties, Chaplin was still an emerging star being tested for her potential iconicity. A film star becomes an icon, P. David Marshall writes, when "what the icon represents is the possibility that the celebrity has actually entered the language of the culture and can exist whether the celebrity continues to 'perform' or dies" (1998: 7). An icon, as Jonathan Goldman notes, is a screen figure whose very iconicity carries within it a kind of instant recognizability for its audience, "celebrity images, specifically, those legitimated by audiences that grasp their meaning instantly" which "act as transcendent signs of their times" (2012: 127). Some of the stars to whom Chaplin was compared (or with whom she was in competition for parts) in the sixties arguably had this iconic status; certainly the Hepburns and, eventually, Julie Christie, but also stars like Faithfull, Fonda, and Dunaway, all instantly recognizable figures who carry with them implicit historical meaning (Katharine Hepburn, for her challenging feminist image which emerged in films in the 1930s; and Dunaway, for her role as Bonnie Parker in *Bonnie and Clyde* in 1967, and for the late-sixties countercultural cachet the part evokes).

The ultimate icon in cinema, as Goldman reminds us, is Charlie Chaplin, whose screen image serves as a transcendent icon of meaning. "Chaplin's films promote his Tramp as an image that represents more than himself," Goldman writes; "rather, it becomes an emblem of the collective experience provided by his films, proposing that his work unifies everyone in his audience, possibly the largest viewing audience in the world" (2012: 125). Chaplin's iconicity also informs Geraldine's star image in the sixties, as this chapter has already suggested; repeated references to her status as the legendary screen comedian's daughter suggests that she was already understood in relation to a screen icon with which her audience was already familiar. Nevertheless, the industry discourse cited above is also an effort on the part of the star system to find a place for Geraldine's own potential iconicity, drawing parallels between her and other major female stars of the period, as well as other young actors also thought to possess a similar potentiality for cultural significance.

Geraldine did not go on to possess quite this kind of iconicity: unlike her father, and indeed unlike several of the performers mentioned earlier, her name and image do not spark instant or universal recognizability among audience members across the globe. Instead, the transnational trajectory of her career suggests varieties of local iconicities, shifting forms of recognition that differ by context. In Spain, for example, owing to her remarkable collaboration with Carlos Saura, Geraldine Chaplin is an icon; however, in the United States, she is primarily remembered, and even then mostly only by cinephiles, for her collaborations with Robert Altman and Alan Rudolph. Even among those who recognize the iconicity of her name and what it signals, it is only "Chaplin" that functions, globally, in an iconic way; "Geraldine," I suggest, retains the perpetual quality of the indexical. I refer here to the distinction and relationship between iconic images in cinema and indexical ones, concepts from film theory that Goldman employs in his study of celebrity images. Screen figures become iconic when they begin to carry within themselves reference to a historical period of which they initially only served as indexes. Rather than pointing to fleeting, evanescent, or embryonic meaning or phenomena, as an indexical image – a photographic imprint – might, an iconic image, when it becomes a powerful enough image of mass celebrity, synthesizes those meanings and phenomena within that image, carrying implicit meanings of collective significance wherever it goes, an image universally recognized by a mass audience. Iconic images carry historical significance, and they transcend any particular photographic or cinematic trace. The burden of this significance is precisely what Geraldine discovered when she became a public figure in the early sixties: repeated references to the iconicity of her last name, a name already awash with historical and cultural meaning that would appear to have transcended anything she might have achieved in films.

Nevertheless, the fact that, in her name, "Geraldine" retains its indexical charge (where "Chaplin" remains inevitably saddled with its reference to an already-established iconicity), remains important. When a star or public figure functions as an index, not only does this mean that their image fails to carry within itself the weight of historical meaning, as the iconic star does. It also carries a more positive and, especially in Geraldine's case, intriguing value. What it means is that the image of the indexical rather than iconic star, retaining her indexical power at the expense of a potential for iconic transcendence, requires perpetual reencounters with screen performance; every act of viewing Geraldine acting onscreen reopens potential meanings that might exist between her gestures, movements, and expressions and the various historical contexts and phenomena within which they come into contact. While her father's screen persona as the Little Tramp is burdened by historical discourse that now, according to Goldman, determines its significance, Geraldine's presence in front of the camera offers the promise of rediscovery. This rediscovery is sometimes also quite literal in nature, given that many of her films, including several made in Spain and France, remain out of commercial circulation, requiring extra effort to track down and see.

As we have seen throughout this chapter, of course, what I am calling the *indexical* quality of Chaplin's presence in front of the camera – that is, her ability to freshly reorient, through her gestural presence, our perception of whatever phenomenon or situation with which she is engaged – is somewhat constrained, in the sixties, by both patronizing journalistic reportage and by films which repeatedly insist on what is already familiar about her presence (her last name; and the ways in which the films repeatedly position her in relation to her public image, as the spoiled and immature daughter of wealthy and celebrated parents). In this respect, the most striking performance Chaplin gives in the early-to-mid sixties as an actor is not in any film, but rather in front of the camera of photographer Milton H. Greene. Greene is best known for his series of photographs of Marilyn Monroe, whom he befriended in the late 1950s. Many of his photographs of Monroe appeared in a later book by Norman

Mailer entitled *Of Women and Their Elegance* (1980), in which Mailer, writing in fictionalized first person, inhabits a feminine subjectivity modeled on Monroe. The book, however, is less interesting for Mailer's projection of himself into Monroe than it is for his depiction of the relationship between Monroe and Milton H. Greene. Greene is presented in Mailer's text as a man of sophistication and taste, whose ways of viewing Monroe – in life, and in front of the lens of his camera – tutor the actress in her discovery of her own intelligence and individuality. As Mailer tells it, in a kind of semi-subjective discourse meant to evoke Monroe's way of speaking and thinking, Greene's process of photographing stars – and in particular Monroe – is a method whereby the star discovers the means to reveal her personality in front of the camera:

> So I told him about my love for Abraham Lincoln, which I hadn't told anyone else (but Arthur Miller, who held my big toe once for hours on a night we talked). The truth was that I was afraid everybody would laugh themselves to death at the thought of me having a crush on such a famous President. But I truly adored Abraham Lincoln. I used to have dreams that I was his illegitimate great-granddaughter. "Why not legitimate?" asked Milton. Before it was over, I let him talk me into taking a picture with my great-grandfather in my Cadillac car. I must have been in love with Milton right that minute to do something so revealing. (Mailer and Greene 1980: 46)

This prose – whatever its uncertain relation to the actual Marilyn Monroe – recalls the implicit relationship between the photographer and every subject who steps in front of the photographer's camera, and the relationship between the subject photographed and the viewer of the photograph, tangled connections Mailer conjures in his writing. Privileged in this relationship is the idea of revelation and imagination, whereby the star's assumed subjectivity articulates itself in ways unexpected (here, Monroe's desire for Lincoln) and self-conscious (Mailer's Monroe is aware that her crush on Lincoln is likely to appear ridiculous, given its ambiguous relationship to other aspects of her public persona already established).

Greene photographed Geraldine Chaplin in the mid-sixties, just prior to the release of *Doctor Zhivago*. These photographs do not enjoy the same iconic status as Greene's images of Monroe, and they did not inspire a figure with the reputation of Norman Mailer to imagine himself inhabiting her subjectivity. For that reason, however, these images – the most striking of the many photographs of Chaplin taken during this period – retain a powerful charge; they are not historical artifacts but rather ongoingly interesting photographic encounters, in the sense that the performance Chaplin is giving in front of Greene's lens is still "there," still vibrant and alive in front of the beholder, potentially affecting her viewer beyond simple recognition of already-established historical fact or legend. Some of these photographs of Chaplin taken by Greene – twelve of which are reproduced in this book (Figures 1.10–1.21) – accompanied various publicity materials surrounding the release of *Doctor Zhivago* (including "The Two Loves of Zhivago" piece mentioned earlier). Most of them, however, remained in Greene's archives until very recently, and are being published here for the first time.

In some of the images, Greene presents Chaplin in ways that invoke the iconicity of her famous father, dressing her in a fashionable hat and bamboo cane which recall the accouterments of the Little Tramp (Figures 1.10–1.11, and the image accompanying the epigraph to this book), or cracking a smile (Figure 1.12) that endearingly conjures memories of her father's beaming grin. In others, she is presented in the trendy *couture* of the day, as in one image (Figure 1.13) in which Greene fashions her, with cigarette and beret, as an alluring gamine who might have stepped right off the set of a French New Wave film. Some of the more striking images strip away this contextual discourse, framing Geraldine through her own charms, gazing into the camera (Figures 1.14, and 1.15, the former of which is a color image reproduced here in black and white). Another (from the same particular series as Figure 1.15) appears on the cover of this book, and catches Geraldine as she glances out of frame, not quite meeting the eye of the beholder. In others, she is photographed in vivid color: in one (Figure 1.16; reproduced here in black and white), taken on a balcony, her hair wrapped in a bun and decorated with a pink flower, with a polite gaze toward the camera; in another, her eyes cast in shadow beneath a straw hat which she tips with her right hand, her gaze toward Greene's lens now mischievous and shyly playful (Figure 1.17). Another photograph, this one originally in black and white, evokes this same kind of glance, as Geraldine, reclining on a couch, a cascade of black hair masking the left side of her face, glances at the camera with her right eye while a slight smile suggests a pleasure taken in the out-of-focus object hovering midair in her left hand (Figure 1.18). The most striking of these images are the ones which imply a subjectivity that Geraldine withholds from Greene's camera, in which she glances just slightly toward something imagined out of frame (Figure 1.19; and the image on the cover of this book) or downward in contemplation (Figures 1.20 and 1.21).

These kinds of absorbed glances, intriguingly, are also present in the aforementioned photographs that style her so as to evoke her father: although the cane and hat are vaguely reminiscent of the Little Tramp, Geraldine's own glance away from the lens (in Figure 1.10, for example, as she looks out beyond the left border of the image frame) suggests an interiority – a wondering at something viewers do not glimpse – not fully exhausted through reference to her dad's familiar accouterments.

**Figure 1.10** Geraldine Chaplin photographed by Milton Greene (Figures 1.10–1.21)

These images, in other words, frequently convey a performative subjectivity that cannot be *immediately* read: even those photographs which play consciously with references to her father, or with fashion trends of the period, are still nevertheless marked by Geraldine's eccentrically charming presence. These photographs – even the ones that play with iconic aspects of Charlie Chaplin's screen image – do not cue us to simply read a familiar iconicity into them but also stage more uncertain encounters between Greene's camera and Geraldine (and, by extension, between Greene's photographs and the eyes of the beholders of these photographs) that prompt us to wonder what she might be thinking as Greene's shutter opens and closes.

In his writing on star photography in the 1950s and 1960s, George Kouvaros suggests that images of stars like this, images which imply but ultimately withhold subjectivity, are part of a larger tradition of portraiture that functions as the "affirmation of absorption": public displays of private withholding that often involve the photographed figure looking away from the camera lens, engaged with some other object of fascination or thought that, in turn, leaves the photograph's viewer only more intensely fascinated and absorbed. "The trope of absorption," Kouvaros writes, "enables a performance that suits the needs of both the star to realign her screen persona and the photographer to provide an image that satisfies the key criterion of … veracity: the star in private" (2010: 104). This realignment of screen persona through photographic presence is, I think, a sign of the *indexical* quality of Geraldine's figuration onscreen (in both her later achievements in her best films, and in this set of images captured by Greene). The photograph (or film) which prompts the viewer to wonder at the meaning of performative gesture or actorly thought is always enacting a realignment, in which the viewer can no longer depend upon commonplace assumptions about the star or her persona but now must realign perceptions of what the figure onscreen is at any moment taken to mean or convey, and in what processes of thought or imagination her characters are presently immersed. These photographs of Chaplin by Greene, I think, are reminders of the striking fact of Geraldine's presence, and of the fact that the meaning of her presence cannot be exhausted through reference to the iconicity of her last name. Through her striking presence in front of the camera lens, Geraldine, even as her last name still continues to cite a cinematic past that precedes her and at times inflects our reading of her presence, nevertheless redirects our attention to other realities, other ways of moving and being in films.

In these images, Greene recognizes – certainly better than any of the journalistic discourse of the sixties, and more poetically than any of Geraldine's early films analyzed in this chapter – the beguiling qualities key to Chaplin's emergence as a star during this period, and for much of her career thereafter. As mentioned, in several of Greene's images she evokes her famous father (either through the explicit reference to a hat and cane, or through her luminous smile which, inescapably, will sometimes contain within it the ghost of her father), such images pointing to the iconicity she carries in the last name "Chaplin." Others, though, more powerfully contain the indexical charge of "Geraldine," prompting the viewer, with the help of Greene's lens, to encounter a charismatic presence whose qualities of being are not exhausted through references to her dad. In some of these, Geraldine sparks the encounter herself through her gaze into the camera, and at the viewer, as if requesting (often playfully, or shyly) acknowledgement of her unique and distinctive presence. In others, her glance away from the center of the camera lens – particularly in Figure 1.21 – suggests a private, withheld subjectivity.

Geraldine's presence in these striking photographs, in collaboration with Greene's skills of photography, reminds us of her powerful presence as a performer, one whose last name functions as an inescapable historical citation but nevertheless does not determine everything which might be said about her. Even as Greene's imagery evokes familiar tropes of the Chaplin legacy (the hat and cane referencing the Little Tramp), these same photographs also vividly capture Geraldine's playful ability to wield these preexisting tropes in performances that remain ongoingly surprising. Many of the photographs insist on Geraldine's own subjectivity, her performance of a private self absorbed in delights of her own making. The presence of the aforementioned hat and cane in some of Greene's photographs does evoke the iconicity of her father, and in this sense bears traces of the discourse of inheritance that is tethered to her emergence as a star in the sixties. However, Geraldine Chaplin's very name, in its combination of indexicality with iconicity (a combination vividly staged by Greene's photographs), should be understood as part of her creative agency, rather than a limit upon it. By combining the unpredictability of the performative *index* (Geraldine, with all her vivid ways of moving onscreen, and of moving us by pointing to meanings that have yet to be felt) with the historical *icon* (the last name Chaplin, with all the historical meanings it cannot help but cite), Geraldine Chaplin animates a performative encounter that carries within it reference to a historical body of cinema whose very iconicity might take on new meanings as she travels into different corners of the world of cinema. In this, Chaplin achieves her own distinction as a cinematic figure, one who guides her viewer into a performative history alive before our eyes.

# Chapter 2

# The Great Dictator: Geraldine Chaplin in the films of Carlos Saura

> The eye you see is not
> an eye because you see it
> it is an eye because it sees you
> —Antonio Machado, "Proverbs and Songs" (2004: 345)

Geraldine Chaplin's performances for Spanish filmmaker Carlos Saura form part of an intimate and creative collaboration, akin to the cross-national bonds shared between Jean-Luc Godard and Anna Karina in France, and Roberto Rossellini and Ingrid Bergman in Italy. Chaplin's and Saura's work together bridges two periods in modern Spain. The first, from 1967 to 1975, encompasses the final years of dictator Francisco Franco's fascist regime (which began in 1939, at end of the Spanish Civil War); during this stretch, Chaplin and Saura make *Peppermint Frappé* (1967), *Stress-es tres-tres* (*Stress is Three, Three,* 1968), *La madriguera* (distributed as *Honeycomb* in the U.S. and elsewhere; 1969), *Ana y los lobos* (*Ana and the Wolves,* 1973), and *Cría cuervos* (*Raise Ravens,* 1976). These early films, in various ways, resist the repressions of Francoist politics. The second, post-Franco, period, from 1976 to 1979, finds Chaplin and Saura making *Elisa, vida mía* (*Elisa, My Love,* 1977), *Los ojos vendados* (*Blindfolded Eyes,* 1978), and *Mamá cumple 100 años* (*Mama Turns 100,* 1979). These three later films explore questions of personal identity, creativity, and the traumas of the past.

In an early sequence in the first film of the Chaplin-Saura collaboration, *Peppermint Frappé*, a character named Julián (José Luis López Vázquez) drives Elena, played by Chaplin, to a graveyard, in the Spanish province of Cuenca. Elena, something of a tourist, is the exotic new wife of Julián's childhood friend Pablo (Alfredo Mayo), a wealthy industrialist who has lent Julián and Elena his sports car for the afternoon. Placed

**Figure 2.1** Chaplin as Elena, with a mischievous gesture in *Peppermint Frappé*

within this graveyard is a stone cross emblemizing, as Julián explains to Elena, a folkloric maiden who turns to stone after a devil, in the guise of a handsome knight, places a hand on her breast. On the cross is an imprint of this devil's hand, onto which Elena places her own, slyly and mischievously (Figure 2.1). She flutters away from Julián; as he catches up, he tells her he has seen her before – at a religious ceremony in Calanda, not so long ago, he fell in love with a drum-wielding woman with long blonde hair. As conveyed in subjective, unreliable flashbacks, Julián's memory of this woman is also embodied by Chaplin who, as in her role as Elena, wears a blonde wig. Elena laughs at Julián's insistence that they have met before, and as she does so she slips from her Spanish to an impish, British-inflected English ("Good grief!" she exclaims, after learning the fate of the maiden). In contrast to both the maiden of Spanish folklore and the woman Julián insists he remembers from the religious ceremony in Calanda, Chaplin's Elena in *Peppermint Frappé* is the embodiment of a feminine, cosmopolitan modernity, coolly disrupting these late years of the Franco dictatorship in Spain.

She also has a sharp eye. Saura underscores Chaplin's striking way of seeing in his films and in *Peppermint Frappé* especially, in a shot of one of the magnified eyes of Elena later in the film, during a visit to Julián's childhood home (Figure 2.2). *Peppermint Frappé* is in part a film about looking and desire; it is dedicated to Luis Buñuel, and is reminiscent of Alfred Hitchcock's *Vertigo* (1958) in its story of a man whose obsession for

**Figure 2.2** The magnified eye of Chaplin-as-Elena in *Peppermint Frappé*

one woman leads him to imagine her in another. Certainly, Julián wishes to possess Elena, to freeze her movements for his pleasure: later in the film he will surreptitiously photograph her. But, as the Machado poem quoted at the beginning of this chapter suggests and as the striking shot of Elena's magnified eye implies, those who are looked at can look sharply back. Later in the film, when Julián takes Pablo and Elena to his small house for an evening of drinks – the frappés of the title – and murder (the drinks are poisoned, and both Elena and Pablo will die at Julián's hand), Elena spots Julián's book of Antonio Machado poems; like the cross, these poems are emblematic of the great literature of Spain. She hands the book to Pablo, who reads from it in a pompous tone meant to needle Julián's high regard for Spanish tradition. As Pablo reads, Elena mockingly pantomimes the playing of a violin with her hands, her taunting movements now visibly, palpably finding their way under Julián's skin. Chaplin's performance personifies Elena as a modern woman, a tourist in Spain, flirting with Spanish tradition but defiantly uncommitted to it.

Geraldine Chaplin's own place in Spanish cinema, however, contrasts with Elena's touristic, parodic behavior. Having arrived in Spain for the filming of two earlier, international co-productions – *Crime on a Summer Morning* and *Doctor Zhivago*, both released in 1965 – Chaplin would very soon establish herself as a part-time resident and a major figure in this nation's cinema. While her collaboration with Carlos Saura remains central to her work in Spain, her performances in Spanish-language films are varied: for the director Pedro Olea, in 1972, the political thriller *La casa sin fronteras*; in 1974, the drama *¿...Y el prójimo?*, for director Ángel del Pozo; in 1977, the debut feature of Enrique Brasó, the anguished melodrama *In Memoriam*; and in 1979, in Mexico, the screen adaptation of the Gabriel García Márquez short story *La viuda de Montiel* (1979). After her personal and professional relationship with Saura ends in 1979, Chaplin continues in Spanish-language cinema, most notably in Pedro Almodóvar's *Hable con ella* (*Talk to Her*) (2002), in which her casting is an homage to her earlier work with Saura; and, later, in *Dólares de arena* (*Sand Dollars*) (Laura Amelia Guzmán and Israel Cárdenas, 2014), an independent feature from the Dominican Republic.

Her work with Saura nevertheless remains central to her legacy in this cinema, even if she was already known in Spain as a celebrity prior to the release of *Peppermint Frappé*. In journalistic pieces on Chaplin published in various magazines in Spain in the 1960s, around the time of the release of *Doctor Zhivago* but prior to her first performance for Saura, she expresses admiration for the country. "I like Madrid," Chaplin is reported to have said to an interviewer for the Spanish periodical *Blanco y Negro* in 1966; "And I love Andalucia, especially the small towns and white *cortijos* of inland Andalucia, that are sung about with so much love by that great poet of yours, Antonio Machado" (Donald 1966: 103). If her public admiration of Machado prefigures her character's encounter with the same poet a year later in *Peppermint Frappé* (Figure 2.3), it also

**Figure 2.3** Chaplin reads Antonio Machado in *Peppermint Frappé*

marks the distance separating Chaplin herself, whose love for Spain goes beyond the relatively uncommitted, touristic behavior of her characters in the early Saura films, women who are often detached from the country's tradition and custom. Geraldine, far from echoing Elena's mockery of Spanish culture, surprises the interviewer in *Blanco y Negro* with her knowledge of Spanish arts and letters: "On Geraldine's lips forms a *Chaplinesca* smile," the interviewer writes, as Chaplin tacitly declares a love for Spanish poesy: "It is also a tender and slightly malicious smile, which seems to be declaring: 'But what did you expect? I also know and love Spain's great poets'" (Donald 1966: 104).

This popular discourse on Chaplin in 1960s Spain is challenged by the ambiguous nationality of her screen presence (British-American by birth, multilingual and playing in Spanish cinema both domestic and foreign women). Chaplin's presence in the Saura films is all the more slippery given that the ostensibly modern Spanish film culture of the 1960s still bears symptoms of Francoist ideology. In a cover article for another magazine, for example, she is referred to as "Geraldine, la Chaplin española" (1969). This particular identification of Chaplin with Spain has less to do with her own ardor for Spanish culture than with this journalistic discourse's need to fix her identity as an actor in nationalistic terms, one that echoes Julián's attempts to control Elena in *Peppermint Frappé*. In the *Nuevo fotogramas* profile, the Spaniard Saura is given credit for Chaplin's growth, and for her professional and artistic maturation. Contrasting two of her early visits to Spain, the first during the making of *Doctor Zhivago* and the second after her first film for Saura, the article suggests that during her initial trip to Spain, Chaplin arrives "as the daughter of her father" ("Geraldine, la Chaplin española" 1969: 10). However, during the second visit after the collaboration with Saura begins, the article declares that she is now a tourist attraction in her own right, a luminous – if not natively Spanish – celebrity whom a traveler might glimpse in Madrid. Moreover, she has earned this status precisely because, according to this discourse, she has found another identity through Saura:

> But Geraldine is back in Spain, with Saura, and Saura lets himself be tempted by the *Pygmalion* myth. Geraldine ... lets herself be appropriated, aware that only by becoming the other half of Carlos Saura – there is in her a Monica Vitti – ... will she cease to be only the daughter of Charles Chaplin. (11)

These words, which diminish her father's importance in her life at the same time as they amplify Saura's potential power for reshaping her persona, frame Chaplin's discovery of performative identity in Spain through the exchange of one male, authorial figure, Charlie Chaplin, for another, Saura. The way in which this popular discourse frames the meaning of Geraldine's relationship with her father is already limited: as suggested earlier in these pages, Geraldine's inheritance of the "Chaplin" name is creative and imaginative, rather than conservative or reproductive. But it is fairly clear that the article in *Nuevo fotogramas* is reflective of a certain tendency in Spanish discourse of this period to give Saura credit for Chaplin's growth as a performer, as if their collaboration were another iteration of the myth of *Pygmalion*, the story of a sculpture of a woman brought to life through the power of masculine affection. But rather than merely reflect this popular discourse about Chaplin's celebrity in Spain, Chaplin's performances for Saura challenge it, and ultimately move beyond it.

## Resisting fascism

Geraldine Chaplin's cosmopolitan presence in her work for Saura – embodied in her transnational background and her multilingual performative abilities – is key to understanding the meanings of her achievements in these films. "Cosmopolitanism," in terms of performance, refers to the idea that the border-crossing actor recurrently recalibrates persona, gesture, and movement in the context of national and social boundaries that are themselves perpetually shifting. This idea is useful for understanding Chaplin's work in the gradually modernizing environment of late-Franco-era Spain. As a cosmopolitan figure, Chaplin in Spain incarnates what Ian Woodward and Zlatko Skrbis describe as "performative cosmopolitanism," wherein "social performativity … [conceives] cosmopolitanism as an emergent and dynamic dimension of social life valuing openness which is based in sets of cultural practices bounded by temporal, spatial, and material structures" (2019: 127–8). This concept underscores the "emergent and dynamic" aspects of Chaplin's presence in Saura's films, as this actor-director team work to imagine an alternative history – and possible futures – that Spain, and its relatively porous borders in the final years of the dictatorship, can no longer repress.

The dynamism of her performances for Saura, which challenge traditional Spanish typage and suggest a future in which femininity slips away from essentialist ideas of national identity, is also part of Saura's larger, anti-fascist cinematic project. Chaplin herself, of course, also inherits from her father a cinematic legacy of anti-fascism, emblemized by Charlie Chaplin in *The Great Dictator* (1940). While her father's film is often remembered for its final passage, in which Chaplin's barber character (a Jewish man evoking certain qualities of the Little Tramp) makes an impassioned plea for the rights of humanity, what is more notable about Chaplin's performance is his tendency to incarnate anti-fascist sentiment through movement and gesture, in particular through dance. In one scene from *The Great Dictator*, the barber is interrupted in his attempt to remove the word "Jew" from his storefront, slanderously painted there across its windows by fascist troops. Two of these authorities arrive to stop the barber in his efforts. The barber's resistance to fascists is conveyed here through whimsical dance: after being accidentally plonked on the head with a frying pan by his neighbor Hannah (Paulette Goddard), the barber comically hops and zig-zags across the sidewalk, the camera tracking alongside him to reveal, as he dances, storefront after storefront pillaged by anti-Semitic vandalism (Figure 2.4). While expressive of the way in which Chaplin intended *The Great Dictator* as a performative riposte to

**Figure 2.4** Charlie Chaplin, in a performative riposte to tyranny, in *The Great Dictator*

tyranny, Donna Kornhaber notes that, within the totalitarian world of the film, such action, no matter how graceful or comic, is ultimately bereft of agency. "These moments of pure action are as deftly composed and executed as anything that Chaplin would ever put on film," Kornhaber writes, "but they do nothing to affect Hynkel's ascension within the film's narrative . . . these scenes are as futile as any individual act of resistance to the storm troopers; it is all too little too late" (2014: 230).

In Geraldine Chaplin's performances for Saura, a desire for liberation – expressed as a cosmopolitan agency within Spain – is also embodied through movements, including dance. Chaplin dances often in the Saura films: twice in *Peppermint Frappé* (both times to the track "The Incredible Miss Perryman" by the Spanish rock band Los Canarios); again in the post-Franco *Los ojos vendados*, in which Chaplin, playing an actor cast in the lead of an anti-fascist film, engages in a seductive dance with its director; and near the end of *Mamá cumple 100 años*, when Chaplin comically dances with other members of the ensemble cast. Chaplin's performances for Saura nearly always emerge in a context in which fascist structures – or in the post-Franco films, that structure's vestiges – seek to repress her movements. While Charlie Chaplin's *The Great Dictator* ends without indication that the actions of the Barber have done anything to change the course of fascist rule, Geraldine Chaplin's films for Carlos Saura constitute an important intervention into late Franco-era Spain and during the first years after the dictatorship ends. Whether or not this amounts to a performance of agency is a question her work in these films poses.

## A tourist in Spain: *Peppermint Frappé, Stress-es tres-tres*, and *Ana y los lobos*

For Saura – Spain's major film auteur after Buñuel and before the emergence of Pedro Almodóvar – Geraldine Chaplin represented an opportunity to circulate his cinema beyond his nation's borders. During this period of intense creativity, Saura's films are realized with help from the savvy producer Elías Querejeta, whose work in Spanish cinema at this time "was driven by an understanding of how emulation of the aesthetics of quality – filmmaking in Europe – would allow Spanish films to be integrated into European networks," films made by production teams "able to create and consolidate a particular politically oriented aesthetic" (D'Lugo 2012: 53). Querejeta no doubt knew how useful Chaplin would be to his project: as an internationally recognized "name," fresh off her success in *Doctor Zhivago*, she could help Saura's work gain cross-cultural currency that also reflects the way in which Spain, near the end of Franco's regime, was slowly embracing modernization and transnationalism. As Tom Whittaker points out, the casting of Chaplin also fits into the pattern producer Querejeta follows in many of his projects, in which he "frequently cast established actors against type, thereby lending a perverse sense of irony to their roles" (2011: 10). For Whittaker, Chaplin's "cosmopolitan 'Europeanness' figures as an ironic counterpoint to the sham modernity of Spain's miracle years" (2011: 10) in these early Saura films, her characters' attitudes toward traditional Spanish culture serving as an ironic riposte to Francoist notions of repression and cultural propriety.

In a picture taken in July 1968 at the home she shared with Saura in Spain (Figure 2.5), there are three striking visual signifiers surrounding Chaplin, each of which suggests something of interest about her work for Saura. First, above her and left, is an image of the American silent film star Theda Bara (born Theodosia Burr Goodman), whose illusionary transnationalism (as a woman from Cincinnati costumed, in a cycle of films,

**Figure 2.5** Geraldine Chaplin in 1968, in the residence she shared with Carlos Saura

as an Arab villain) figures as an oblique parallel to the British-American Chaplin's transformation into ostensibly Spanish women in some of Saura's films (particularly the later works, in which the tourist persona of Chaplin's early characters for Saura is gradually discarded). Second, and directly above Chaplin in this photo, a familiar image of her father as the Little Tramp, something of an occasional phantom presence in her performances for Saura, whose cinema is itself obsessed with the question of inheritance and the ongoing presence of the past in the present. Finally, above Chaplin and right, a portrait of Chinese Communist leader Mao Zedong, whose political philosophies were antithetical to Spain's dictatorship and suggestive of Chaplin's and Saura's critique of Franco in the films they make together.

The exchanges between transnational, performative, and political allusions in the images inscribed within this photograph of Chaplin are suggestive of the general nature of her participation in the films of Carlos Saura during this period. For Saura, she crafts performances that explore questions of national identity and creative inheritance, in a combined address to both liberal viewers in Spain – prepared to read the films as rejections of Francoism's repressions – and a larger, international audience receiving the films as art cinema. When Chaplin makes *Peppermint Frappé*, the first of her films with Saura, she performs slippages between cross-national notions of feminine identity during a period in which Franco's Spain begins opening its borders to foreign influences. Scholar Justin Crumbaugh has explored the cultural impact of the boom in Spain's mass tourism, beginning under Franco during the late years of his regime and reaching a peak in 1967, the year *Peppermint Frappé* is released. A crucial figure in discourse about tourism in 1960s Spain is the female foreign traveler, or *sueca*, a word typically used, in this context, to identify a vaguely (and frequently blonde) Northern European woman whose appearance and norms of behavior contrast with nationally sanctioned ideas about traditional Spanish femininity. As Crumbaugh shows, the *sueca*, a key figure in Spain's tourist boom of the 1960s, also becomes a crucial figure in popular Spanish cinema of the period, serving in melodramatic plots as a metaphor for "Spain's ... integration into consumer capitalism, a process the [Franco] regime itself had engineered despite some misgivings" (2010: 90). In her first two films for Saura – *Peppermint Frappé* and *Stress-es tres-tres* – Chaplin performs a variation upon this figure of the foreign tourist, challenging both traditional and modern stereotypes of feminine identity circulating within Spanish film culture.

## Elena in *Peppermint Frappé*

In *Peppermint Frappé*, Chaplin plays two characters: Ana, the mousy, brunette, Spanish assistant to the doctor, Julián; and Elena, a blonde, modish tourist (her native country is never specified, but given that Chaplin is playing her Elena is legible as British-American). For Julián, Elena comes to embody his vision of the ideal *sueca*, an embodiment of the women in his cut-up fashion photographs that Saura shows the viewer in the film's opening montage. But onto this vision of a modern, transnational woman Julián projects his own notion of a purely traditional, Catholic femininity, his imagined Elena a fantastical synthesis of the traditional and domestic and the modern and foreign.

A striking moment in Chaplin's performance challenges Julián's fantasies about the modern *sueca* at the same time as it addresses the international audience for Saura's film. In this scene, Julián, Elena, and Pablo have arrived at a museum exhibiting modern Spanish art. Julián has arrived here to share with Elena the photographs he has taken of her while she was dancing in an earlier scene. In contrast to these photographs that freeze her movement, Elena moves freely across the exhibit, and often in a direction diverging from that of both Julián and Pablo. Saura, as the scene unfolds, repeatedly associates Chaplin with modern art. When, for example, a man asks Elena what she thinks of the exhibit, she smiles from within an internal frame composed of the lines of an artwork, as if she were the living embodiment of the modernity it represents (Figure 2.6).

**Figure 2.6** Chaplin as Elena, a living embodiment of feminine modernity in *Peppermint Frappé*

Later, as Elena strolls into a black room displaying several brightly lit paintings, Julián pursues her, apologizing for confessing his fantasies to her in an earlier scene. But Chaplin, abstracted in silhouette against the museum display, says nothing in response, resuming her solitary walk through the exhibit.

These moments align Elena with a modern art that disrupts traditional methods of interpretation, in turn skewering Julián's and Pablo's stodgy ways of seeing and interpreting feminine identity. These men are unable to "read" Elena as either a traditional Spanish woman – which Julián tries to do through his fantasies of the Easter celebration – or as yet one more stereotypical *sueca* figure. But the scene also addresses an international audience, linking Chaplin to another celebrated female actor in European art cinema. After Chaplin leaves the dark room, the camera eventually picks up with her again as she approaches a large painting hanging on a far wall. Then there is a cut to a wider, high-angle shot of Chaplin standing in front of the painting as Pablo, in the foreground, ruminates on developments in both art and tourism in Spain. The camera tracks backward past the entryway into another room, once more framing Chaplin internally in the image as she contemplates the lines and forms of the painting in front of her, a painting that, as we look on with her, manifests a strangely human figuration (Figure 2.7). As she looks at the title card accompanying the painting, Saura cuts to a close-up of the text she reads:

> Antonio Saura
> BRIGITTE BARDOT
> Oleo sobre lienzo (250 × 200 cms) (1958)

The cut reveals that this work is an abstract rendering of Brigitte Bardot, painted by Carlos Saura's older brother, Antonio, a major figure in postwar Spanish art. A cut from the title card takes the viewer back to Elena as she continues to gaze at the painting; and a subsequent pan of the camera implies a connection between Elena and the figure in the painting. After a moment, Julián approaches. But now, rather than greeting him with the nonchalance characterizing her attitude earlier in the scene, Chaplin rejects him brusquely, leaving the frame.

The painting Elena is looking at is part of a series of images of Bardot created by Antonio Saura in 1957 and 1958. In her study of the pin-up in postwar popular culture, Maria Elena Buszek contrasts Antonio Saura's depiction of Bardot to Willem de Kooning's earlier and "comparatively sweet handling of the quintessential postwar pin-up, Marilyn

**Figure 2.7** Chaplin gazes upon a painting of Brigitte Bardot by Antonio Saura in *Peppermint Frappé*

Monroe – all smiles, colorful curls, and windblown locks" (2006: 267) – a celebrity image that, like Bardot, is much closer than Geraldine Chaplin to the typical vision of the blonde *sueca* tourist at play in Spanish popular culture of the period. Buszek, however, and in contrast to the fetishizing of femininity circulating in Spain via the image of the blonde tourist, credits Antonio Saura with finding in his images of Bardot "an anxiety about a new kind of woman – complex, tempestuous, unruly... increasingly politicized, [demanding her] freedom to interpret as well as create" her own sense of self (2006: 267). A similar kind of anxiety might also be found in a comparatively angular and similarly abstract portrait of Chaplin herself completed by Antonio Saura the same year (1967) of *Peppermint Frappé*'s release, a work entitled "Geraldine Chaplin en su sillon" ("Geraldine Chaplin in her armchair") (Figure 2.8). In his film, Carlos Saura, with Chaplin, sets this anxiety about a new kind of woman into more concrete motion in a story about a man desperately trying to fix a female tourist into a traditional image. This scene in the museum exhibit, in which Elena gazes at an aggressive rendering of another transnational cinematic figure, presents Chaplin as a figure contemplating possible new directions her performance might take, a prefiguration of the more active creative role Chaplin herself would assume in the scripting and realization of her subsequent films with Saura later in the decade.

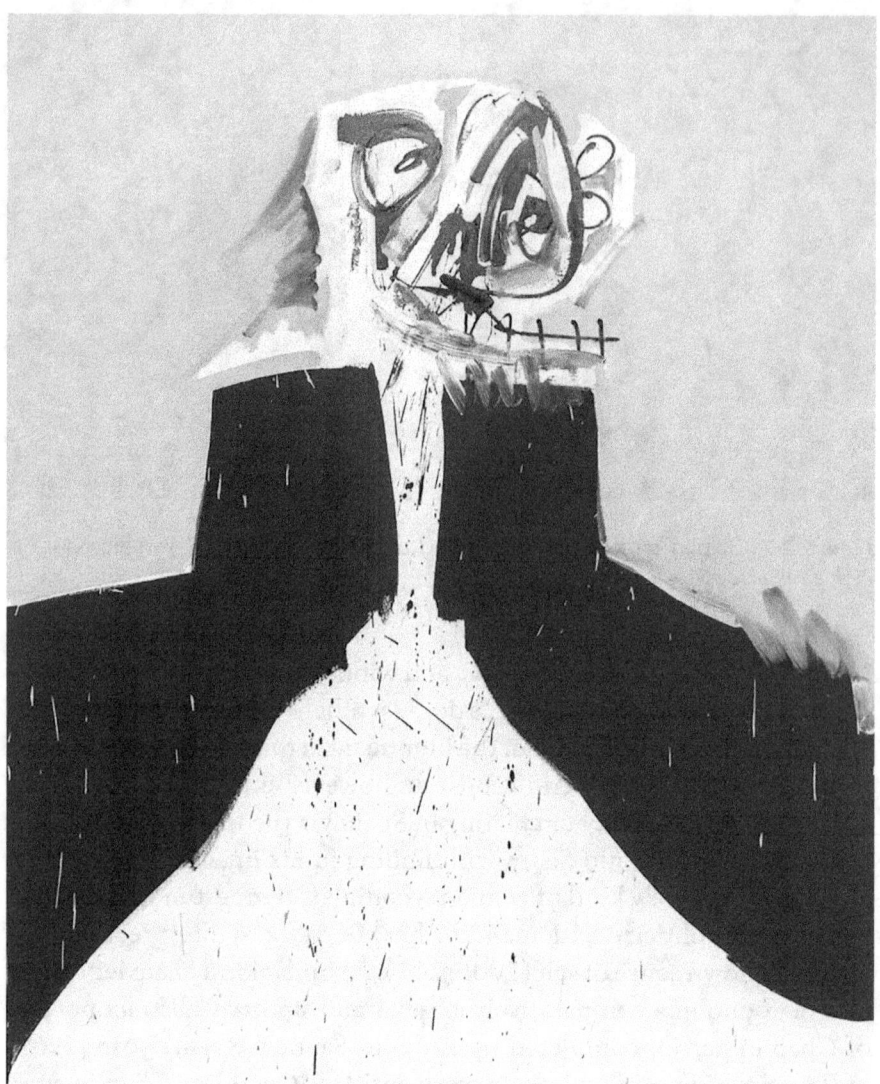

**Figure 2.8** "Geraldine Chaplin en su sillon" ("Geraldine Chaplin in her armchair"), by Antonio Saura, 1967. Author's collection

## The Spanish *acousmêtre*

In her first two films for Saura, *Peppermint Frappé* and *Stress-es tres-tres*, Chaplin's voice is post-synchronized: in *Peppermint Frappé* her voice as the blonde tourist Elena is Chaplin's own, dubbed after the shooting of the film; her role as the Spanish Ana in the same film is dubbed by another actor, a vocal contrast intended to be illustrative of the cultural differences between the two characters. In the subsequent *Stress-es tres-tres*, Chaplin's lead performance (as a character, Teresa, once again in a blonde wig) is dubbed by another Spanish vocal performer, creating an intriguingly strange contrast between the bodily presence of Chaplin onscreen, who reminds us of the cosmopolitan *sueca* of the earlier *Peppermint Frappé*, and the vocal indication of Spanish nationality. It is not until *La madriguera*, in 1969, that Chaplin begins speaking with her own voice in Saura's cinema – on-set, in English (the language in which the film was shot, owing to the inability of her Swedish co-star, Per Oscarsson, to speak Spanish) and, in post-synch, in her own Spanish (tinged with shades of her own distinctive accent). Beginning with 1973's *Ana y los lobos*, Chaplin's speech would become fully her own in her work for Saura, her Spanish as recorded on-set preserved in the released version of the film.[4]

Chaplin's voice, and the way in which her voice is at times inhabited by ghostly offscreen speech (either her own post-synched voice, or that of another voice performer), is important to an understanding of her work in these films. In his book *The Voice in Cinema*, Michel Chion writes of the "magic and power" of a sonorous figure he calls the *acousmêtre*, the voice heard but not yet incarnated in an onscreen cinematic body:

> When the acousmatic presence is a voice, and especially when this voice has not yet been visualized – that is, when we cannot yet connect it to a face – we get a special being, a kind of talking and acting shadow to which we attach the name *acousmêtre*. A person you talk to on the phone, whom you've never seen, is an acousmêtre. If you have ever seen her, however, or if in a film you continue to hear her after she leaves the visual field, is this still an acousmêtre? Definitely, but of another kind, which we'll call the already visualized acousmêtre. It would be amusing to invent more and more neologisms, for example to distinguish whether or not we can put a face to the invisible voice. (Chion 1999: 21)

In her performances as Ana in *Peppermint Frappé* and as Teresa in *Stress-es tres-tres*, Chaplin's presence onscreen is accompanied throughout by a partial-acousmêtre: in the diegetic worlds of the films, both Ana and Teresa are embodied with voice, and heard speaking Spanish by the people surrounding them. But in our experience of the films themselves, Ana and Teresa are each incarnated by a voice other than Chaplin's. (Her performance in *La madriguera* and her role as Elena in *Peppermint Frappé* are somewhat different, given that the post-synchronized voice, although still technically acousmatic in its cinematic properties, belongs to Chaplin.) To some extent the acousmètre inflects Chaplin's performances as Ana in *Peppermint Frappé* and Teresa in *Stress-es tres-tres* with a haunting quality. But I would not go so far as to suggest, as other commentators have, that this acousmatic dimension strips her work in the early Saura films of artistic agency (de Montero 2014: 1–2). Chaplin's achievements of movement and expression often work as a counterpoint and commentary on the acousmatic Spanish words, spoken by a native Spanish actor in post-production, that in the finished film she is made to speak.

## Ana in *Peppermint Frappé*

The character of Ana, in *Peppermint Frappé*, brings these questions of performative agency to the forefront. Ana's presence in the film is a combination of submissiveness and modernity: in Chaplin's first appearance in the film as Ana, she is maneuvering a large radiological device and assisting Julián with the filing of medical documents, while her eyes are kept in a downward glance, in seeming deference to Julián's professional authority. But as Julián leaves the examination room, Saura holds on a shot of Ana's gaze, an initial indication of her relatively autonomous subjectivity.

As the film goes on, Ana's subjectivity continues to emerge from within restraints. Chaplin's performance suggests that it is Ana, rather than the tourist Elena, who ultimately incarnates a vexing synthesis of traditional and modern Spanish womanhood. Later in the film, Ana, lying on Julián's bed after work one evening, surprises the doctor. She is listening to the same pop song by the band Los Canarios to which Elena dances earlier in the film. She lies on the bed, resting against the headrest, her left arm languorously raised, in knee-high fishnet stockings, her pose generating an erotic charge in striking contrast to her earlier, quotidian appearance in the doctor's office. All of this would appear in accord with Julián's desires (earlier in the film, he has been trying to shape Ana into his fantasy of Elena). However, what disturbs Julián is that this is an erotic charge Ana creates; Chaplin's performance characterizes Ana as a woman who is performing sensuality – trying it out for herself – rather than incarnating it exactly as Elena has done earlier in the film. Julián, trying to take control over the situation, turns off the record player, and guides Ana to a nightstand, where he will instruct her on the method of wearing false eyelashes. As he does this, Saura films Chaplin's eyes in extreme close-ups that recall the fragmented images of the female body in Julián's scrapbook of fetishes, glimpsed at the beginning of the film. Here, for Ana, what began as a moment of imaginative self-creation slowly slips into submissiveness. But it is the last time in the film that Ana will be under Julián's control. A moment later, Julián leaves the room and Ana discovers a folder of the photographs Julián has taken of Elena dancing. This discovery provokes a change in Ana. When Julián returns to the room, she slowly turns around in her chair to meet his gaze, her motion implying that she is now actively, unpredictably performing the femininity Julián has fetishized in his photographs. His photographs are the mere residue of Elena's movement; Ana's performance, by contrast, is a mobile incarnation of a living, feminine subjectivity. As Chaplin characterizes her, for Ana this becomes a performance that combines traditionalism (signified again by the Spanish voice dubbing Chaplin's performance) and internalized cosmopolitanism, a synthesis that – as the end of the film, in which the newly incarnated Ana appears in a blonde wig, ready to assume a performance as the modern *sueca*, makes clear – ultimately baffles Julián.

## Teresa in *Stress-es tres-tres*

In Saura's next film with Chaplin, *Stress-es tres-tres* ("Stress is three, three"), Fernando (Fernando Cebrián), a wealthy industrialist and amateur photographer, journeys with his wife Teresa, played by Chaplin, and his business partner Antonio (Juan Luis Galiardo), to an undeveloped stretch of the Andalusian coast, where Fernando plans to build a new tourist complex. Fernando eventually begins to suspect that Antonio and Teresa are lovers, and he attempts to surveil their behavior at various points through his camera lens. Chaplin's character, through her relationship with the businessman Fernando, is in this film more firmly a part of "the new technocratic bourgeoisie which had become wealthy over the previous ten years in Spain" (de Montero 2015: 92), even as her character continues to embody touristic traits. But as *Stress-es tres-tres* nears its conclusion, Chaplin begins to shed some of the traits of the *sueca* tourist embodied in her earlier performance for Saura in *Peppermint Frappé*, revealing more ambiguous facets of subjectivity.

In this advancement beyond the type of the *sueca*, and in the vivid way of seeing the world that Chaplin bequeaths to Teresa near the end of the film, *Stress-es tres-tres* marks a substantial advancement in the nature of Chaplin's contribution to Saura's cinema. In *Stress-es tres-tres* Chaplin gives to Teresa something that goes beyond what Saura himself is able to conceive in a female character. As Saura himself has said, Chaplin's presence in this film is crucial because

> she provides me with a vision, an enrichment, certain remarks, indeed a range of things which I don't know, or rather which I can guess but which I do not really know … it is more than the performance of an actress … it goes much further than that; it goes as far as debates about certain scenes, because on several occasions I think that she was right and I have adjusted … (quoted in de Montero 2015: 97)

As in her doubled performance as both Ana and Elena in *Peppermint Frappé*, Chaplin portrays Teresa as a modern woman whose vivid ways of moving and seeing act as a counterpoint to conventional expectations of femininity. Teresa in *Stress-es tres-tres* is a synthesis of Elena and Ana from the earlier film, embodying the image of the *sueca* tourist while nevertheless finding herself in a relatively more domesticated romantic relationship with a Spanish man. For the first hour of the film, Chaplin is dressed in a blonde wig, resembling Elena's in *Peppermint Frappé*. The acousmatic properties of her dubbed voice on the soundtrack, meanwhile, continue to signal the way in which this fantasy of the *sueca* figure is coupled with a lingering desire to hold onto traditional ideas of Spanish womanhood. Ultimately, however, Chaplin's performance in *Stress-es tres-tres* moves toward other ideas and positions.

Near the end of *Stress-es tres-tres*, playful qualities emerge in Chaplin's performance that convey her character's gradual shedding of the *sueca* persona. Through shifting the tenor of her appearance, Teresa becomes, like Ana at the end of *Peppermint Frappé* but in a different key, a threatening synthesis of cosmopolitan traits that defy the attempts of traditional Spanish men to control her behavior. This becomes especially apparent in the long final sequence in the film, in which the threesome arrive at the coast to survey the land Fernando intends to buy for his tourist resort. Fernando's car gets stuck, which gives Teresa the opportunity to abscond from the automobile in which she has been seated for most of the duration of the film up to this point. Here, Chaplin makes expressive and pointed use of performative accessories – props and costumes. While the two men squabble about the car, Teresa slips into a bikini, for a moment her beach-blonde image matching the typical mid-1960s Spanish fantasy of the *sueca* tourist (an especially potent fantasy in *Stress-es tres-tres*, given that this "sueca" is in this film an ostensibly domesticated foreigner, married with children to a Spanish industrialist). But as quickly as she has changed into her swimwear, Teresa, in a close-up, tosses aside her blonde wig (Figure 2.9), first revealing and then tossing left-to-right her shoulder-length black hair, a smile of pleasure cracking across her face. At this, Saura's camera tracks backward, reframing Chaplin in a long shot before she walks away from the lens toward the water. Her character relatively free of Fernando's gaze, Chaplin throws her arms out wide as she plays along the shoreline, darting away from the focus plane of Saura's camera as her arms extend like propellers, while her acousmatic Spanish voice imitates the sound of a plane engine. This moment falls short of performative freedom: the sounds Teresa makes here are still generated by an offscreen voice not Chaplin's own. But as image, Chaplin projects a figure of unbridled energy, and free of the blonde wig which up to now has signaled a kind of "European exoticism" in her performances for Saura, she darts past *sueca* fantasy.

Still alone, Chaplin walks along the beach, framed from the knee down as the camera follows her feet to a spot in the sand. Stopping for a moment, she spies sheer, black fabric partially buried in the ground. Kneeling down, she begins to tug on it, eventually revealing a single

**Figure 2.9** Chaplin as Teresa, shedding an identity in *Stress-es tres-tres*

nylon. She puckishly unfurls the hose and wraps it up the length of her right leg. Antonio approaches, carrying a portable radio, which emits the kind of innocuous Spanish pop music often heard in these early Saura-Chaplin films. Here, Saura cuts to a shot of Fernando again spying on his wife and Antonio with his camera lens, this time from inside his stalled car. Teresa, meanwhile, happens upon a latex glove, wraps her right hand in it, and then walks along a wooden plank like a model on a catwalk. Shortly thereafter, she makes a pact with Antonio to perform the reality Fernando expects – to make as if the two of them are having an affair. After a moment, having abandoned the glove, but still wearing the nylon, she plays an improvised game of hopscotch in the sand. Fernando, unsettled, walks over and orders her to take the nylon off – at which point she mockingly asks him if he finds her attractive in it. Here, on this shore where Fernando imagines a profitable future peddling tourism, Teresa strikes a figure not understandable as either a traditional Spanish wife on the one hand, or exotic *sueca* tourist on the other.

Flaunting her sexuality, which in this scene makes ironic use of old, discarded feminine accouterments, Chaplin's Teresa – her voice still animated by acousmatic sound – is a figure both national and foreign, at once domesticated and relatively free. She escapes Fernando's limited way of seeing the world; but Chaplin herself also here begins, in the evident performative pleasure she takes in this last sequence, to explore liminal corners in the pre-determined symbolic structure of Saura's cinema, an intriguing development that continues in their subsequent films. Increasingly, Chaplin's personality in these films cannot be contained by the fascist cultural mechanisms diagnosed by Saura's allegory. But likewise, the very force of her performative personality, as this collaboration with Saura goes on, begins to transcend even the allegorical and symbolic strictures of the films themselves.

## Ana in *Ana y los lobos*

In *Ana y los lobos* (*Ana and the Wolves*, 1973), Chaplin is cast as the second of the three characters named Ana she will play in Saura's cinema. At the beginning of this film, Ana ventures to rural Spain to begin a job at an isolated estate. She will be a nanny for a very strange Spanish family, headed by an ailing matriarch, Mamá (Rafaela Aparicio) and her three sons: José (José María Prada), Juan (José Vivó), and Fernando (Fernando Fernán

Gómez), each of whom has a specific function in Saura's narrative. In Saura's allegorical structure, José is linked to the military, Juan is the embodiment of lust, and Fernando symbolizes religious mysticism (D'Lugo 1991: 108). Jose recruits Ana to help him care for his collection of military uniforms; Juan desires her in ways alternately aggressive and childish; and Fernando engages in mysticism in an isolated cave on the estate, briefly luring Ana into his ritualistic practice near the end of the film.

Chaplin's presence in *Ana y los lobos* embodies the kind of border-crossing, liberated spirit that fascistic forces work to contain; in the film, these forces are the military, predatory lust, and religion (all of which converge around the traditional Spanish family, clearly situated as a repressive mechanism in the allegorical structure Saura employs). But her very worldliness also guarantees that Ana is not a character – and Chaplin is not an actor – who can be contained by fascism *or* allegory. Chaplin creates her Ana as a dynamic, alive woman, one who creatively responds to – rather than one who is subjected by – forces of repression.

The handling of objects is key to Chaplin's performance during Ana's scenes with José. Early in the film, José takes Ana on a guided tour of his collection of Spanish military artifacts: gas masks, regal uniforms, swords. As he guides Ana through the room, Chaplin follows from behind, as José explains his desire to complete the collection. After they climb to a second level connected by a spiraling staircase, José directs Ana to the cloth of a uniform he particularly admires. Just as Elena, when guided by Julián through the artifacts of Spanish folklore in *Peppermint Frappé*, takes her own touristic pleasure in historical artifacts, so too does Ana stop to admire the beautiful surfaces of objects. While José continues to move forward, Ana caresses the textures of a navy blue uniform, guiding her hands through the luxurious feathered plum at the tip of a bicorne helmet adorning the mannequin. Ana soon catches up with José, walking past several displays before stopping at another dummy dressed in the gray, steely garb of a military uniform. She places her left hand on this plastic soldier, guiding her right finger to a hole left by a bullet in its helmet. Her hands circle around these crevices on the head of the mannequin, before José guides her to the next artifact. This pattern – Ana stopping to touch and wonder, José moving forward with pre-determined purpose – shapes the scene, and is a gesture toward the way Chaplin herself performatively slips beyond the pre-determined purpose of the very film she is in. Ana's gestures and movements suggest a desire not simply to preserve but instead to linger on the qualities of these objects, an imaginative tourist daydreaming about what new meanings her movement through space might reveal.

Chaplin's characterization is sharpened in Ana's scenes with Juan and Fernando, the two characters who are meant by Saura to represent lust and religion. Chaplin's work here implies the ironic pleasure Ana takes in her encounters with these men, even as they attempt to contain – or, more precisely, avoid the implications of – her subjectivity. If Chaplin expresses Ana's fascination with José's military collection through the way she guides her hands along the surface of objects, in the scenes with Juan she conveys Ana's bemused, ironic detachment through movement and various ways of positioning herself in the frame. In a later scene, she arrives to confront Juan over a badly tattered doll that the three younger children in the family have unearthed in the back yard. In Saura's allegory, this doll represents "the history of human generations who have been progressively deformed by the cultural patterns that will gradually transform them into the monsters who initially seem so harmless but who, in the final analysis, are predators" (D'Lugo 1991: 115). Doll in hand, she approaches Juan near a window, and when he moves to the other side of the room she glimpses a female foot under a curtain, failing to make itself invisible. Ana, it turns out, has interrupted a tryst. Playing with the newfound knowledge that Juan is hiding another woman in the room, Ana, as Juan approaches her, moves back to the window, leaning against it while looking up and down the length of the window curtains with a sidelong gaze. Resisting, now, another of Juan's amorous propositions – he is shifting back into the predatory behavior D'Lugo suggests is embodied by the fate of the doll – she moves to the other side of the room. Refusing finally his advances, she uses her knowingness to wring out of Juan the revelation that it is Fernando who mutilated and buried the doll.

In her character's subsequent interactions with Fernando, Chaplin's attitude and poise shift notably, from ironic detachment to a measured fascination with Fernando's obsessive religiosity. Early on, the film suggests Fernando is tempted by Ana's erotic presence: as conveyed by a shot inserted by Saura upon Fernando's first meeting with Ana, Fernando is haunted by the image of Ana's long, flowing black hair, possessed of the kind of natural, unconscious sensuality and presence that he is bent on renouncing through his religious practice. Midway through the film, Ana happens upon Fernando in the middle of a seance. He explains his unyielding commitment to a disciplined life bereft of the sins of the flesh, and at this Chaplin moves closer, kneeling down next to him. In a reverse shot, still kneeling next to him, Chaplin questions this commitment, reminding him of the family he is renouncing. In response, he quotes from his book of devotions. Chaplin in turn quotes these; Ana is attempting to possess their meaning. But she cannot quite make the words work, and at this Fernando asks her to leave: to achieve purity, he needs to be alone. She remains, and, after a moment, begins to twirl her fingers through her long hair, the same hair that, as it was seen to blow through the wind earlier in the film, seems effortlessly suggestive of the sensuality Fernando means to renounce through his repressive asceticism. But the gesture stops short of mockery; Ana is treating Fernando more seriously than she has Juan or José, perhaps because he has so far not posed any threat to her. Chaplin's running of her fingers through her hair, to that end, is a gesture that positions Ana somewhere between self-conscious seduction and effortless naturalism. At the same time, Chaplin eschews full disclosure of her character's intentions; if Ana intends to entice, this motivation is hidden behind a facade that is subtler than Fernando's pained piety.

Chaplin pushes further this aspect of her characterization in later scenes involving Fernando, sequences that continues to balance Ana's sexuality – condensed, again, in both Saura's imagery and in Fernando's repressed mind's eye, by her flowing black hair – with a certain self-conscious knowingness of the challenge her presence might pose to the ascetic, repressed Fernando. In the first of these two scenes, Ana returns to the cave with food and wine. Fernando is annoyed by this, but it is Ana's physical, sensual presence that provides the greatest obstacle to his concentration. Chaplin's very manner of presenting her character in this scene expresses an awareness of the effect her presence has; wearing a short black dress that seems like an extension of her black hair in the form of fabric, Ana's simply being there constitutes a challenge to the renunciation of life and desire, of Eros, that Fernando declares. He explains to Ana his recent success at levitation, which he describes as "the leaving behind of all weaknesses," a floating wherein he finds a "suspension of the senses, of the physiological reality . . . One forgets about his body, and rises. Weightless: air of air." Chaplin, still in the center of the frame and facing away from the camera, in a medium shot, is a cascade of black hair; as Gomez circles around her, he expresses Fernando's desire to touch her, for it is Chaplin who ultimately embodies, more vividly than Fernando's old religious books, the combination of ethereality and physicality he seeks through his acts of levitation. Ana seems genuinely curious about this supposed act of levitation, though, and just as Fernando gestures to touch her hair, she turns to face him, asking if perhaps she might levitate too. At this, Chaplin smiles, and moves over to the altar, where she kneels before Fernando's modest shrine, the light from an opening at the top of the cave shining on her face, a challenging combination of both the spirituality Fernando seeks to achieve and the physicality he struggles to reject.

Ana returns, later, for one final sequence in the cave. In this last scene, it is clear she intends to stay for a time; she is sewing together a brown robe she will wear while in the cave, a robe signaling, if only momentarily, her own renouncement of the desire and life her very presence embodied in the previous scene with Fernando. As she sews together this robe, Fernando moves over to her, reading from his religious texts as he sits down next to her. Ana, glancing offscreen at Fernando as he reads, brings the needle and thimble she uses to sew to her mouth; she then glances downward as she continues to guide the edge of the thimble and needle around her lips, shyly looking away at Fernando before returning her gaze to his eyes (Figure 2.10). Chaplin's movements here call up a memory: earlier in the film, Mamá has revealed to Ana, while going through Fernando's old childhood belongings, that she placed a spiked thimble on the child Fernando's hand in an effort to curtail his habit of sucking his thumb. In that scene, Ana reacts with disgust and concern at Mamá's revelation, and her gesture here with the thimble and needle seems, in its transformation of a painful gesture into an erotic one, an effort to correct

**Figure 2.10** Chaplin as Ana, calling up a memory through gesture in *Ana y los lobos*

this childhood trauma, a deft combination in one image of the maternal and sensual qualities at play in these scenes with Fernando. As Chaplin begins to guide her finger fully inside her mouth, Fernando reacts with the repressive fervor the viewer, at this point, has come to expect from him, declaring that they must burn every material possession in the cave.

The challenge Ana poses to all three of the brothers – her modern femininity; her ironic detachment and bemusement in the face of their obsessions; and her sexual agency, which expresses, at various points, autonomous desire and curiosity – is ultimately that against which José, Juan, and Fernando react violently. In Chaplin's characterization, Ana's subjectivity forms an important intervention in the life of this family (even as they fail utterly to comprehend it and ultimately work to punish it). Within the frame of the allegory of *Ana y los lobos*, the vanquishing of Ana at the end of the film points brutally, forcefully, and allegorically to the misogynistic power of the fascist regime that is the subject of Chaplin's and Saura's critique. Nevertheless, Chaplin's performance in *Ana y los lobos* conveys a rich and emotional complexity that exceeds not only the limited view of the three brothers her character encounters, but also the limits of the pre-determined symbolic allegory in which Chaplin as actor and Ana as character are contained.

## Interiority within interiority: *La madriguera* and *Cría cuervos*

During the Franco era, Chaplin also plays Teresa in the earlier *La madriguera*, in 1969, and two characters – María, the suffering mother of Ana, a child whose future self is also played by Chaplin – in *Cría cuervos* (filmed in 1975, during the last year of the Franco regime, and released after Franco's death in 1976). In these films, Chaplin portrays women more firmly a part of the domestic world of bourgeois Spanish life. Gone, in these performances, are the blonde wigs of Chaplin's modish tourist characters in *Peppermint Frappé* and *Stress-es tres-tres*. In *La madriguera* and *Cría cuervos*, Chaplin – speaking Spanish, in her own voice, for most of the duration of both films (dubbing her own performance in the case of *La madriguera* and recording her Spanish on set as the mother in *Cría cuervos*) – plays permanent residents of Spain. (The origins of these characters are nevertheless ambiguous, as Chaplin's Spanish continues to be inflected by her British-American lilt.) Here, her women are fully situated in Spanish domestic life: in both films she plays the wife of a powerful male figure (in *La madriguera*, a factory owner, and in *Cría cuervos*, a decorated general). If Chaplin's other performances for Saura during this period grapple with the consequences of external appearance and perception as well as the inherent border-transgressing aspects of her presence, *La madriguera* and *Cría cuervos* explore, more surrealistically than her other films with Saura of this period, questions of interiority.

## Teresa in *La madriguera*

In *La madriguera* (the title loosely translates to *The Burrow*), Chaplin is cast as Teresa, the wife of a successful industrialist, Pedro, played by Per Oscarsson. Teresa and Pedro have moved into a modernist house, designed by the architect Carvajal, on the outskirts of the Madrid suburbs. At the beginning of the film, furniture trucks deliver old relics that once belonged to Teresa's deceased parents. Amongst these objects are papers revealing their early deaths, when Teresa was a child. These family belongings spark hallucinatory memories in Teresa. Saura's films often incorporate images expressing a character's waking dream or memory: Julián's fantasy of the blonde woman at Calanda in *Peppermint Frappé*, or Fernando's obsession with the affair he imagines his wife is having with his friend in *Stress-es tres-tres*. In *La madriguera*, much of this dream-like, imaginative subjectivity is, for the first time, tethered to Chaplin's character.

*La madriguera* is the only Chaplin–Saura collaboration on which Chaplin receives a screenplay credit. Chaplin's participation in the writing of the film is especially intriguing given its theme of inheritance. In her performance Chaplin makes use of particular objects from her character's childhood, including old photographs, notebooks, and baby teeth she finds amidst the relics. While none of Teresa's photographs are of Geraldine herself (in contrast to *Cría cuervos*, in which we see pictures of a younger Chaplin serving as mementos of her character's personal history), *La madriguera* is nevertheless a film about how the past lingers in the present. In playing Teresa, Chaplin conveys how Teresa incarnates multiple versions of herself, variations of selfhood that seem to emerge from some disturbing dream or memory.

Chaplin's performance in *La madriguera* involves throughout the touching and wearing of textiles, fabrics, and clothes, expressive objects which become intertwined with questions of interiority. On the second evening after the delivery of the family artifacts, Teresa gets up from bed (in her second bout of hallucinatory sleepwalking in the film) and returns to the basement to look through her deceased parents' belongings. Gesturing for Pedro's attention, Chaplin has Teresa guide her fingernails along the surface of her pillow and bedsheet, clawing at fabric like a cat beckoning its distracted master. A cut to the basement: Saura's camera tracks along the wall, looking for Teresa, who has gone missing among these musty objects. Pedro eventually finds her hiding in a tall armoire. He gives her a shawl to wear, to ward off chills; but rather than wear it around her shoulders or torso to protect from the cold, Chaplin wraps it around her neck like a scarf.

Just as she wraps this scarf around her neck, Teresa is gradually enfolding herself, and us, in another reality in these scenes. As the sequence in the basement goes on, Teresa exclaims her desire to play "Sleeping Beauty" with her husband. Arranging an old mattress pad with bedsheets on the floor, Chaplin prepares another mise en scène of fabric and cloth, where she will play Beauty while Pedro incarnates the Prince who wakes her. Saura's framing complements Chaplin's play with clothing; as Chaplin lies down on the mattress, the shawl given to her by Pedro, which she has removed and placed over the edge of a chair, is framed by Saura in the foreground of the shot. Chaplin, meanwhile, poises Teresa as the choreographer of this scene-within-the-scene. Having instructed her husband not to touch her during this performance, Teresa carefully covers herself with her white nightgown, a chaste rendition of the Sleeping Beauty myth that befits the child-like regression into which Teresa now slips. Having arranged the light in the basement to her liking – above Chaplin is a toplight that almost magically transforms this basement into a theatre stage – Teresa cues her husband to begin his share of the performance ("Okay! I'm dead now!"). Childhood has become theater, theater childhood; and in the metaperformance of *La madriguera*, Chaplin creates Teresa as both its central actor and its desiring auteur.

This surreally charged moment presages the next extended passage of the film, another sequence of waking dream in which the couple begins to burrow further into their isolated, repressed psyches. Sending away the cooks for the day, Teresa busies herself in the kitchen; she aggressively kneads bread while Pedro ambles about, looking for coffee. After a large, pleasurable meal, Teresa and Pedro, now in their living room, drink wine. Fabric again weaves its way through Chaplin's performance: her red dress and red belt match the flow of red wine she drinks. As Pedro lies down on the couch, Chaplin goes over to the window and closes the blinds, masking out the light from the outside world – and also preventing, a moment later, a disruptive band of visitors (Teresa's friend, Carmen, Carmen's husband, Antonio, and their two children) from seeing that the couple is at home. Here, Chaplin's performance switches from slightly soused languorousness to a sprightly impishness, as she playfully flits across the living room to avoid these unannounced visitors attempting to peek through the curtain. Through an intercom, Teresa and Pedro listen to the gossipy prattle of Carmen and her husband, still lingering outside the house: Carmen says she suspects Teresa is having an affair, and her husband accuses Pedro of treating Teresa like a caged animal.

Although both are at first distressed by this chatter, a moment later Teresa and Pedro channel it into play, in which they enact parodic versions of Carmen and Antonio's bourgeois decorum. Chaplin, re-entering Saura's frame as if from the wings of a stage, now appears with her long, flowing hair buttoned back (in imitation of Carmen's restrained, respectable appearance), and with a large pillow simulating a pregnancy under the midsection of her red dress, a caricature of Carmen and Antonio's normative tendency to link romance to reproductive sex ("I'd like to have seven babies at the same time!" Teresa squawks, in mocking imitation). Chaplin in this scene travesties the self-satisfied security of a traditional housewife: clutching her protruding pillow-stomach with delight, rocking the baby carriage, and twirling between her fingers the faux pearls hanging around her neck. While she does this, Saura's camera pans to follow her, and she looks directly at the camera itself, as if soliciting the film's viewer (and perhaps the film's female viewer in Franco's Spain in 1969) to join her in the farce. She also bids a reluctant Pedro to join her in this performance, which he does only when she begins to enact the ritual of childbirth: heaving, sweating, her buttoned-up hair coming undone, she produces a porcelain baby wrapped in bedsheets and straw. Pedro chucks the fake infant across the room, the two of them embracing in convulsive laughter.

These games, and Chaplin's manipulations of fabric and clothing, continue as the film nears its end. As if in response to the earlier revelation of the possibility that Pedro might have committed marital infidelity, Teresa suggests that he might have another "type," an idea she links to a black dress he has always wanted her to wear and which he gave her shortly after their wedding. While this conversation unfolds, Saura cues a series of images (suggestive of a memory Pedro had long ago buried) of an apparently dead woman wearing this same dress. Cutting back to the present, the film rejoins the couple at a later moment: Chaplin, after putting on the black dress and contemplating herself in a mirror (Figure 2.11), slowly walks out from behind a partition, wearing lipstick, rouge, and powder. "Stop!" Pedro says, upon seeing her, freezing Chaplin momentarily in a kind of tableau, positioned in-between two other sculptures (relics from her family inheritance) that evoke her posture. Oscarsson's hand jutting into the frame, he gestures for her to come forward, almost as if he were a fashion designer controlling the movements of his latest creation on a model (Figure 2.12). Chaplin circles around his chair, guiding her fingers

**Figure 2.11** Chaplin in *La madriguera*, frozen momentarily in a tableau

**Figure 2.12** Per Oscarsson, offscreen, gesturing toward Chaplin in *La madriguera*

along its edge, all the while defusing the erotic charge of the moment through an acknowledgment that these gestures are not fully her own: "What else does she have to do?", she asks Pedro, sharply, pointing to her lack of control over this fantasy. However, it is precisely her defusing of Eros which allows Teresa to claim control over this hallucination, as she spits in Pedro's face after he leads her to bed, proceeding then to destroy this dress in the garbage disposal.

Marvin D'Lugo has suggested that *La madriguera* ultimately gives centrality to "Teresa's growing consciousness of her entrapment in a constructed social identity" (1991: 88). But the sharpest motif of Chaplin's performance in the final stretch of the film is not growth but destruction: Teresa seeks to eviscerate – rather than simply grow within – the very structures surrounding her. Rather than merely becoming conscious of her "constructed social identity," Chaplin's Teresa uses performance to generate new possibilities and positions, setting different gestures and poses into motion in order to gradually deconstruct the physical reality of the film. To this end, accessories important throughout this performance – fabric, clothing, and make-up – continue to be employed by Chaplin in the film's final scenes. Receiving an invitation from Pedro to join him in the basement, Teresa does so, and is greeted by Pedro, now enacting the role of her authoritarian father. Teresa coquettishly assumes the role of docile schoolgirl while Pedro berates her about her poor marks. Dressed in a yellow turtleneck and plaid dress that evokes a slightly modern variation of a Catholic schoolgirl's uniform, Chaplin has Teresa enact submission, kneeling down before Pedro as she recites a lyric about Santa Catalina. But rather than position Chaplin determinatively, this performance of a repressive rite, remembered from her childhood, initiates a series of destructive gestures: first, a cascade of feathers, falling onto Chaplin as Oscarsson rips apart pillow fabric; Teresa's mounting of Pedro's back as if he were a large dog, reimagining what was a moment ago an act of submission into one of domination; and, one final performance on the main level of the house, as a married couple, gathering for dinner, dressed in traditional, bourgeois garb, a meal which culminates in a series of stylized deaths. First, Pedro discovers Teresa, apparently shot in the head, pretending at suicide; then, Pedro himself is shot down by Teresa at gunpoint outside the home, after he threatens to leave her; and, finally, one final gunshot is heard offscreen, in the film's concluding sequence, from inside the home, presumably Teresa's actual suicide after her apparent murder of

Pedro. That these violent acts remain, on the level of Saura's hallucinatory film, games – rather than verifiable facts within a narrative "reality" – is confirmed by Chaplin's use of make-up in these final sequences: a carefully applied streak of painterly red across the left side of her face, and slightly dashed near the right edge of her mouth. This performative accessory, applied with careful but not verisimilar care to Chaplin's face, serves not as a sign of the character's "real" shedding of blood. The vivid, artificial red of this play-acted "blood" instead reminds us of Jean-Luc Godard's famous dictum that blood in cinema "is not blood, it's red." In *La madriguera*, resistance against the domination of the Franco regime does not happen through finalized narrative resolution or unambiguous political statement. Rather, movement, color, gesture, and – in this film – the touching of fabric, create a playful and stylized aesthetic violence that works to deconstruct – and ultimately, within the bounds of the film, destroy – the demands that a fascist regime places on the body (in *La madriguera*, the body of a woman, but also the body of an actor). Of all these early, Franco-era Saura films, *La madriguera* – less stridently allegorical than *Peppermint Frappé*, *Stress-es tres-tres*, and *Ana y los lobos* – is the greatest, precisely because Chaplin's character's own efforts to slip beyond and ultimately destroy pre-determined structures are at one with the film's own violent, alluring, energetic modernism.

## María and Ana in *Cría cuervos*

In *Cría cuervos*, Chaplin plays two characters, neither of whom exist except as the vision, memory, or possible future of a child. The viewer mainly knows Chaplin in this film as María, mother to three daughters and the suffering wife of a proud military man, Anselmo (Héctor Alterio). One of María's daughters is Ana (Ana Torrent), from whose eyes – for Torrent's large, receptive eyes are a signature feature of her presence in the frame – seem to emerge memories of the mother Chaplin plays. The year is 1975: Franco is dead (at the time of filming, he was still alive, but his demise was everywhere anticipated in Spain, so to some extent *Cría cuervos*, and the performative work that courses through it, are artifacts of that anticipation); and Ana's father is likewise deceased (he has suffered a heart attack in the opening sequence of the film; Ana erroneously believes she has successfully poisoned him with laced milk). Chaplin's character, María, is also dead, although whenever she appears onscreen in *Cría cuervos* she will seem to be alive: for Ana she lives in memory, and so Chaplin, in her performance, invests María with life. This conjuring is an act of memory, one that refuses to let a mother who suffered, under a regime about to be ousted, be forgotten; and in the way *Cría cuervos* is colored by both Torrent's and Chaplin's performative subjectivity, the film anticipates Spain's future while also refusing to forget those who have suffered under its past.

Chaplin's performance in this film also has a pointed political dimension. In *Cría cuervos* Chaplin also plays, in two brief sequences that frame the film as a memory of a childhood experience, the adult version of Ana, in flash-forwards set twenty years after the film's making, in 1995. In a stark, undecorated sequence shot in which the young Ana absconds to her hideaway near the family home, the camera pans away from Torrent and toward the adult version of the character she is playing, as Chaplin's incarnation of Ana in 1995 stares directly into the camera, recounting childhood memories of her mother. Her embodiment of this vision of a "future Ana" creates vertiginous effects in our experience of Chaplin's performance – in this film she is at once María *and* Ana, the very embodiment of a matri-lineage in the body of a single actor. In appearing as both Ana's remembered mother in the 1975 scenes and the future Ana in 1995, Chaplin's presence in the film insists on a future shaped not by Francisco Franco but rather by a woman and the lineage she represents, and by a cross-cultural performer, Chaplin, continuing in Saura's cinema to incarnate an open-bordered Spanish femininity beyond the strictures of nation and tradition.

Photographs are a primary motif of *Cría cuervos* and Chaplin's performance in the film is poetically linked to them. They serve as the backdrop for the film's opening credits, and they are also occasionally glimpsed at various points in the narrative: when the adult Ana, played by Chaplin (her voice dubbed by a native Spanish performer during these moments), begins speaking of her past, Saura cuts to several of these photographs; and at various points the child Ana will guide her grandmother's wheelchair to a wall of photographs so that they may look at them in quiet contemplation. The viewer of the film sees two types of photographs of Geraldine Chaplin in these moments. The first are those from Chaplin's own past, contextualized for the film as part of María's fictional autobiography: from her early society years, before she met Carlos Saura, in which she is gathered around flashing lights and with bouquets of flowers in her hands (for Chaplin, the celebration of a young performer, beginning to step out of her father's limelight in the early 1960s; for María, an early life before a commitment to conventional marriage and children – she was once a celebrated young pianist with a promising artistic future). The other group of photographs are those that have been staged and taken expressly for this film, in which Chaplin assumes various kinds of poses: at the piano, looking toward the camera, in the act of playing María as a young, musical ingénue (Figure 2.13); her arms warmly embracing Ana Torrent; alongside her husband at social events, she the polite bourgeois wife, he dressed in military garb.

Something Roland Barthes says about photography evokes the different levels of performance Geraldine Chaplin projects in these still images:

> Lineage reveals an identity stronger, more interesting than legal status – more reassuring as well, for the thought of origins soothes us, whereas that of the future disturbs us, agonizes us; but this discovery disappoints us because even while it asserts a permanence (which is the truth of the race, not my own) it bares the mysterious difference of beings issuing from one and the same family ... (Barthes 2010: 105)

Chaplin's own lineage is evoked by these images, through those photographs of her, from the early 1960s, that the film re-presents to us as images of María's shortened music career. The presence of Chaplin's

**Figure 2.13** Chaplin posing as María in her days as a young musical ingénue in *Cría cuervos*

own lineage in the frames of these photographs in *Cría cuervos* suggests that something of her own personal history slips into the film. Yet in those other photographs in which she is clearly performing, for the sake of this film, a stilled moment from María's earlier life, the "soothing origin" Barthes speaks of above is strangely, hauntingly absent. María's abandoned ambitions, performed by Chaplin in her frozen gestures at the piano, are a melancholic sign, a future unrealized, and a past that the young child Ana will struggle to understand. But what does issue forth in these still photographs of Chaplin as María is the "mysterious difference of being" of which Barthes speaks: this mother, a voice and body from the past, who lived in an earlier moment, speaks to Ana from within the frame of these old photos, silently. Chaplin's performance in the rest of the film, as the María of whom Ana dreams and wonders, is the film's moving incarnation of the past, which is palpably present even as it is entirely absent within the reality of the film's world.

Given the way ghosts of the past flit through memory in this film, what initially appear as the most virtuosic moments in Chaplin's characterization of María are in relatively melodramatic sequences in which Chaplin commands the tableaux of the frame and expresses suffering. In these striking tableaux, Chaplin comes across as less a ghost in young Ana Torrent's memory and more a figure witnessed by Torrent, who always remains apart from Chaplin during these intense sequences. The mother's suffering is also of a different kind than the child's: Chaplin writhes in pain on the bed, dying and pale, her eyes demonic, speaking in an emaciated rasp of "the lie" that is the reproductive, heterosexual family in the context of this fascist regime, as her daughter looks helplessly on. Or, elsewhere, María lowers her head in tearful, convulsive anguish when she confronts the family patriarch about his amorous liaisons (another moment Ana witnesses from a distance). In such moments, Chaplin's performance in *Cría cuervos* works with a kind of centripetal effect not unlike that of the aforementioned, staged photographs (and similar to the allegorical, tableaux effects in certain moments in her earlier films for Saura): she is positioned centrally in the frame and the anguish of the Franco regime and its brutalities enacted upon women powerfully converge in her anguished expressions.

While such moments in the film unavoidably stand out precisely by virtue of their melodrama, Chaplin is ultimately most memorable in this film during quieter moments of intimacy – moments in which she is much more intimately involved with Ana Torrent. During such scenes, Chaplin has María inhabit, disappear beyond, and reappear along the edges of the film frame and across the more subtle borders of internal frames created by Saura and Chaplin in their collaborative staging of the image. In counterpoint to her work in the film's melodramatic, tableaux-style frames, Chaplin in these other scenes playfully slips in and out of view and in-between visibility and invisibility, incarnating María as an ambiguous but palpable presence in Ana's imagination and memory. Chaplin, in these moments, moves back-and-forth between an ethereal haunting of the edges of the film frame and more intimate, direct, gestural contact with Torrent's character. No longer a witness to Chaplin's performance in these scenes, Torrent is now intimately bonded with her, and in this way *Cría cuervos* becomes a delicate duet between an experienced adult artist and an inexperienced, but preternaturally gifted, child performer.

The first of these moments occurs early in the film. Ana, in the kitchen, is removing some lettuce and chicken's feet from the fridge. From behind her, Chaplin enters the edge of the shot, moving into an internal frame (formed by the edge of the refrigerator on the left and a set of water pipes on the right), her hand raised to her chin in contemplation – Saura cuts to a brief close shot of the chicken feet, suggesting the intertwinement of Ana's subjectivity and her mother's – before María clears her voice and commands Ana's attention. This is a bit of play: María, of course, already has this attention, for she is already here Ana's memory, and unfolds before us a private recreation of lost moments of intimacy. "You can't sleep," Chaplin says, repeating the words Ana has just spoken and now moving further toward the right edge of the frame, now internally re-framing herself on the other side of the image. In addition to her movements across the edges of these internal frames, Chaplin also plays with her glances: her eyes first cast down as she speaks to Ana, she then raises them sharply as María admonishes Ana for being up so late. As Chaplin's performance conveys, this is a mock punitiveness, a playful admonishing betrayed by the warmth and intimacy she expresses toward Ana. As the sequence ends, this playfulness culminates in an intimate embrace between Chaplin and Torrent, in a brief close-up that now elides our awareness of the frame's edge that otherwise serves as such an essential accessory to Chaplin's performance in the scene.

In Chaplin's next appearance as María, she creatively explores the possibilities of an ethereal in-betweenness in a closely framed two-shot. The family housekeeper, Rosa (Florinda Chico), is combing Ana's hair, preparing the child for her appearance at her father's funeral (in the film's opening sequence, the family patriarch has died while in bed with his mistress). Saura frames this action in a frontal shot, with both Torrent and Chico looking directly at the camera in close-up, which doubles here as an implied mirror. Chaplin soon enters from the left, lingering in thoughtful contemplation. Then, after approaching the foreground of the frame, she asks Rosa – a Rosa who now clearly exists only in Ana's waking dream – for the comb. Rosa departs and María begins stroking Ana's hair (Figure 2.14), ostensibly preparing her daughter for the duty of attending the funeral; but Chaplin converts cold duty into warm intimacy, tenderly dipping her face into Torrent's neck and gently biting it, and then asking her, with a whisper, "what if I gave you a big loud kiss on the ear?" Such gestures could be understood as the wish of a ghost to make herself incarnate again, through touch and voice; but Chaplin's whisper also suggests these words are for Ana alone, and the performance's effect here is to create a shared, private bond.

Visions of María usually appear in the film when Ana cannot sleep. It is not surprising, then, that she becomes a more frequent presence in the second half of *Cría cuervos*, as Ana becomes more and more sleepless and haunted. Chaplin's presence in these passages takes on the shape of a lullaby, as María works to coo Ana, frightened by these family tragedies, into dream. At times Chaplin will be seen once more lingering around the edges of the frame, and of internal frames in the image, during Ana's

**Figure 2.14** Chaplin and Ana Torrent, in a moment of intimacy in *Cría cuervos*

sleepless moments, as in a sequence late in the film in which Ana, wide awake in bed at night, imagines seeing her mother walk back and forth in a hallway outside her bedroom, a play of absence and presence that intensifies the ghostly qualities of María. In another sequence, Ana, wandering around the house at night, happens upon her mother writing in a notebook, seated in a chair at the edge of a family room. This is a different staging strategy than in other scenes, in which María emerges from the edge of the film frame, or the edge of an internal frame formed by the mise en scène: here, Chaplin is seated, centered, in repose, as Ana approaches her mother as if encountering a memory (perhaps Ana, by this point in the film, is learning how to face memory directly, rather than have it only well up and surprise). Instructing Ana to go back to bed, María soon realizes that Ana will not do so without a song; at this, Chaplin moves to the piano, tinkling the film's title music. Saura keeps this moment in a long two-shot, so that we may see Chaplin play the song as Ana drifts into sleep. Music is key to Ana's memory of her mother; at other moments, when María is absent, Ana will repeatedly, obsessively spin on her record player the pop song "Porque te vas?" ("Why are you leaving?"). This infectious, yearning pop music is sung by Jeanette, a Spanish-language singer, born in London, whose voice – a Spanish lilt inflected by an English accent – suggestively resonates with the transnational inflections of Chaplin's own presence. In the context of *Cría cuervos*, the song's vocal mix of Spanish and English becomes especially poetic, as Ana uses it to remember the voice of her mother.

Chaplin steps down from the piano to meet Torrent, whose now-sleepy head is resting on the side of a chair, in another intimate two-shot as the camera moves closer; the music has succeeded as lullaby, but before sleep there is another moment for shared intimacy, as Chaplin and Torrent mimic affection. María and Ana perform three varieties of kisses:

> María: "Kiss me like in the movies." [*a peck on the lips*]
> María: "Now like the eskimos." [*Chaplin and Torrent rub noses*]
> María: "And now kiss me –" [*interrupted*]
> Ana: "Like a bear!" [*Chaplin engulfs Torrent in a hug, with laughter*]

These moments of casual and apparently completely natural intimacy may be the most marvelous achievements in the film. And they *are* achievements: as Chaplin reveals in an interview, the child Torrent seemed to despise her on set and it was frequently difficult for the two of them to work together in conveying a mother–daughter bond (see

"Interview with Geraldine Chaplin," *Cría cuervos*, Criterion DVD, 2006). That the two of them nevertheless conjure a very intense intimacy onscreen remains one of this film's marvels.

Chaplin, in these moments when she performatively works the edges of *Cría cuervos*'s frame, again slips beyond the allegorical limits of Saura's cinema, implying a de-centered, feminine future that resists the vestiges of fascism even as it remains undetermined by any kind of simple social message. In this sense the performance is somewhat similar to her work in earlier films with Saura, most especially *Ana y los lobos*. But where in *Ana y los lobos*, and indeed most of the earlier Saura films, Chaplin's performative playfulness mostly involves sexual agency and erotic energy, in *Cría cuervos* her play takes the form of a dreamt message to a young girl, a daughter whose future in Spain will be shaped by what she does with this memory.

## Generative performance in *Elisa, vida mía* and *Los ojos vendados*

Chaplin's performances in *La madriguera* and *Cría cuervos* are engaged with complex questions of interiority and personal memory. Her performances in *Elisa, vida mía* (*Elisa, my life*) and *Los ojos vendados* (*Blindfolded Eyes*) continue that thread, now in relation to themes of creativity and personal authorship. In these films, Chaplin's characters seek new lives through artistry: Elisa, from whom emerges a creative impulse in *Elisa, vida mía*; and Emilia, a shy bourgeois woman, who attempts to become a professional actor in *Los ojos vendados*. These performances frame creativity as a way to imagine new, possible futures, shaping life itself into a kind of artwork.

### Elisa in *Elisa, vida mía*

In his reading of Saura's poetic approach to cinema, Krzysztof Ziarek suggests that *Elisa, vida mía* offers not a literal representation of post-Franco Spain but rather a meditation upon the potential of a creative life at that historical moment. Ziarek writes of how the film keeps "scenes open to a future reemergence, whether as an alternative rendition, a corrected version, or simply as a reimagined occurrence, that gives the film its characteristically open rhythm, a rhythm whose force is that of 'making possible'" (2008: 74). In Chaplin's performance, this "making possible" is felt through her character's encounters with the world around her, as she puts into play words and objects that function for her as totems of generative self-discovery.

At the beginning of the film, Elisa journeys to Segovia, in Castile, with her sister Isabel (Isabel Mestres), along with Isabel's husband and child, to visit their father, Luis (Fernando Rey), on the occasion of Luis's birthday. Luis, twenty years before the events of the film begin, left his life with Elisa, Isabel, and their mother (also played, in stylized flashbacks at various points in the film, by Chaplin), absconding from Madrid to a solitary, ascetic life of writing, translating, and teaching. After Isabel and her family leave, Elisa remains with Luis. Soon thereafter, Elisa begins to undergo her own transformation, as she contemplates leaving her husband after learning of his affair with a close friend of hers. From here, Saura's film explores the intersubjective and poetic relationship that gradually emerges between Elisa and her father. As Luis continues to work on his memoirs and his translations, these writings intersect with Elisa's own discovery of an artistic, poetic sensibility. At various points in *Elisa, vida mía* Luis's writings are spoken aloud in voice-over, occasionally read by Fernando Rey, and at other points by Geraldine Chaplin. Through this mix of voices, Elisa discovers her own poetic authority, although the extent to which this discovery remains finally separable from her father's voice is one of the film's ambiguities.

*Elisa, vida mía* begins with a voice-over by Luis, reading from his writing. His words, although spoken by Luis, are written from Elisa's perspective, which suggests that the character played by Chaplin could in fact be something of a ghost conjured by Luis's prose. The ending of the film loops back to this same voice-over, now spoken by Elisa; this in turn suggests the possibility that Elisa, and not Luis (who has died, Elisa tells us, by the end of the film), might be the authorial source of onscreen events, her father a kind of ghost conjured by her own creative account of her life. The penultimate shot in the film underscores this idea, showing us Elisa sitting at her father's desk, writing her own continuation of a story she inherits. Further, at various points in the film, Chaplin's voice-over will give way to Fernando Rey speaking, and vice versa, while various gestures of writing and art-making by both actors imply that the events in the film are a product of their intermingling aesthetic consciousnesses (at one point, Chaplin is glimpsed assembling a collage of colorful cut-outs, suggesting Elisa's artistic ambitions go beyond literature). Chaplin's performance creates a character whose very existence vibrates with poetry: Elisa might be a figure imagined in her father's private, writerly reverie, or she is perhaps the artist whose imagination weaves together the events of the film. This latter interpretation implies that, within the fiction, Chaplin's presence is itself a poetic achievement born within Elisa's self-reflective, artistic imagination.

The theme of intersubjectivity in Saura's film also invites us to think about the extent to which Chaplin is an autonomous creator of her performance in *Elisa, vida mía* – and by extension, in all of Saura's films – and to what extent Saura's strategies of poetic authorship (which, with *Elisa, vida mía*, have moved beyond allegory) inflect the way Chaplin's movements and gestures are understood. In *Elisa, vida mía*, the poetic relationship between Chaplin's performance and Saura's film style corresponds to the emergence of a connection between Elisa and Luis: just as it is difficult to cleanly separate Luis's writing of his memoirs from Elisa's discovery of personal creativity, so too is it tricky to distinguish between Chaplin's achievements of performance and Saura's achievements as a director. This close link between Saura's role as director and Chaplin's position as actor derives from one of the inspirations for the film, an artifact from Geraldine's childhood. Saura describes seeing "a childhood picture which Oona, Geraldine's mother, gave me (you could see two little girls in the woods and one of them full of emotions, ghost-like) . . ." (quoted in Brasó 2003: 46). This description of the image of the child Geraldine as ethereal and haunting resonates with the theme of a continuity between the past and the present in *Elisa, vida mía*, and implies an intimate connection between Saura's film style and Chaplin's performative work. Just as Luis's writing appears to touch Elisa and draw her into new, creative possibilities, so too do Saura's techniques of framing, staging, and cutting develop complex relationships with Chaplin's gestures and movements, paralleling – if not exactly mirroring – the authorial intersubjectivity at play between Elisa and Luis.

This parallel is introduced when Elisa encounters her father's prose for the first time. While her father is away on a bike ride, Elisa explores the house, finding a small room devoted to writing. It is here that the creative relationship shared between actor and director begins to generate a series of images and gestures that inscribe the mysterious, poetic connection between daughter and father in the story. (This sequence is softly inflected by the lilting presence of Erik Satie's piece "Gnossienne

No. 3" on the soundtrack.) Upon seeing this writing room – internally framed by the curtains, it is presented here as a separate, private space – Chaplin begins to slowly walk toward it. A cut to a tracking shot moves us into the room, showing us its contents: a writing desk, with books and papers scattered upon it. Here, the moving camera serves momentarily as a metonymic embodiment of Elisa's own movement, an early example of the way Chaplin's performance and Saura's filmmaking are joined in the creation of Elisa as an onscreen figure. The camera, after arriving at the room's threshold, stops, as Chaplin picks up the movement of her character, stepping first into the frame and then into the room. The camera shortly resumes its movement, tracking toward Chaplin as she moves near the desk, eventually stopping at the typewriter. Here, the camera again assumes Elisa's point of view as it pans across the contents of Luis's workspace: pens, books, a framed picture of Elisa and Isabel as children, a lamp, a calendar, paper. The camera, and Elisa's eyes, land on several pages of writing. We cut back to a shot of Chaplin as she begins to read these writings, their words now heard by us in her voice-over.

The words Chaplin reads in this sequence speak of disillusionment, personal fatigue, and the desire to begin anew. At first, the words heard in voice-over appear to be tethered to this moment of reading, but as the sequence continues, the precise spatial and temporal source of Chaplin's voice becomes ambiguous. While Elisa reads these lines in a sanguine, unaffected monotone on the voice-over track – it is quite a detached reading of her father's literature – Chaplin's embodied presence in the frame conveys something like anxiety: as she reads, her breathing is visibly deeper, the expression on her face serious and focused. Chaplin's voice-over continues to "read" Luis's words even after she takes her eyes from the page, looking away from the writing and toward a framed photograph of Elisa and Isabel as children. In a reverse shot, Saura shows the photograph, the adult Elisa reflected in the glass frame of the picture. As seen in this reflection, Chaplin is now visibly speaking the words heard on the voice-over, complicating the relationship between vocal performance and bodily gesture, and further muddying the precise source of the words. Are these lines the product of Luis's writings (which we never actually see onscreen, as precise text), or of Elisa's memories of her childhood? Then, a cut back to Elisa at the desk, no longer reading aloud, her eyes darting away from the pages as the voice-over continues to intone Luis's words, glancing about herself as Chaplin's voice continues speaking Luis's words. The orchestration of Chaplin's presence in the frame in relation to Saura's cutting, framing, and camera movements work in concert to "create" Elisa as a figure here and elsewhere in the film, and this collaborative authoring of Elisa as a character parallels the intersubjective authorship at play in the world of the film. These words are not simply "written by" Luis and "read by" Elisa, but seem to emerge from an imprecise space in-between them, just as Chaplin's voice-over seems to float around these objects, any one of which – the writings, her reading, her reflection upon the childhood photograph – might be its source, or its object of fascination.

This connection between father and daughter is also at play in the next sequence when Elisa shares a cup of coffee with Luis and Isabel. The cups and saucers on the table remind Elisa of a dream she once had, of a family dinner in Madrid. As she begins to recount these visions, Saura's camera tracks in slowly toward Chaplin, her eyes gazing offscreen, as if toward a dream space her ensuing words conjure. Elisa tells of how the teacups, saucers, and chandeliers in this dream were quivering, as if stirred by unspoken emotions. Chaplin's voice becomes a voice-over as the film cuts to a tableaux of the dream Elisa is recounting: an image of her mother, her father, and Elisa and Isabel at dinner in their elegantly appointed home in Madrid. In these images, Chaplin plays Elisa's mother (Ana Torrent plays Elisa as a child), sitting silently with her family at the table, reaching out a hand to Luis and gazing up at the ceiling, out-of-frame, at a silver chandelier, which shakes quietly. The repetition of Satie's music strikes a parallel with the earlier sequence, framing Chaplin's words, glances, and gestures in poetic reverie. The character of Elisa created here by Chaplin and Saura, as in the earlier sequence, is a woman whose emotions and reflections are stirred by *things*: just as she was moved by written words on a page in the previous sequence, so too is this dream sparked by coffee cups – and in the dream itself, Chaplin, playing a vision of Elisa's mother, is moved in turn by the quivering objects of the world. Chaplin's Elisa is a character we largely understand through our perception of her emotional and physical reactions, emotions and actions provoked by her encounter with various objects in the narrative (Luis's writings, childhood photographs, cups and saucers) and generated by Chaplin as an actor in conjunction with Saura's filmmaking choices.

But if Elena begins by reacting to the surrounding world, her poetic discovery of self is ultimately tied to her newfound ability to creatively incarnate past memory in an embodied, present moment. Shortly after deciding to stay on with Luis after her sister heads back to Madrid, Elisa goes to sleep while her father stays up writing. Fernando Rey's voice-over, as he works at his desk, recounts Elisa's mother's melancholy life. Elisa's powers of recollection are expressed not through writing but through movement. Music from the opera *Pygmalion* now cued on the soundtrack, Saura cuts to a traveling shot that eventually lands on Elisa in bed. Chaplin is wrapped tightly in the bedsheets, with only her head visible; she is awake, gazing out of frame. The camera panning with her movement, Chaplin crawls under the sheets and squirms to the other side of the bed, one hand slowly emerging from under the bedspread. "I can't make any noise," she whispers, as if she were a child again, carefully creeping about so as not to wake up her parents, lifting the sheets above her head, and very slowly crawling onto the floor. Lying prostrate on the ground, Chaplin, with her hands serving as support, gradually raises her head and her torso up to the air; eyes still closed, a shaft of moonlight from the window illuminates her face and the vertical line of her body (Figure 2.15). She slowly stretches her left hand to the post and sheet of the other bed in the room, letting it rest on the top sheet. Opening her eyes, she turns her head left, with gentle expanses of breath, now guiding her hand across the surface of the bed. This cues a camera movement which reveals Elisa's sister Isabel, as a child, calmly sleeping under the sheets. At this, Chaplin raises her head and looks into the mirror on the other side of the room, her own childhood self (embodied again by Ana Torrent) now occupying the bed. She slowly edges herself over to the bedroom door, and proceeds into the hallway, but this is now the hallway of her childhood home, in Madrid. Guiding her hands along the walls, she eventually lands upon a door: in this room she finds another tableau

**Figure 2.15** Chaplin, awakening from sleep in *Elisa, vida mía*

of her family's past, with Elisa again figured as her own mother, and with Torrent again as the child Elisa.

These moments of Elisa waking, lifting herself up off the ground, and encountering her childhood through a waking manifestation of a dream are not presented as sudden flashbacks or memories. Elisa is not merely "reacting" to a sudden emergence of a memory. As Chaplin's performance carefully conveys, these are memories conjured – reimagined and newly incarnated – by Elisa through her movement and gestures. The crawling out from under the bed, the lifting of her body, the caress of the bedsheets, the touching of the hallway walls: these do not suggest a character under the spell of memory, but rather one who is working to generate some understanding of a memory that she might dream within, walk through, touch. This marks a significant development in the Chaplin–Saura films: in the earlier, Franco-era work, no matter the vividness of subjectivity and personality of Chaplin's characters, they were often contained, subject to, and sometimes victims of, history and memory. By contrast, in *Elisa, vida mía*, Elisa moves through the world, and the world of memory, in ways that give her creative agency over her life – her decision to leave her husband is cemented shortly after the moment described in the previous paragraph. For her, the past is not something to which she will be subject but with which she will tangle poetically. Likewise, if this moment of performance is also partially shaped by Saura's movement of camera and choice of music, this is nevertheless *not* an instantiation of a director "shaping" his actress, his muse, to suit his vision, à la *Pygmalion* myth. As Elisa discovers herself, so too does Chaplin perform this moment with assurance, with the authority of a performer who can now no longer be taken as anything other than her own creation, an established citizen of Spanish cinema.

And so it is suitable that Elisa's gradual transformation of her life is conveyed as a discovery of performance, an active and imaginative inhabitation of the fluid boundary between waking life and memory. Part of the gift Elisa discovers, a gift any aspiring writer or artist longs to have, is her ability to conjure and inhabit several different subjectivities at once. If Elisa will, in the penultimate image of the film, take up her father's authorship, assuming after his death a position at the writing desk which is her inheritance, her own creative voice is expressed by Chaplin through her poise of body and its styling. After she returns from a final meeting with her husband, Antonio, Elisa breaks down emotionally in front of her father before retreating to her bedroom in solitude. In the next sequence, as the sounds of the *Pygmalion* opera again waft in on the soundtrack, Chaplin, facing the camera in a medium close-up shot frontally framed by Saura, pulls off a thin exfoliating mask (Figure 2.16). A jump cut transitions to another shot of Elisa, framed from the same position, putting on one of her mother's elegant dresses, tossing her hair before tying it back. Then, Elisa puts on her mother's shoes; in the next shot, she begins applying eyeliner, drawing connecting lines from her eyelids to her eyebrows and with these gestures transforming her face into another kind of mask (Figure 2.17). In this striking shot in which Elisa paints her face,

**Figure 2.16** Chaplin, facing the camera in a medium close-up shot frontally framed by Saura, pulls off a thin exfoliating mask in *Elisa, vida mía*

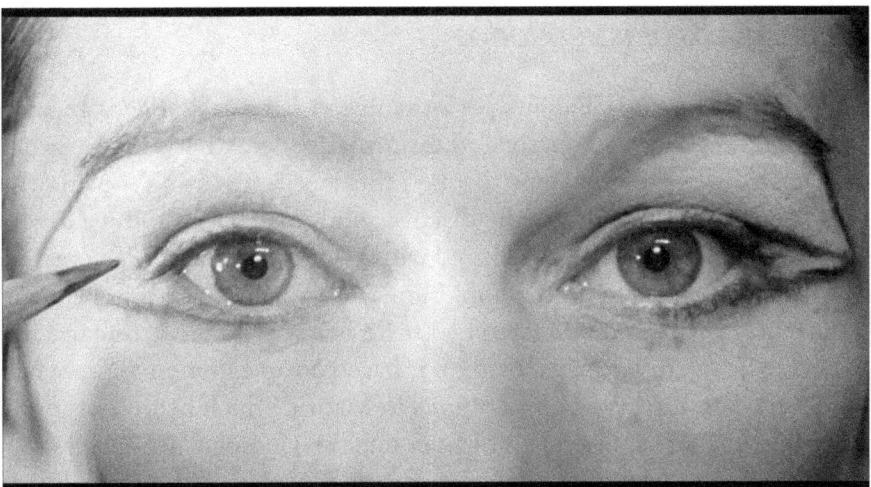

**Figure 2.17** Elisa applies eyeliner, transforming her face into another kind of mask in *Elisa, vida mía*

Chaplin's eyes momentarily inhabit the entirety of Saura's frame, the two familiar beauty marks under her eyes now decorated by Elisa's theatrical make-up. Glancing into a mirror, as if at another self, Chaplin then takes a glass of water and begins to walk – almost catatonically, her gaze fixed out of frame – toward Luis's study, her lip beginning to mime the opera *Pygmalion* playing on the soundtrack.

But again, here she is no figure brought to life by a Pygmalion. When Elisa arrives in her father's study, she shuts off his cassette player (the source of the opera heard on the soundtrack), bringing an end to the opera and its various implications. No man has wrought these changes in her person: they are Elisa's own theatrical stylings. And a transformation is clearly evident here, although who Elisa is precisely becoming is ambiguous – a future version of herself? An incarnation of the memory of her mother? The vision of the murdered woman whose bleak end was earlier narrated by Luis? The answer is less important than the very act of creative becoming witnessed here, the use of gesture and movement and make-up to inhabit another personality, to create another way of living. This is what Chaplin, the actor, does for a living: and, now, for Elisa, it is her life. With these striking images lingering in memory, it is certainly possible to imagine Elisa at her desk, after her father's death at the end of the film, writing away the hours, inscribing with ink on paper new women and new subjectivities, possible future lives that Chaplin herself has inscribed performatively throughout the film.

## Emilia in *Los ojos vendados*

As in *Elisa, vida mía*, Chaplin's performance in *Los ojos vendados* engages with questions of generative, transformative creativity. The earlier film explores these questions through the motif of writing – using the performing body to express the discovery of a writerly self. But *Los ojos vendados* is more directly concerned with performance as itself a creative act. Chaplin's character in the film, Emilia, is an aspiring actor rehearsing a stage play written and directed by Luis, a playwright and acting teacher played by José Luis Gómez. The film is based on an experience Saura had in 1977, when he served on a tribunal in Madrid which heard testimony from victims of right-wing political torture (D'Lugo 1991: 147–8). In the opening sequence of *Los ojos vendados*, Luis listens to similar testimony, from a woman named Inés (Gabriela Roel), a political activist who delivers an account of her kidnapping and torture at the hands of domestic terrorists. It soon becomes clear that Luis is himself facing intimidation from these same brutes, as he attempts to stage his version of Inés's story. Developing alongside this narrative is Luis's budding romance with Chaplin's Emilia. Emilia desires to act, and she sees her relationship with Luis as an opportunity to discover a more authentic identity after several years in an abusive and unsatisfying marriage with her husband, Manuel (Xabier Elorriaga). While Emilia does appear to discover a more liberated self through her relationship with Luis, the film also suggests that personal, expressive desire does not necessarily square with the making of political art. In *Los ojos vendados*, it is precisely the liberated self Emilia discovers in her rehearsals with Luis that becomes restrained and repressed as she incarnates Inés on the theatrical stage. In this, Chaplin's performance in *Los ojos vendados* reflexively explores the unintentionally repressive aspects of well-intentioned political art.

From her first appearance in the film, Chaplin's performance develops parallels with the figure of Inés whom Emilia will eventually play on stage. When first glimpsed in the film, Inés, during her testimony, is seen wearing reflective glasses, in which the viewer glimpses reflections of the public audience before her. In her first appearance as Emilia in a subsequent scene, Chaplin appears similarly wearing glasses, but their black shades, rather than reflecting what is before it, mask her eyes. Further, while Inés speaks of her eyes being blindfolded by the terrorists who kidnap her, Emilia, after she removes her glasses during a conversation with Luis, also draws attention to her eyes. She wants him to notice that she has had work done, wrinkles removed around her eyelids (she is anxious about appearing too old to begin an acting career). "Ta-da!" Chaplin announces, after removing her glasses and raising her hands in the air like a magician, conjuring a new face on a private theatrical stage meant for Luis's gaze; to him, she looks the same, but she is attempting here to mold herself into a possible actress, which requires more self-conscious self-presentation. As the conversation continues, and as Emilia discloses her acting ambitions, she knits, her eyes drawn back and forth between this activity and Luis: she is giving a tentative performance for this director, edging herself into a public persona, even as the knitting needle and thread pull her back from a social disclosure of self, as she busies her hands with a solitary, domestic task.

Chaplin here is developing intriguing parallels between the violent political repression of Inés and the oppression of Emilia, who is stuck in an abusive relationship with her husband and whose anxieties about her physical appearance suggest an inherent sexism in the theatrical world in which Luis operates. After this initial encounter with Emilia, as Luis continues to think about his stage play about Inés, he begins to imagine her possibly playing the main role, as subjective shots imagine Inés's torture, suggesting the mind's eye of Luis as he contemplates his stage creation, with Chaplin now embodying Inés. But Emilia has some work to do before she is herself able to incarnate this character quite so fluidly. Emilia joins the first rehearsal of the play after it is already in progress, as Luis's students (most of them younger than both Emilia and Luis) practice a series of contorted physical exercises designed to generate a malleable, flexibly performative body. When Emilia arrives on this scene, Chaplin's turtleneck sweater and tightly wrapped hair suggest a private figure uncomfortable in this new social world. Emilia's reserve – her stillness, her withheld gestures, her pinned-back hair – is placed in sharp contrast to the freely flowing limbs of the confident students. Emilia soon joins in the exercises; but the staccato rhythm of Chaplin's bodily movements – rigidly alternating between jutting, forward gestures and reserved stillness – are thrown into relief against the fluid convulsions of the bodies surrounding her.

As the film progresses, Emilia's relationship with Luis becomes crucial in her gradual liberation from an unsatisfying life. Nevertheless, Chaplin's performance in *Los ojos vendados* underscores how Emilia's discovery of creativity is the product of her character's individual strength and vision. Ironically, though, it is precisely this expressive individuality that is ultimately restrained by the allegorical conception of Luis's stage play. (In this sense, *Los ojos vendados* is something of a self-reflexive meditation on Saura's own earlier strategies of containing Chaplin's performances in predetermined allegories.) During a subsequent rehearsal scene in which Emilia reads her part as Inés in public for the first time, Luis reminds her that she does not need to exactly follow the script, inviting improvisation. Here it is implied that Emilia has creative agency in the co-creation of this stage play with Luis, a reflection of Chaplin's own creative participation in the authoring of these films with Saura. But Emilia's own "ad-libbing" in the rehearsal room does not take the form of a physical expressivity of gesture: in the sequence, Chaplin remains absolutely still, looking past the edge of the frame as if in contemplative reverie, perhaps imagining the scene she is to rehearse in her mind's eye. Standing in front of a lectern while she embodies Inés recounting her capture and torture at the hands of terrorists, Chaplin remains still while Saura cuts to a series of subjective shots showing us what Emilia imagines as she reads these words. These subjective images, which unfold like a film-within-a-film, present for us a visceral, emotional reenactment of Inés's story, distinct in its immediacy from the rather Brechtian stage play Luis will eventually mount. In these images, Chaplin plays an Emilia now fully imagining herself as Inés, acting out her attempted escape from her kidnappers as Emilia reads the words from the script describing these events in the rehearsal room. Notably, in these subjective shots – which represent only how Emilia, practicing her part in the rehearsal room, imagines they might have played out – we are shown Chaplin-as-Emilia-as-Inés running away, screaming for help, and begging her captors for mercy, even as Emilia in the rehearsal room stands perfectly still. The dramatic and physically expressive performance is a product of Emilia's mind's eye, a sign of the creative vision she has within her to take on this character. But in contrast, Emilia's own "performance" in the rehearsal room within the diegetic world of *Los ojos vendados* requires stillness, restraint, and an almost trance-like lack of expressivity.

In this way, *Los ojos vendados* – the penultimate film of the Chaplin and Saura collaboration, before the end of their personal and professional relationship the following year – functions as a reflection upon their artistic partnership, which has balanced the work of a remarkably expressive actor with the allegorical conceptions of a politically astute filmmaker. The final scene of this film ends this reflexive exploration on an ambiguous note: Luis's stage play premieres, with Emilia playing Inés – now quite like the one played by Gabriela Roel in the first sequence of the film – and with her eyes now hidden behind reflective glasses and with her face and head wrapped in a shawl. Here she speaks at the lectern about her character's political kidnapping and torture, a repression that is matched by the restraint required of Emilia as she keeps her own face nearly hidden, her body free of flowing movements. Near the end of the diegetic scene, two gunmen erupt from the audience and apparently shoot Emilia, Luis, and nearly everyone else on stage and in the audience dead. Is this part of the performance within the diegetic world of the film, or an actual and fascistic disruption, within that same diegesis, of the theatrical work Luis and Emilia have strived together to create? In either interpretation, Chaplin's Emilia finds herself physically restrained and restricted: either by the allegory of Luis's stage play, which, in the physical and expressive restraint it demands from Emilia as she embodies Inés, restricts how Emilia might "author" this work through the movements of her body; or by a devastating act of violence in the fiction itself, which brings Emilia's life to an end.

But an earlier, and much more apparently straightforward scene, is perhaps the film's secret coda to the Chaplin–Saura relationship. This scene is difficult to experience today apart from the knowledge that, shortly after this film was made, Chaplin and Saura's private and professional relationship would end. In this bedroom scene, ostensibly separate from the public world of the theater and rehearsal space in which Emilia and Luis are at other points involved, Emilia recounts for Luis a dream she has had. Chaplin sits up in bed and against a wall (as Gomez gets up and walks offscreen), carefully and with a half-awake soft-spokenness, describes in words the moving pictures that have flitted through Emilia's dreamy sleep. She describes the images she has glimpsed while dreaming, as Saura's camera begins to slowly track toward Chaplin as she speaks (the shot begins in a long medium shot, and ends in a shot of Chaplin in close-up; see Figure 2.18):

> How would I put it? They looked liked pictures where people had been surprised mid-walk. The people were there, but they looked surprised, with their usual gestures frozen … as if life had been stopped in time. I started walking down the street. I went into a fashion boutique. It was such a bizarre place. A really weird place. Huge, very big. And there wasn't a soul there. I was walking around inside, like I was looking for something, someone, but there was no one there. So then … I stuck my head out over some hangers and I saw a curtain that was cracked open, and inside there was a mirror where I could see the reflection of this really beautiful young woman. A really beautiful young woman who was trying on a skirt and was looking at herself in the mirror. She had an amazing body. Her skin was … so … I approached the changing room, and she was there looking at herself in the mirror. I felt like touching her. So I reached out my hand and suddenly I look into the mirror, and I can't move. The young girl starts moving like everything's fine. She finishes putting her skirt on, then she puts on a blouse, she leaves, and I stay there … paralyzed. Looking at myself in the mirror …
> [*Luis, from offscreen, asks who the girl was.*]
> She looked like someone, but I don't know who.
> [*suddenly*]:
> She looked like one of your students. They're all in love with you, you know? She looked like one of your students.

No other moment of Chaplin's performance in *Los ojos vendados* is more moving than this one; it is Emilia's most stirring ad-lib in the entire film. Freed entirely of Luis's script, and now exploring her own dream, her account of the images she saw while sleeping reflects many of the

**Figure 2.18** Chaplin as Emilia, recounting a dream in *Los ojos vendados*

themes of the film: the anxiety about aging; the potential pitfalls of a male–female collaboration in the performative arts, when the male is the director and the female is the actor; an anxiety over other accouterments of appearance (it is notable that this dream occurs in a fashion boutique); and the ongoing fear of being replaced by a younger, newer performer.

That eventually Saura himself moved on to collaborations and personal relationships with other female performers gives this moment, in retrospect, a sharply reflexive and autobiographical tinge; and it suggests how much *Los ojos vendados* is also about Chaplin herself working through the complex implications of her work with the director. It is notable that, in Emilia's account of the dream, gestures are frozen, movements stopped, all except those of the younger actress (whom Emilia, with a little jealousy, compares to Luis's students), who moves freely. The moment reminds us again of the limits of performative expression in Saura's allegorical works, limits Chaplin tests and expands, to various degrees, in all the films, where her gestures and movements work in creative counterpoint to conceptual schemata set in place largely before gesture and movement have even begun.

## Ana in *Mamá cumple 100 años*

Six years after the completion of the 1973 film *Ana y los lobos*, and one year after *Los ojos vendados*, Geraldine Chaplin makes *Mamá cumple*

*100 años* (*Mama Turns 100*, 1979), her final film with Saura. Rather than functioning as a straightforward sequel to or simple continuation of *Ana y los lobos*, *Mamá cumple 100 años* works instead as a more complicated aesthetic reimagining of the earlier work. At the beginning of the film – which is set some eighteen years after the events of *Ana y los lobos*, meaning still some eleven years ahead of the year of release of *Mamá cumple 100 años* itself – Ana returns to the same family estate. But *Mamá cumple 100 años* seems to occur throughout in some alternative timeline that acknowledges the world of *Ana y los lobos* even as it changes and revises the rules of its own narrative game. In contrast to the serious detachment of the earlier *Ana*, the tone established throughout *Mama cumple 100 años* is mostly one of comedy (for Saura on this subject, see Castrow 2003: 53).

Likewise, Geraldine Chaplin's performance in *Mamá* is one that thoroughly reincarnates and reconceptualizes an earlier character and her possibilities. As if to foreground the idea that *Mamá cumple 100 años* is a new imagining, rather than a literal continuance, of the earlier mise en scène of *Ana y los lobos*, Saura begins and ends the film with a *pasodoble*, a modern, formal presentational arrangement that reflexively acknowledges its self-conscious embodiment of archetypes. Given this, a traditional auteurist perspective might take *Mamá cumple 100 años* as one more in a series of "studies" of Geraldine Chaplin by Carlos Saura, amplified by the fact that individual films in this series are themselves preoccupied with the idea of doublings and repetition: in *Peppermint Frappé*, Chaplin plays "doubled" characters; in *Cría cuervos* she plays the adult versions of both a mother and a daughter; in *Elisa, vida mía*, she is both the subject of her father's narration and, it is implied, the eventual author of a narrative that includes her father as a character; and in *Los ojos vendados*, she is both an actor in a film about political reality *and* an agent in political reality itself. These repetitions undoubtedly serve a meaningful function in Saura's work as auteur, functioning as temporal signposts that chart the director's work across a quickly changing social reality.

But Geraldine Chaplin does more in *Mamá cumple 100 años* than serve as object of repeated study for an auteur's musing. More profoundly, through her act of revisiting the same character seven years later, Chaplin is studying *herself* through her performance in this film, becoming an actor who now takes herself as her very muse. Throughout the film, this new Ana, upon her return to the family's estate, will experience moments of sudden, performative *déjà vu*, that underscore the idea that this film is not only Saura's reshaping of his earlier conceits, but also Chaplin's own reflection upon her very presence in the frame, and upon the nature of her performative body and its various capacities for resurrecting and reshaping earlier poses and postures. Something like this idea is a key motif of this book, which has suggested that Chaplin creatively reshapes her father's cinematic figurations. But in this work with Saura this reshaping and reimagining are now more about how she inherits her own earlier, past work. That her character is aligned with properties of reflection and reflexivity is underscored in Chaplin's very first appearance in *Mamá cumple 100 años*, in which Ana snaps a Polaroid of the family estate upon emerging from the car. In terms of the character, it reminds us that Ana is still something of a tourist, taking snapshots of a Spain to which she only tangentially belongs. But in the larger frame of Chaplin's work as a performer, this moment of photographic preservation and preparation for future remembrance frames this performance by Chaplin in the ensuing film as one acutely aware of its place in time, as if she were self-consciously creating a performance meant less for the audience of 1979 than for a future audience – one that might even contain Chaplin herself – contemplating her past presence, and her retrospective place in a larger cinematic history.

This idea becomes crucial at one moment in the film, in which Saura cuts to a flashback from the earlier *Ana y los lobos*. Mamá and the entire family are visiting the grave of her deceased son, José. There is already a self-reflexive tinge to this moment, given that the actor who played José in the earlier film, José María Prada, died the year prior to the filming of this scene. As Mamá speaks of José, the camera begins to slowly track in toward Chaplin, who stands near the back of the gathering, eventually resting in a close-up of her intense gaze upon José's tombstone. At this, the film cuts to a flashback directly taken from a sequence in the earlier film, described earlier in this chapter, in which Ana helps José with his collection of musty military uniforms. There is an appropriately recursive quality to the selection of this particular flashback, for in the scene Ana and José are preoccupied with the fitting of an old uniform on the bust of a dummy, gestures which foreground, in ways the earlier film (and performances) could not possibly anticipate, the obsession in *Mamá* with the way in which a present-tense body begins to take on qualities of the past. The moment is perfectly readable as Ana's own remembrance of her earlier, and haunting, interaction with the departed José. But the direct juxtaposition of Chaplin's visage, at the time of filming in 1979, with footage from her performance in this earlier film, also means that, in its final constructed form, this sequence in *Mamá* is also presenting us Geraldine Chaplin reflecting upon an earlier incarnation of herself. This is intensified later in the film when Fernando, sitting alone in his bedroom, begins once again, as he does in the first film, to pine for Ana. As he yearns, the film cuts to a shot of Chaplin, in a dress with arm-length sleeves that flow like leaves in the breeze, arms outstretched as if in flight (Figure 2.19). (Fernando yearns to achieve flight in this film, but in this image his desires for aviation are conflated with his desires for Ana.) Remarkably, however, this is *not* a flashback from the earlier film. Instead, the film presents new footage, filmed for *Mamá cumple 100 años* in 1979, of Chaplin reincarnating a vision of her earlier Ana. Both of these "flashbacks" to *Ana y los lobos* – one in which Chaplin is confronted by footage of herself from the earlier film, the other in which Chaplin herself reanimates the presence of the same character – are sharply self-reflexive moments, implying a relationship between Chaplin and her earlier performances, and suggesting Chaplin's ability to reflect upon, and even reincarnate, aspects of that earlier work.

But unlike the rather serious *Ana*, the later *Mamá* is a comedy which, from the outset, acknowledges that Ana is herself a completely fictional

**Figure 2.19** Chaplin, in a dress with arm-length sleeves that flow like leaves in the breeze, arms outstretched as if in flight, in *Mamá cumple 100 años*

and aesthetic creation, subject to perpetual reincarnation by the actor who embodies her. This conceit frees the viewer of *Mamá cumple 100 años* to appreciate Chaplin's performance less for its accrual of psychological or narrative meaning than for the ongoing variation of her presence: for the way in which Chaplin now takes Ana less as a legibly "psychological" incarnation of a possibly existing human person, and more as a point of departure for the ongoing freedoms possible in posing, gesturing, and moving in cinema – freedoms that, in post-Franco Spain, are felt in new and potentially liberating ways.

In the recursive framework of this film, Chaplin comes to represent nothing less than cinema itself, or an idea of the cinema as a source for performative freedom. As the film continues, it becomes clear that Saura's conception in *Mamá* is, as in the earlier *Ana*, still largely an allegorical one, in which specific characters, as in the earlier film, fulfill pre-determined symbolic functions: Mamá (Rafaela Aparicio) represents the memory of the past; her granddaughter Carlotta (one of the children from the earlier film, now grown, and played by Ángeles Torres) is associated with José's musty old uniforms, suggesting the dangerous residue of fascism in a member of the younger generation; and her other, now-grown granddaughter Natalia (Amparo Muñoz), with whom Ana's husband Antonio (Norman Brisky) has an affair, represents the sexual liberation of post-Franco Spain. But Chaplin, who again speaks Spanish with her own distinctive inflection, tends, as she always does in these films, to represent something that slips beyond the borders of Saura's schema. In one sequence, the family is gathered in the basement of the house, prowling through old clothing Mama has kept in boxes. While Carlotta tries on José's old military uniforms and as Natalia unearths skimpy lingerie, Chaplin unearths a feathery, ostentatious hat that would not be out of place in a society comedy from the 1930s. "Fred Astaire!" Norman Brisky announces, as he tries on an aristocratic tuxedo that here matches Chaplin's try at a kind of Ginger Rogers. Where the other characters in this sequence are associated with clothing that symbolically aligns them with sex, politics, and religion in a changing Spain, Chaplin, in her final film with Saura, is associated instead with something more expansive, something more difficult to pin down: the cinema itself. Whatever else Chaplin represents in Saura's cinema, as this moment in the film makes clear, she also *is* cinema, a fact that becomes especially important in some of her other collaborations (including especially her work in the modernist films of Jacques Rivette, explored in the fourth chapter). This aspect of Chaplin's last performance for Saura ultimately reminds us that her work for this director, while still very inscribed in his allegorical narratives, ultimately gestures beyond that framework, developing an interfilmic resonance with her other performances that functions relatively autonomously from Saura's work as auteur.

# Chapter 3
# The Circus: Geraldine Chaplin in the cinemas of Robert Altman and Alan Rudolph

"This isn't a circus, it's a wedding!" So exclaims, to baffled waiters and chefs, wedding planner Rita Billingsley, Geraldine Chaplin's character in Robert Altman's *A Wedding* (1978). Hurriedly arranging food and flowers like a beleaguered film director might attempt to organize chaos into ordered mise en scène (Figure 3.1), she also prefaces each of the ceremonial events – the cutting of the wedding cake, the throwing of the bouquet – with a loquacious description of that ceremony's purported historical significance and meaning. She directs people, too, humorously assembling servers and cooks to double as wedding guests when it becomes apparent that a good number of those invited will not be attending. But despite Rita's toil, the wedding in *A Wedding* is a glorious disaster, and Chaplin's characterization of Rita's organizational failure a source of humor.

Chaplin's function as a kind of surrogate director in *A Wedding* recalls her character of Opal in her first film for Altman, *Nashville* (1975).

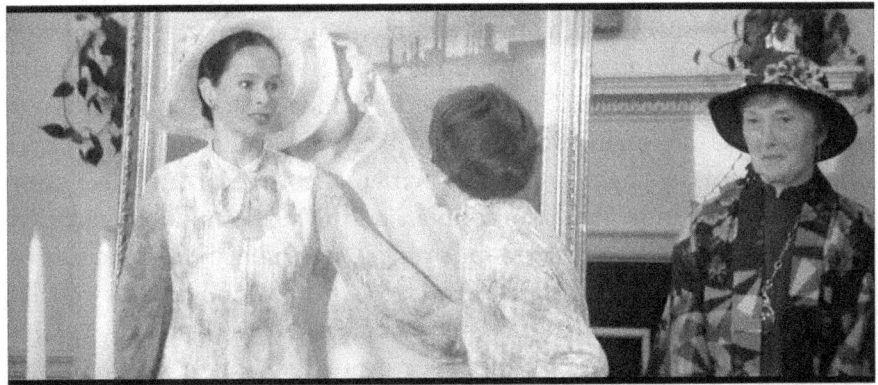

**Figure 3.1** Chaplin, as wedding planner Rita Billingsley, in *A Wedding*

Altman's mosaic sardonically depicts both the country music industry of Nashville and a political campaign for a fictional presidential candidate who has made the city his latest stop. The film is a sprawling ensemble, and Chaplin's role in it has been described as a kind of implicit "tour guide" (Stuart 2000: 65) for viewers. The chatty Opal, who fools nearly everyone into believing she is a reporter for the BBC, is the single character in *Nashville* who, at one point or another, encounters nearly all the others. But the first thing she guides us toward, in this film about the American obsession with celebrity, is herself: "I'm Opal!" she gleefully exclaims, from behind the glass in a recording studio as an annoyed recording artist, Haven Hamilton (Henry Gibson), orders her out of the room. Her performance throughout underscores Opal's amusing efforts to attain a position of knowledge as she attempts to craft something of a narrative in her "reporting" about the various events and people she witnesses. And, just as Rita fails to successfully organize mise en scène in *A Wedding*, so too does Opal fall humorously short of narrative authority in *Nashville*.

As the previous chapter has suggested, Geraldine Chaplin achieves substantial creative agency in her performances in Spain for director Carlos Saura. In her three films in the United States for director Robert Altman – *Nashville*, *A Wedding*, and *Buffalo Bill and the Indians, or Sitting Bull's History Lesson* (1976), in which she is cast as Annie Oakley – Chaplin also attains notable creative control over her characterizations. A performative freedom is likewise at play in her three films for Altman protégé Alan Rudolph – *Welcome to L.A.* (1976), *Remember My Name* (1978), and *The Moderns* (1988). The methods of both directors privilege the creative contributions of actors. Altman's films, in particular, enable actors to improvise, revise dialogue, and invent character traits, freeing them from the shackles of a pre-determined conception (see, for more on Altman's use of improvisation and his appreciation for actors, Wexman 2015: 372–4). But where Chaplin's performances in her films with Saura draw us *inside* (sensually, erotically, and psychologically) the worlds of her characters, immersing us in complex cinematic images that reflect upon the place of the individual, the couple, and the family under a repressive dictatorship, her performances in Altman tend to begin from a position of emotional and ironic distance. And from this position, at least initially, a viewer is free to laugh at Chaplin's characters, as they comically occupy ostensible positions of authority (surrogate director in *A Wedding*, a "narrator" in *Nashville*, and performer in a theatrical production in *Buffalo*

*Bill*). All of this, of course, happens precisely because of Chaplin's own performative ability, the improvisational skills she uses to make us laugh.

In the introduction, I suggested that Charlie Chaplin's direction of his daughter in *A Countess from Hong Kong* – a film that takes a droll perspective of its maker's own tendency, in his earlier sound films and in *The Great Dictator* especially, to earnestly speechify – could be understood as an instruction in the value of performative irony. In her films made in the United States that I will discuss in this chapter, Geraldine Chaplin's powers of performative irony and reflexivity are strengthened and sharpened. Her attractive but unconventional screen presence did not lead to major stardom in mainstream Hollywood after her initial breakthrough in the international coproduction *Doctor Zhivago*. Nevertheless, she found her place in American cinema – in particular the films of Robert Altman and Alan Rudolph – through performances that are legible as critiques of the very star system that, in Hollywood at least, kept her at the margins. Her performances in these films for Altman and Rudolph suggest a model for an alternative and sharply sardonic variation upon American stardom, one shaped less by glamour and national identity, and instead shot through with reflexivity, eccentricity, and ironic play.

If the viewer begins in a position of distance and detachment from Chaplin in her films for Altman, her performances do eventually find – in tandem with Altman's filmmaking strategies – ways of connecting us emotionally to what turn out to be, finally, very human characters. A reverse sort of logic informs her films for Alan Rudolph. There, the viewer often approaches her daydreaming characters from a close and intimate point of view that only later gives way to understanding and narrative revelation. At least one of her characters for Rudolph – Emily in the remarkable *Remember My Name* – achieves what Rita in *A Wedding* and Opal in *Nashville* could not: a kind of diegetic and authoritative performativity that enables her to authorize her place in the film's world in the form of covert, sly manipulations of mise en scène. Her performance as Emily in *Remember My Name* is one of Chaplin's great achievements in cinema, all the more so for being Chaplin's only leading role in a major American film.

This chapter focuses primarily on Chaplin's work in films for Altman and Rudolph, but it ends with a discussion of her remarkable performance in the role of Lily Bart in a 1981 telefilm adaptation of Edith Wharton's *The House of Mirth*, broadcast on PBS in the United States. Chaplin's Lily vividly desires a theatrical and artistically defined life, even as she remains subject to a patriarchal society which sets limits around her pleasure; Chaplin's incarnation of Lily is another of her remarkable – and in this case sadly underseen – achievements in American cinema.

## Acting in Altman's circus

Geraldine Chaplin's first appearance for Robert Altman, in *Nashville*, as the logorrheic Opal – "reporter for the BBC" – carries autobiographical resonances. The screenwriter of the film, Joan Tewkesbury, reports that Chaplin's characterization of Opal is largely based on the actor's own experiences as a celebrity: "I was in Cannes with Geraldine in 1974, and every time she would walk down the street there'd be ten or fifteen Opals chasing her with tape recorders," Tewkesbury recalls. "Her whole life she'd been pursued by people following a famous man's daughter, trying to take a picture or ask her a question. So what she did really was show what she's been plagued with all her life" (quoted in McGilligan 1991: 412).

Altman's improvisatory methods as a director – which give great freedom to actors in the interpretation and execution of roles – enable Chaplin to find her own relationship to the material, creating a comical character the audience is meant to understand as absurdly in thrall to celebrity culture. This method involves incorporating unexpected aspects of the actor's life into the performance. For example, when Chaplin revealed to the director, just prior to the start of filming, that she was pregnant (with Shane Chaplin, her son with Carlos Saura), Altman did not miss a beat. "I was pregnant – I thought I'd be fired for that," Chaplin recalls. "Bob said: 'That is just something Opal would do'" (quoted in Zuckoff 2010: 280). In his typically generous way, Altman gave Chaplin the freedom to define her character, which in this case partially involved making her own decisions about the clothing in which Opal was to appear, a wardrobe that also served to mask the pregnancy.

Although rarely noted in Altman scholarship, the journalist most strongly evoked in Geraldine's characterization of Opal (always with tape recorder in hand, ready to record the answers she hopes her obnoxious questions will receive) is a figure Chaplin herself encountered during her emerging years as a star in the 1960s. The notorious Oriana Fallaci was a controversial Italian writer whose profiles of and interviews with celebrities often took the form of catty descriptions of stars whom Fallaci sought to cut down to size, even as she exploited their celebrity for her own gain. Fallaci interviewed Chaplin in Madrid in 1964, during the filming of *Doctor Zhivago*. As her description of Geraldine in the published interview demonstrates, Fallaci trafficked in the kind of pretentious reportage ironically embodied by Chaplin in her later characterization of Opal in the Altman film. One can almost imagine Opal herself intoning the words from this interview into her tape recorder:

> On that beautiful face of hers ... Geraldine Chaplin has three beauty spots, forming a triangle ... The one above her mouth she manages to conceal, more or less, with make-up, but not the ones beneath her eyes and, as they are actually adjoining her lashes, they look like two little black tears: the motionless, continual, heartrending tears of a little clown ... During our conversation I never took my eyes off those two beauty spots, those two black tears, and even if she hadn't been so touching, so sincere, they would have been enough to cancel out the scant indulgence with which I had approached her, this twenty-year-old who has everything: charm, beauty, illustrious name, success, easy career. Without so much as raising her little finger, let's admit it, she has got where other people fail to get after years and years of effort. (1967: 165)

This sort of gossipy celebrity journalism – which both depends upon and at the same time attempts to deconstruct the allure of a star – is not far away in spirit from Opal's own amusingly vacuous descriptions of the various phenomena surrounding her as she travels through the Nashville music scene.

Midway through the film, Opal happens upon rows and rows of discarded automobiles in a junkyard on the outskirts of Nashville, and offers her own absurd commentary on these objects she has "discovered":

> I'm wandering in a graveyard. The dead here have no crosses, no tombstones, nor wreaths to sing of their past glory, but lie in rotting, decaying, rusty heaps, their innards ripped out by greedy, vulturous hands. Their vast, vacant skeletons sadly sighing to the sky. The rust on their bodies is the color of dried blood. Dried blood. I'm reminded of – of an elephant's secret burial ground. Yes. *Cette aire de mystère. Cette essence de l'irréel.* These cars are trying to communicate! O cars, are you trying to tell me something? Are you trying to convey to me some secret ...?

Altman's camera, framing Chaplin in long shot as she walks past junked cars, remains critically detached from Opal, even as her delivery of the lines amuses us. At the same time as Altman distances us from the character Opal, however, his film brings us *close* to the actor Chaplin, her amusing commentary and performance drawing us to her (even as we remain distanced from Opal the character), leaving us amused by Chaplin's characterization and in admiration of her comic skills.

In that sense, in *Nashville*, Geraldine Chaplin creates a character and simultaneously a commentary on the character she plays. Her performance invites us to recognize all that is ridiculous about Opal, even as Chaplin's own clever embodiment of the character provokes delight. The viewer laughs at Opal as she becomes distracted by any hint of celebrity that falls within her purview. Chatting with Haven Hamilton's son one minute, Opal, her attention drifting away to something else at this gathering of local celebrities and political figures (Figure 3.2), looks past the camera and notices enchantment offscreen: "Elliott Gould!" Spying Gould, the frequent Altman collaborator who makes a cameo appearance in *Nashville*, Opal cannot contain herself: she is a celebrity gadfly, and lives giddily for these moments in which she spies a luminary. We watch on, sharing Altman's slightly detached perspective of Opal, bemused.

That Opal can be read as a rejoinder to all of the carping, prickly journalists Chaplin herself encountered during her early career makes the charms of her performance even sharper. But despite its ironic view of the world, *Nashville* is not without its allurements, and even a certain kind of odd, earnest romance. Romance is a part of Opal's experience of the narrative world of *Nashville* and of Geraldine Chaplin's characterization. And this is appropriate, for in Altman's universe, allure is often conveyed through eccentric means. Virginia Wright Wexman has suggested that Altman's films, in contradistinction to most Hollywood cinema, "depict a world in which romantic bonding is no longer seen as providing the core

**Figure 3.2** Chaplin as Opal, spying Elliott Gould offscreen, in *Nashville*

of social stability" (2015: 375). This focus on ensembles and communities rather than star couples is paralleled by Altman's style, which tends to reject the lush forms of cinematography that typically serve to glamorize and accentuate star presence. However, as Helene Keyssar suggests in her reading of Altman's films, Altman's rejection of mainstream forms of star coupling does not entail a wholesale rejection of intimacy; instead, it opens up an unconventional kind of eroticism: "The promiscuity of camera and characters," she writes, "becomes central in the audience's relationship to the film and the characters' relationships to each other," a form of viewing and being that only rejects commitment, not intimacy itself (1992: 152). If Chaplin, in her performance, is to ultimately move us from a position of detachment to one of closeness, it will have to be through an expression of her character's promiscuity – that is, delighting us through the very expression of caprice and inviting pleasurable reflections on flirtation in ways that rhyme with the whims and impulses of Altman's camera.

Tom, the country singer played by Keith Carradine in the film, flirts with a quartet of women over the course of *Nashville*. The first of these is Opal. One of Tom's songs ("It Don't Worry Me," sung by Carradine) plays on a two-reel as the camera pans to the couple in bed, passing over as it does various objects associated with the characters (Opal's clothing and her tape recorder; Tom's records). The camera joins them during the morning after; Tom smokes a cigarette while Opal sleeps. After nudging her awake – he wants her to leave, because he is thinking of another girl – she tells him she has been dreaming of Israel, and of a kibbutz and her romantic feelings about socialism. "I thought I'd like to have a bash at it," she says, as if an entire political ideology were another lover she might hook up with for an evening. Opal's discursive nonsense, however, when set against Tom's philandering – while she is talking, we see that he is calling another woman – is charming, as are the toeless red socks she wears as she walks across the room (in this moment, the camera shows us only her feet) to retrieve her clothing. Altman's framing of the shot, focusing on socks and other odd objects in what might be for another director an opportunity for conventional eroticism, is as altogether capricious here as Opal herself, who has her own penchant for focusing on irrelevant details in her amusing narration.

Opal's flirtation with Tom here involves a recorded song, but soon he will serenade her – and several other women – with the crooning of another tune. Later in the film, Opal arrives at a small venue to hear Tom and others play music. Unknowingly, she joins here Tom's other various paramours – L.A. Joan (Shelley Duvall), Mary (Cristina Raines), and Linnea Reese (Lily Tomlin) – each more or less unaware of Tom's involvement with the others. Presented through Altman's widescreen imagery, which makes salient use of pans and zooms across the room, the moment draws invisible connections between women, each of whom assumes she is the object of Tom's lyrical affections. They have varied, individual reactions to Tom's "I'm Easy," a ditty which sings of the sort of commitment it may be difficult to imagine promiscuous Tom ever wanting finally to achieve:

> Don't lead me on if there's nowhere for you to take me
> If loving you would have to be a sometime thing

"Let me watch you from a distance," Tom croons, as Opal – visibly touched at an earlier moment in the song, thinking he sings for her (Figure 3.3) – now looks around the room at these other women those words might be for, as if in sudden realization that the yearning expressed in the song is in fact sung by a man who has demonstrated no capacity for prolonged intimacy. The cutting underscores the ambiguous mix of sentimentality and doubt at work in the scene. Carradine occasionally looks up from his guitar and into the audience, but his eyeline is not clearly matched to any of the women presented to us in the corresponding reaction shots; and Altman includes no master shot that would clarify the object of Tom's look (even as the sequence eventually rests on Lily Tomlin's character). This strategy allows us to imagine that Tom might be singing indeed to any of these characters, an alternative formation of erotics in cinema that

**Figure 3.3** Opal listens to the crooning of Keith Carradine in *Nashville*

links intimacy and musicality to a kind of democracy of spectatorship: as Carradine sings of commitment we are free to link the sung words to any one of these attractively eccentric women in the audience, or to none of them. The moment at once exploits the machinery of performative desire through its play of gazes, at the same time as it rejects romantic cinema's typical conventions and obvious pathways. Through this strategy, it places Chaplin (and, surprisingly, Opal) as a *possible* object of loving fascination, but does not determine our gaze toward her as might a conventional film in Hollywood's star system.

Altman's approach to filming Chaplin, in this way, begins by distancing us from her character, but as *Nashville* progresses, it opens up opportunities for unexpected moments of connection. A somewhat different method informs Chaplin's next performance for Altman, which also constitutes a self-reflexive investigation of the star system. *Buffalo Bill and the Indians, or Sitting Bull's History Lesson*, released in time with America's bicentennial in 1976, is a revisionist account of "Buffalo Bill" Cody, a showman whose mythologizing of the American West took on theatrical form. A performance unfolds within the film, as *Buffalo Bill* follows the behind-the-scenes machinations of Cody's Wild West Show, and Cody's desire to incorporate Sitting Bull and his tribe of Native Americans. Geraldine Chaplin's Annie Oakley is a part of this show, amusing the crowd with her sharpshooting skills in-between dramatic reenactments of standoffs between "Buffalo Bill" and bands of Indians.

During the filming of *Buffalo Bill*, Chaplin fell off a horse and broke a shoulder bone. When asked who would replace her, Altman insisted that Chaplin should remain in the role, wearing a cast. Her injury, then, became part of the character, just as Chaplin's pregnancy prior to the filming of *Nashville* prompted changing the wardrobe of Opal (Zuckoff 2010: 280). As if taking her cue from Altman's insistence that actors should play a creative role in the authoring of films, Chaplin's Annie Oakley also resists Bill Cody's attempts to rule as authoritative "master" of the Wild West Show. When Cody threatens to remove Sitting Bull and his tribe from the performance, Oakley threatens to leave, in a scene in which she is seen giving away her costumes and dresses to Native American children. The moment reflexively recalls Chaplin's own creative agency in her performances in Altman's improvisation-driven films, this time again in relation to costume. The way in which the film aligns Chaplin's Annie Oakley with the Native Americans also gives the character an ethical dimension entirely lacking in Opal, demonstrating the range of personality Chaplin projects in Altman's cinema.

As Annie Oakley, Chaplin performs several trick shots throughout the film, which mostly involve her firing at objects held at varying degrees of distance away from the body of Frank Butler (John Considine), her manager, husband, and rather nervous co-star in their sketch in Buffalo Bill's spectacle (Figure 3.4). Near the end of the film, in a performance for the visiting spectator President Grover Cleveland (Pat McCormick), Chaplin and Considine give a bravura show, spinning around one another in playful use of Altman's widescreen frame. (Oakley's and Butler's performance in this sequence is not in any of the various drafts of the *Buffalo Bill* scripts that I have examined in the University of Michigan's Robert Altman archives; it seems likely that it is an improvisatory invention created by Altman and the two actors on the set.) This lighthearted twirling comes to a sudden halt when Oakley misses her shot at a playing card held in the air by Butler; she tags his shoulder instead. Just as Chaplin went on with the production of *Buffalo Bill* after injuring her shoulder, so too do Oakley and Butler here continue with their show, attempting to mask the injury for the sake of the spectators (and for the President of the United States in particular) before exiting the stage. Oakley's theatrical flub here is the product of Chaplin's comic success: Altman's film punctures the illusions of spectacle and star performance just as Chaplin has us take delight in performative failure. The signature achievement of any actor in a Robert Altman film is to make moments of performance individually memorable in films known for their ensemble casts. Chaplin's comical performance of failure in this sequence is one of those moments.

**Figure 3.4** Chaplin as Annie Oakley in *Buffalo Bill and the Indians, or Sitting Bull's History Lesson*

## A desire for performance: three characters for Alan Rudolph

Shortly after completing her role in *Buffalo Bill and the Indians*, Geraldine Chaplin began a collaboration with Robert Altman protégé Alan Rudolph (the co-screenwriter of *Buffalo Bill* and assistant director on *Nashville*) that extended to three films: *Welcome to L.A.*, in 1976; *Remember My Name*, in 1978; and *The Moderns*, in 1988. As head of Lions Gate Studios, Altman produced both *Welcome to L.A.* and *Remember My Name*; but despite this professional partnership, Rudolph's filmmaking approach distinguishes itself from Altman's, necessitating a slight reframing of my discussion of Chaplin's performances here. Where Altman perches himself slightly above his characters, seeking to understand, from a detached view, the worlds they populate, Rudolph meets his figures at eye level, dreaming alongside them. His characters still behave in quite theatrical ways, performing selfhood more or less flamboyantly. But in Rudolph's films this performative reflexivity is approached intimately, only later building out to a fuller picture that even then never quite results in the mosaic view with which Altman begins.

Rudolph himself suggests that the difference between Geraldine's performances for him and her performances for Altman is not the result of any substantial shift in her performance style, but instead emerges because of a difference in how that performance style is approached by the director:

> The main difference in Altman films and mine are the differences between Bob and myself. Most Altman projects started from large subject perspectives, working into details through characters. Mine were mostly conceived from situations or character details. However, Geraldine remains constant. Were *A Wedding* about the planner [Rita, Geraldine's character], Geraldine would have been the same character but with more exposure. More revelations. (Rudolph, email correspondence with the author, 2017)

In a Rudolph film we begin not from a position of distance, but rather in a moment of intimacy from which point the film proceeds out to a larger picture.

Despite their closeness to Chaplin's performances, however, Rudolph's films also show us the influence certain forms of media have over her characters' behavior. All three of the characters she plays for Rudolph are passionately and also somewhat eccentrically engaged with various forms of art, media, and popular culture. There is frustrated mother and wife Karen Hood in *Welcome to L.A.*, who daydreams of Greta Garbo instead of facing her marital problems directly; jilted lover Emily in *Remember My Name*, whose anxiety is paralleled and amplified by the old Hollywood melodramas buzzing on her apartment's television screen, and who herself seems to regard the revenge she seeks on her ex-husband as a kind of carefully orchestrated, partially improvisatory performance; and society woman Nathalie de Ville in *The Moderns*, who desires to possess the paintings that strike her fancy. All of these characters are finally creatures of cinema. And they might all be said to *desire performance*: they yearn for theatrical lives, giving Chaplin's work for Rudolph a metaperformativity.

## Karen in *Welcome to L.A.*

In *Welcome to L.A.*, Geraldine plays Karen Hood, a housewife who spends her days driving around in taxicabs, playing at Greta Garbo. According to Rudolph, the idea that Karen would imitate Garbo was Chaplin's own (Rudolph, email correspondence with author). In the opening shot of the film, the camera is placed in the interior of a moving taxicab, arcanely focused on an empty passenger seat and the view outside the rear-view window. Chaplin's voice is heard before she is seen: "People deceive themselves here, don't you think? Yes, and that's how they fall in love." As the camera pans right to reveal Chaplin seated in the adjacent seat, it becomes clear that she is talking to herself, looking out the window and then down at her notepad, on which she documents the name of the street the cab passes as she reaches a satisfactory answer to her own question (she records that they've just passed Van Nuys Boulevard). She next gazes into the camera, now confidently, even defiantly, addressing us, as if just becoming aware we have joined her in the backseat: "I don't need to be loved by anyone," the desire for solitude expressed in the dialogue belied by her gaze toward the camera, and toward us. Her eyes, a beat after this line, gently return back down to her notepad, losing a bit of her insolent edge as she returns to scribbling. When she looks up to meet the camera's gaze again, and once more speaks, she is now a bit less defiant, a touch more vulnerable: "I don't mind waiting." Rudolph's camera, as if in response to Karen's suggestion that she might be willing to wait for love, begins now to move a little closer. "It's how you wait that's important, I think," Chaplin says – her eyes, still in the general

**Figure 3.5** Chaplin as Karen, in her first appearance in *Welcome to L.A*

sightline of the viewer's gaze, now just slightly glancing past the camera as Karen drifts into private reverie. But even as she detaches herself slightly from our gaze we remain attached to her, through Rudolph's close framing (Figure 3.5). Even when aloof or at their most arcane, Chaplin's characters in Rudolph's cinema are kept close to us, weirdly stirring us even as we are kept at arm's length.

The subtle rhythms created here between Chaplin's eyelines and her words, and the interplay between Chaplin's performance and Rudolph's filmmaking choices, set the tone for Chaplin's work in *Welcome to L.A*. Her subsequent scenes continue to incorporate self-reflexivity, involving not only additional references to the gaze of a camera but also to Chaplin's own history as a performer in film. When we next see Chaplin she is camped outside the office building of her husband, Ken Hood (Harvey Keitel). She is glimpsed from above by photographer Nona (Lauren Hutton), who takes a series of pictures of her. (This gaze of a female character's camera toward Chaplin prefigures her performance in Michel Deville's *Le Voyage en douce*, which will be discussed in the next chapter, and in *Sand Dollars*, discussed at the end of the book.) Karen's relationship with Ken is strained, as a subsequent scene in the Hood home suggests. Karen is cooking in the kitchen, cutting the feet off raw chicken while she speaks in affectionate Spanish to her son, who is brought briefly into the room by the nanny. The language spoken in the scene and the food in the kitchen here function, in Chaplin's performance, as references to *Cría cuervos*, which she made with Carlos Saura a year before *Welcome to L.A.* and which also incorporates chicken's feet as a motif. Ken Hood will soon arrive in the kitchen and demand that Karen speak English, a moment that suggests ongoing tension in this marital relationship.

The fact that Chaplin was near the end of her own nearly decade-long personal and creative partnership with Saura at the time *Welcome to L.A.* was made gives Karen Hood's struggle to connect with her husband in the Rudolph film an additional poignancy. A little later in the scene, Ken, at work, will call Karen to tell her he will not be home for dinner. She then tells him, with the same vulnerability at play in the earlier taxi scene, that she loves him, but in response to this he can only complain about her failing to call the plumber. After Ken hangs up, Chaplin picks up the phone again (as Rudolph zooms into a close, intimate framing). Falling to her knees and looking to the ceiling as she speaks to a stuttering dial tone, Chaplin again has Karen intone the words "I love you" – but now with grand melodrama, a stylization of her everyday being that recalls her earlier play-acting in the taxicab.

As *Welcome to L.A.* progresses, Chaplin creates a character who uses performance as a way to imagine a more satisfying kind of life. Her self-styled personal drama eventually finds an audience in Carroll Barber (Keith Carradine), a playboy songwriter who is in Los Angeles to attend to the recordings of a few of his songs. If the opening sequence finds Chaplin looking to the audience for a partner, in the diegetic world of the film it is Carradine's Barber who becomes the viewer of her eccentric, performative mannerisms. Carradine first encounters Chaplin on the side of the street. As he drives up, she's jotting something down in her notepad, wearing the same red beret and fur coat she always wears in her taxi (Figure 3.6). He's curious, so he pulls up beside her. Rudolph frames much of their conversation from the passenger side of the car, as Carradine looks out the window at Chaplin. Carradine asks if she wants a ride – a simple enough question, met with artifice. Chaplin first has Karen pretend not to hear, and then claims she can't go with him because she can't drive. Karen, rather than communicate directly, prefers instead to perform, soon sliding into her Garbo cough – in homage to the film she adores, *Camille* – as she looks back down at her notepad.

"I've just been to a movie and I was the only person there," she tells him. "It's nice when you're by yourself," Carradine suggests. Karen is not quite sure if it is nice. "Well – men always have a better time," she answers; "Maybe it's because they understand the situation." Rudolph

**Figure 3.6** Keith Carradine and Geraldine Chaplin talk about Garbo in *Welcome to L.A*

cuts to a shot of Carradine, inside the car; Barber is carefully contemplating her words – she is saying more than she had a good time at the movies. *Camille* is a part of her, and she would have liked to have had someone with her there to share the emotions radiating from the screen. Here, as Carradine lingers on Chaplin's words, it becomes apparent that Chaplin's Karen is performing Garbo mannerisms so as to hold onto the passions of *Camille* she caught while watching it. Perhaps, in lingering on and with her now, Carroll is trying to catch a few of Karen's feelings, too. She continues coughing; he offers her a drink of whisky, extending this moment of encounter but also perhaps trying to help her out with her cough – maybe he wants to ease it, so he can find out who Karen Hood really is. But she insists on Garbo; the drink has merely improved her coughing, which she performs again. "It was so sad when she died at the end – Camille," Karen tells him; "she said – *Nanine* . . . . *Nanine* . . ." As Karen cries for Marguerite's maid, Carradine watches, bemused.

Chaplin does not imitate Garbo to suggest that her character is masking her real self from others. The impersonation instead functions as a kind of mechanism Karen uses to draw Carroll close and then push him away, as if testing him against the husband she is, in the end, only fantasizing about leaving. And although Carroll is initially perplexed by Karen's behavior, the way Karen imitates the legendary Swedish film star leads to as many revelations as obscurities. Carroll takes Karen back to his home, playing pool while she sits and observes. Distracted by the billiards table, she is not quite yet holding his attention. So Chaplin stands up, removes her fur coat, and drops it to her side, revealing a red velvet dress. She stands silent and vulnerable, nervously waiting for the sort of adulation with which she has appreciated Garbo in *Camille*. A moment later, she shyly sits down, coughing again – the Garbo impersonation begins afresh, as Carroll joins her by her side. They share swigs of Carroll's Southern Comfort as Chaplin looks him over as he drinks, her glancing suggesting both a possible wariness as well as a desire to see what effect her performance is having on him. He moves back over to the pool table, but she draws him back with her impersonation and he leans down to kiss her. "I'm married," she says, ending the intimate moment as soon as it began: and with a forlorn look he walks back to the pool table. Imitating Garbo again, Chaplin gets up, slides over to the pool table, and sits on its edge before lying down on it, gazing up at the ceiling while quoting dialogue from *Camille* ("I've always wanted to see the inside of a chateau"). Carroll leans down to embrace and kiss her but the moment ends quickly, with Chaplin retreating to retrieve her fur coat and return to her husband.

The scene suggests Karen is incarnating Garbo in order to work out her own emotions, casting herself in a variation of *Camille* in which the Carradine and Keitel characters compete for her affections. But her final sequence with Carroll also finds Karen relinquishing, momentarily, these performative mannerisms, removing all of her clothing and standing in front of him, naked, as if stripping away every affectation she has embodied throughout the film. Chaplin is rarely nude on film – besides other, brief moments of performed lovemaking, in *Remember My Name*, *Le Voyage en douce*, and *Elisa, vida mía* – and when she bares herself in this way in front of the camera it is almost always in order to suggest a kind of desperate vulnerability in her character. Mediating our gaze toward Chaplin's nudity in this scene is the manner in which Rudolph films it. The arrangement of this shot of Chaplin removing her performative accouterments from her body evokes Henri Matisse's various paintings of nude women, in which the naked figures are associated with flowers (so too here does Rudolph place a floral arrangement to Chaplin's left), and to other Matisse works in which goldfish bowls figure centrally (to Chaplin's left in this shot, in the middle ground of the frame, there is a goldfish bowl, strangely empty of fish). In Matisse the relationship between nude women and surrounding flora and fauna is, according to one critic, meant to suggest "the exchanges of energy between beings and things, to suggest how they can interact with each other conceptually, physically, and spiritually" (Flam 2012: 138).

Certainly Chaplin's discarding of clothing seems a charged declaration of the desire to connect, vulnerably and nakedly, with another self.

After she removes her clothing, Carroll walks over to Karen and, cradling her head in his hands, embraces her for a moment, the two of them held, for a few seconds, in a motionless tableau, allowing us to momentarily scan the image for Rudolph's painterly associations. Nevertheless, in this complex image, Karen withholds her vision, as if protecting herself from all this complexity: she brings her hands to her eyes, covering them while Carradine approaches her. When Ken calls on the telephone a moment later (he has found Carroll's number among Karen's things), the moment with Carroll is interrupted. Over the phone (and now draped in bedding), Karen speaks to Ken and reaches a kind of temporary reconciliation with him, while Carroll looks forlornly out the window. The moment in which any conceptual, physical, or spiritual connection he might find with Karen is now over.

Before we leave Chaplin in the film she is again imitating Garbo, suggesting that her character's diegetic melodrama will be ongoing. Carroll, seeing no future here with Karen, leaves, but before he does Linda (Sissy Spacek) arrives. We know – Karen does not – that Linda is Ken's lover (she is also Carroll Barber's maid, and has returned to get her things). Once Linda realizes Karen is about to reconcile with her husband, she unplugs the phone. Karen, realizing Ken is no longer on the other end, briefly pauses – but after a beat resumes the conversation over a disconnected telephone line. What began as a potential reconciliation with Ken now drifts back into solitary performance. As the shot ends she gazes into the camera again, a moment that rhymes with our introduction to the character in the first scene in the film and which again suggests that Karen is still very much performing, searching for a viewer who might give her the response, an accompanying performance, she seeks.

In Chaplin's final moments in *Welcome to L.A.*, Karen saunters out of the bedroom to join Linda, lying down across from her, wrapped in bedding, as if she were Garbo reclining on a chaise lounge. She continues her performance for Linda, imitating Garbo but now also imitating Carroll Barber, quoting his earlier, eccentric pick-up lines ("the sleep of reason produces monsters") as if Linda herself were now her object of affection and reminding us again that Karen is a woman who soaks up everything in the world around her, sensitively incorporating others' words (whether those words belong to Garbo or Keith Carradine) into her own performance. As the camera tracks in, framing Chaplin in a two-shot across from Spacek, the film leaves Chaplin in the same sort of performative bubble in which we met her – but now, alongside another woman, carving out a different kind of performative space. This brief moment between Chaplin and Spacek prefigures the queer textures of the central female relationship in *Le Voyage en douce*, which Chaplin makes five years later, with director Michel Deville, in France.

## Emily in *Remember My Name*

> The woman stands motionless. We hear breathing and see her flushed face. The air is exceptional to her, she is fresh from a cocoon. This is EMILY.
> – Alan Rudolph's shooting script for *Remember My Name* (1977)

Chaplin's next film for Rudolph, *Remember My Name*, places her at its very center. No longer part of a shifting ensemble, and uniquely in her American work, this film belongs to Chaplin, with her co-stars – Anthony Perkins, Berry Berenson, Moses Gunn, Jeff Goldblum, Alfre Woodard – in support of her starring performance. Although *Remember My Name* received mixed reviews in the United States upon its release in 1978, Chaplin's performance met with wide acclaim and the film has become something of a cult object among cinephiles over the last forty years. Some of the early writing on the film captures the tenor of its more ardent admirers. Michael Ventura, writing in *L.A. Weekly*, suggests that Chaplin in this film creates "a sonata of gestures, actions, and expressions that build upon each other, set each other off, blend in discords as well as harmonies" (1979: 18). In France, the film was a hit (Jonathan Rosenbaum, in a review of the film written from Paris, attests to its success at the local box office).

After working with Chaplin on *Welcome to L.A.*, and also as assistant director on *Nashville* and as co-writer of *Buffalo Bill and the Indians*, Rudolph was moved to write the part of Emily in *Remember My Name* for her. Or, as he puts it, Chaplin *embodied* Emily before Rudolph had even conceived of the character:

> She was Emily before a word of *Remember My Name* was written. I wanted Geraldine Chaplin to be at the center of whatever film I wrote next. I started mentally exploring a genre story by thinking of moments of truth and madness a Geraldine *femme fatale* might experience. Geraldine loved the script but was unaware at the time it was crafted expressly for her. (Rudolph, email correspondence with author, 2017)

*Remember My Name* is devoted to Chaplin with nearly its every frame, and in a way that is unique among her American films. In its ambiguous approach to narrative, the film is much closer in spirit to Jacques Rivette's abstract and experimental *Noroît* (discussed in the next chapter), which likewise utilizes Chaplin's gestures, movements, and expressions not as vehicles for a pre-illustrated plot but as discrete aesthetic entities that make relatively autonomous interventions in our interpretation and experience of the film. In his appreciative review of *Remember My Name*, Rosenbaum also notes Rudolph's devotion to his star, calling the film "a concerto for Geraldine Chaplin." Remarking that the film is "the most exciting Hollywood fantasy to come along in quite some time" precisely because of its parallels to Rivette's experimental works, Rosenbaum emphasizes the way in which "*Remember My Name* deliberately suspends narrative clarity... and never entirely eliminates the ambiguities that keep it alive and unpredictable" (1979: 55). A film structured in response to Chaplin's every movement and gesture, *Remember My Name*, even more than her other films for Rudolph, and more than any other American film she has made, is a film which exists as a kind of shrine to the attractive eccentricity of its leading actor.

The film begins, in its opening credit sequence, with a shot of a highway curving around the mountains, as the smoky blues of Alberta Hunter's soulful songs – which accompany Chaplin's performance throughout the film – fade in on the soundtrack. A cut to inside the car then introduces Chaplin through her hands, which clutch at the steering wheel as the camera looks on over her shoulder, from the passenger's seat in the back of the car. (The shot is a neat inversion of our introduction to Chaplin in *Welcome to L.A.*, which figures Karen Hood as a passenger.) A wedding ring is visible on her left hand, while her right hand pinches a burning cigarette between her fore- and middle-finger. Even before her face, which is initially kept out of frame, is seen, the viewer knows her through her hands, which manipulate the steering wheel and hold a cigarette, two expressive actions that signify a tension between moving forward and waiting languorously (the handling of the cigarette gestures toward her willingness to wait and breathe it in, to time her revenge to just the right moment). Chaplin pulls over to the side of the road and gets out of the car, ambling over to the side of the mountain: but we stay in the same shot, as Rudolph keeps the camera in the car, peering at Chaplin now through the driver's-side window. Cigarette now in her mouth, Chaplin surveys the mountains – which lead on to Southern California – as a performer

**Figure 3.7** Chaplin surveying the landscape in *Remember My Name*

might contemplate a stage from the wings just a few minutes before the beginning of a show (Figure 3.7).

It is part of Rudolph's sly work as a filmmaker in these opening minutes to align our perspective with Chaplin's character. His method attaches us to her gaze and her way of moving, and we are witness to the way she can haunt an environment, before we know anything about her motivations. When the film first presents Neil Curry (Anthony Perkins), driving to his job on a construction site, we are not so much introduced to him as a character as we are introduced to the way Chaplin gazes at him: from behind her wheel, her eyes – now visible to us through the rear-view mirror of her car – are intently focused on him and his car. And when Chaplin makes the first of several telephone calls to Curry's residence, Rudolph's camera is already lingering inside the home, like the intruder Chaplin will shortly become, before Neil's wife, Barbara (Berry Berenson), who has just pulled into the driveway, arrives inside to pick up the phone. Rudolph's approach establishes the camera as a silent dance partner, moving in rhyme to everything Chaplin does: the film is with her, on her side, devoted to her every gesture even before the ends to which those gestures are directed are revealed. Throughout the film – and well before we learn her reasons for wanting to confront and harass Neil and Barbara – Chaplin crafts a portrait of a woman refashioning and continually modulating her self-image as the situation demands it (precisely in order to create the situation she demands); and a woman who carves out a way of moving through a world, a world that she approaches with a heady cocktail of tension, apprehension, vengeance, and pleasure.

The film's opening scenes give us only a hint of the Chaplin character's purpose: she is quietly following Neil and Barbara, for reasons not yet clear. But what is clear enough, at this point, is that she is shedding a skin. Wardrobe and fashion are important accouterments to Chaplin's performance in *Remember My Name*, and we know her character through her decisions about clothing even before we know her name. Introduced in a plain beige top and functional blue pants – inexpressive threads that communicate little of the angular personality Chaplin's sharp handling of cigarettes, in the first few minutes of the film, has already implied – her first order of business will be to refashion herself with new clothing. She visits a boutique store to look at new clothes, drawn inside by a dummy in the window; motionless and eyes masked by a black cloth, the mannequin is already an oblique objective correlative of the tightly bound movements of Chaplin's character, shielded as she is from the world's glare by a pair of dark sunglasses. Once inside, Chaplin seeks out not a particular dress but a price tag: money is a concern. Wary of interaction with the sales staff, her gaze perpetually returns to the masked mannequins that stand immobile around her, themselves entrapped; her eyes linger on one figure, again blindfolded by a black mask, handcuffs dangling off the end of its hands. An elliptical cut – Chaplin has somehow finally made contact with a human in this alienating space – takes us to the dressing room, where a saleslady fashions her hair, dress, and kimono in ways aimed to please. "My husband likes me in loose-fitting clothes," Chaplin intones without affect, staring into a mirror as the saleswoman continues to modulate her appearance, as if she were another of the mannequins, or as if another mannequin were staring back at her (Figure 3.8).

Rudolph describes the moment in the screenplay – which reveals the name of Chaplin's character before the film or the character herself does – in this way: "Emily is caught between the image of herself and the physical closeness of the Saleswoman" (Alan Rudolph's shooting script for *Remember My Name*, 1977). It will be the work of Emily in this film to turn the image she sees before her in the mirror, and around and about her in this fashion store, into a lived reality – to become like one of these mannequins come alive, ripping off its blindfold and discarding the handcuffs, but without giving up a certain capability to freeze motionless in space in creation of or in response to a situation, when it might help her

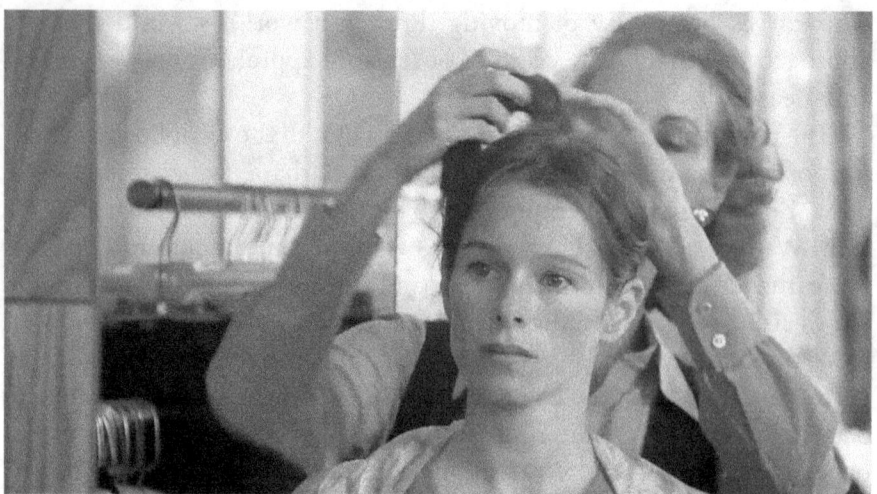

**Figure 3.8** Chaplin as Emily, with a saleswoman, in *Remember My Name*

to improvise a response to or keep at bay the physical closeness of others. Stillness as part of the repertoire of performance is difficult to achieve. As Dan Kamin describes in his study of Charlie Chaplin's use of stillness in the film *One A.M.* (1916),

> Standing "still" is an illusion that doesn't exist in real life. We balance the wildly different shapes of our body – on the two narrow platforms of our feet. Standing is in fact a continuous process of falling and catching ourselves. (Kamin 2011: 45; see also Figure 3.9)

The point of stillness in Geraldine Chaplin's characterization of Emily is to convey the sense of a woman who wishes some modicum of control over how her moments in-between falling and catching herself might be used, what effect they might come to have on others. She characterizes Emily as one who desires agency over the falling and the catching: as someone who no longer is pushed or is caught, but one who decides how to fall and how and when to catch herself.

With Chaplin cast here as someone who inhabits the world like a mannequin imbued with the potential for motion, wardrobe and tightly bound gestures are the template against which everything else she does in *Remember My Name* is measured. And most of what we see her character do in the first stretch of the film is work to prepare for a kind of social performance, modulating the presentation of her self (her wardrobe, her hair, her walk, her gestures) in the isolation of her tiny, run-down

**Figure 3.9** Charlie Chaplin's use of stillness in *One A.M*

apartment, before confronting Neil and Barbara. Returning from the shop to her apartment, Chaplin lays out her newly purchased attire neatly across the bed, delicately unwrapping a black nightgown and laying it before her. A cut to a close-up draws our attention to her hair, as she hovers her hands, without making contact with her own skull, around the sides of a pile of black curls that she keeps neatly tied up. There is a sense here of a character discovering, or rediscovering, a piece of herself at a time – the black nightgown first, the hair next – but not yet sure how to combine wardrobe, coiffure, and other pieces of socially presentable selfhood into a whole person. Returning to Emily's apartment in the subsequent scene, Chaplin is introduced to us through the shards of a broken mirror: Rudolph's framing, camera movement, and cutting fragment and, in the mirror imagery, double Emily's self-image, suggesting a psychological fragmentation (as mirror imagery often does in cinema). But the approach also has the effect of isolating the distinctiveness of Chaplin's discrete gestures: the focus on her lighting of the cigarette; the slightly wobbly steps, as the camera pans down from the mirror to her feet, in her new red shoes; the profile of Chaplin against the shadowy apartment, cigarette raised, as she paces back and forth (Figure 3.10); her knee and thigh,

**Figure 3.10** Chaplin's Emily privately rehearses her gestures and movements in *Remember My Name*

momentarily exposed from under her dress as the character examines her effect in the broken mirror; the crumbling of the cigarette in an ash tray before she moves over to the bed; the rehearsal of lines of dialogue she will later speak to Neil – "I didn't cry when you disappeared," intoned twice. Emily hasn't quite mastered all of these gestures – when she lies down on the bed she forgets to let down her hair, and the pin in her bun jabs her in the back of her head when she puts it onto the pillow. But the jazz playing on her stereo in the background underscores the total effect here of a woman rehearsing a series of discrete, abstract "beats" – her gestures and movements – into a performative repertory that can later be used and varied in improvisatory situations.

These private scenes of intimate rehearsal in Emily's apartment do not have a definite ending point; and for the most part, the film as a whole eschews structuring its sequences with clear beginnings, middles, and endings, preferring instead to present Emily as a person who either jaggedly interrupts a setting or who abruptly departs from it. The scene described above ends with Emily, face first on her bed, continuing to rehearse dialogue for her eventual meeting with Neil – and then Rudolph cuts abruptly, in the middle of one of her lines, to a sequence with Perkins and Berenson. A few perceptive critics upon the release of the film noticed the way Rudolph's film style works not simply as a kind of visual container or stage for Chaplin to act within but rather as a kind of perceptual surrogate, operating in concert with Chaplin's acting. "Scenes are frequently chopped sharply," Mark Rowland notes, "while others unravel in agonizingly slow motion" (the apartment scene I've described above, notably, manages both tempos at different times). "The pacing is hardly frenetic," Rowland goes on to observe – "just quirky, like Emily" (1979: 11). "Emily is trying to become the heroine of her own personal, private movie," Michael Ventura (1979: 19) suggests, pointing to how the film we are watching is so intimately bound with its main character's psyche that every aesthetic choice Rudolph makes – at least in the scenes that feature Chaplin alone or in control of a situation – is in fact the kind of choice Emily herself might make in framing her self-presentation in the film of her fantasy. Rudolph's approach to filming Chaplin is not to begin by looking at her (as part of an ensemble, or from a slight position of distance, as Altman does in his films) but rather by looking with her, the gaze of the camera in *Remember My Name* becoming a kind of ideal vantage point in the character's own unfolding realization of vengeance and fantasy.[5]

Up to this point in my discussion of Chaplin's performance in *Remember My Name*, I have set narrative motivation to the side. This is precisely because this is what the film itself – and what Emily herself – does, for a time. However, once Emily is ready to re-enter the social world – equipped now with the performative repertory she's been honing in the private space of her apartment – she is ready to confront Neil and Barbara, and initiate a kind of trajectory of narrative and revelation. This confrontation involves Chaplin's nimble manipulation of screen space, working in concert, again, with Rudolph's own stylistic strategies, suggesting again that the film we are watching is itself a poetic evocation of a world Emily herself might create. Important here is the idea of control, deciding when and how she will be seen. Early in the film, Emily furtively stalks the Curry home, trampling flower beds, chucking a rock through their window, and continuing the harassing phone calls. Such moments present Emily to us but she is absent to the gaze of others in the social world of the film itself; she works throughout most of the first half of the film to conceal her appearance. In a scene in which Rudolph films a conversation between Neil and Barbara from inside the home, we see Chaplin, almost mechanically (and quite comically), duck below a window frame (Figure 3.11). When she walks down the corridor of her apartment building, she holds up a grocery bag to prevent her neighbors from seeing her (of her apartment's denizens only the building's super, a character named Pike played by Moses Gunn, will connect in any

**Figure 3.11** Chaplin comically ducking below a window frame in *Remember My Name*

way with her). And when Neil and Barbara venture to the department store where Emily has scored a temporary job, she ducks to avoid their gaze at the checkout line (later, Neil will reveal that he remembers Emily as a blonde, which clarifies his inability to recognize her here).

But Emily is soon ready to emerge from her cocoon, and Chaplin's performance expresses this readiness through her character's control over the timing of her appearance and disappearance to our view and to the view of characters in the frame. Her careful orchestration of how she now appears to others has a kind of hallucinatory control over Rudolph's camera and his cutting, both of which work at every moment in concert with her gestures. Midway through the film, the camera joins Barbara as she readies the kitchen for cooking. We spy her through a door frame as the camera pulls back. Barbara walks over into another room as Emily, outside the house, stealthily peeks through the side of a window. A cut joins Barbara in her walk to her bedroom, before the film cuts back to our previous view of the kitchen: Emily is now inside, stepping silently across the kitchen, clutching her black handbag to her torso, gesture and movement kept carefully bound. Chaplin slides carefully to the edge of the dining room, before hearing Berenson emerge on the other side of the frame. Chaplin, at this sound, slips offscreen, the camera panning left to focus now on Berenson, its movements working in accord with Emily, who for the moment wishes to disappear. Returning to the kitchen, Berenson retrieves something from the refrigerator, while Chaplin reemerges again on the left side of the frame to our view, but clear of Berenson's. Chaplin moves to the very edge of the entryway leading into the kitchen, darting her head back and forth to catch glimpses of her prey while still keeping out of sight. It is a moment of suspension: Chaplin appears about ready to reveal her presence to Berenson, but not quite yet. She pulls back, sneaking into another room (a sitting space decorated with illustrations of the new home Neil plans to build for Barbara), and eventually again slipping out of frame, into offscreen space.

Emily's surreptitious journey through the house continues. While Barbara slices lettuce in the kitchen Emily looks over photographs of the couple, and peeks in drawers, in the bedroom. A cut back to the kitchen, a close shot of a knife slicing a vegetable. The camera remains on Berenson as she turns around, panning leftward with her movement and her gaze to reveal Emily, watching in stillness, now seen by Barbara who stands in terror on the other side of the frame. Barbara grips the knife she has used to prepare food, and threatens to call the police: she would appear to have the upper hand. But Chaplin has Emily take control of situation and space through movement and speech. "So, you got a name?" Emily intones, almost catatonically – we have heard her say this before, to Pike; it is one of Emily's automatic utterances, something prepared and rehearsed, at the ready. Barbara threatens that her husband will be back soon. "Neil?" Emily says, keeping the upper hand – she knows the husband's name. Emily backs up a step, and then holds up an illustration of the log cabin she has pilfered from the other room: if the entire trajectory of the sequence is for Emily to temporarily control the private space of the Curry home, here she literally holds their dream home in her hands. "This for you? Barbara?" In the subsequent exchange of dialogue Chaplin's staccato repetition of Berenson's lines suggest again her ability to take on the guise of others –

> Barbara: How do you know my name? How do you know Neil?
> Emily: How do you know my name? How do you know Neil? ... Butterfly.

– before Barbara interrupts this exchange with a jab of the knife in the air, toward Emily. That Emily knows her nickname, too, is too much. Chaplin, after a beat, lets the illustration of the Curry dream home fall to the floor. She looks Berenson up and down, her eyes landing on the knife her prey holds. After a beat, Chaplin pulls out her own knife, jutting toward Barbara with a scream. Berenson shrieks. Emily can no longer repress the absurdity of the situation: she laughs, and then places both knives on a mantle. Hearing Neil's car in the driveway, she slips away furtively from the room.

Emily, by disturbingly intervening in the lives of the Currys, provokes the film's gradual revelation of more narrative information. We learn, after Barbara demands of Neil knowledge of who this woman harassing them is, that the twelve-year prison sentence Emily has just finished at the beginning of the movie was given to her as a result of the murder of her ex-husband's – Neil's – lover. Emily has done her time: waiting to leave prison; waiting to journey westward to Los Angeles (she has been in prison in New York City, where the murder occurred); waiting patiently (but with her own arcane methodology) and now arriving here before our eyes to enact revenge on Neil, the husband whose jilting motivated her act of murderous passion.

Sequences like the scene between Emily and Barbara in the kitchen not only serve Chaplin well in creating a character able to continually orient herself in surprising and new physical figurations and appearances; they are also intriguingly evocative of the work of her father, while also taking that performative inheritance in an intriguing new direction. Key to the performance style of Charlie Chaplin is an ability to fuse new life into a range of everyday objects. The most celebrated example of this is his refashioning of dinner rolls into a pair of dance shoes during the dream sequence in *The Gold Rush* (1925). Such creative gestures implicitly give Chaplin's Little Tramp a measure of control and agency in a social world in which he is otherwise marginalized, while at the same time establishing Chaplin the actor as a master of shaping a harmonious relationship between his performing body and the objects available in the frame at any given moment. Although always at the center of our film experience, in other words, this centeredness is used to convey his character's marginality; Chaplin's Tramp, although the focus of our sympathetic eye, is cast away from the mainstreams of the social worlds depicted in his films. But by placing his Tramp at the center of the film itself, Chaplin reveals his character's vulnerability within a larger, threatening world. In *Remember My Name*, Geraldine Chaplin is, likewise, very much at the center of our experience of Rudolph's film, which takes her as the driving force behind its rhythms and a central participant in the authoring of its form; but in the film's reality, she is no less marginalized than the Little Tramp, a wronged woman and ex-convict who stealthily inhabits the edges of her social world even as she remains at the center of Rudolph's film frame.

And as with her father, Geraldine Chaplin repeatedly, in *Remember My Name*, finds new use for objects – we've seen this already in her manipulation of clothing, and the knife in the kitchen scene – that give her a measure of control in a world otherwise inimical or indifferent to her presence. Later in the film, we will see her pose, as if in a fashion shoot, in front of the wooden frames of the homes her ex-lover Neil, a construction worker, is tasked with building. While attracting Neil's gaze through this performance, Emily's dress-up as a tempting femme fatale is also delightfully awkward, an attempt at fulfilling a pre-existing feminine model that serves only to highlight what is inimitably sharp and original about Chaplin's inhabitation of the film frame. That Emily only needs these feminine accouterments long enough to first tempt and then rid herself of Neil is figured in the film's final shot; we see Chaplin comically kick a box of clothing over a cliff, ridding herself of her these old clothes as she heads, out of frame, to her new life (Figure 3.12).

In *Remember My Name*, Chaplin, in her characterization of a woman who is wary of establishing relationships with others, operates relatively autonomously from Anthony Perkins and her other co-stars, using them as figures around which her own performance mysteriously orbits. Emily has no interest in re-forming a couple with Neil, as might be suggested in the film's repeated motif of house frames undergoing construction; these homes the Perkins character is helping assemble in the film are never

**Figure 3.12** Chaplin as Emily kicks off a new stage in her life in *Remember My Name*

completed, and the home Neil lives in with his current wife is presented only as an object of Emily's vengeful gaze, a private space into which she will intrude. All of Chaplin's movements and expressions in *Remember My Name* are ultimately geared towards her eventual, ambiguous departure, in the final shot, from the narrative space the film has worked so patiently to establish: if she is going to build any sort of new home, it will be entirely on her own terms, outside even the frame of the film's sympathetic vision.

## Nathalie in *The Moderns*

Her third and, to date, final film for Rudolph, *The Moderns*, returns Chaplin to a supporting role in an ensemble cast; of the three films for Rudolph, it is the closest to possessing an Altmanesque sensibility in its depiction of an entire society (the 1920s Parisian literati and art cognoscenti). In this heavily stylized depiction of the Parisian art world of the period, Chaplin plays Nathalie de Ville, an art collector who has learned her husband is leaving her for another woman. She concocts a scheme whereby struggling American painter and caricaturist Neil Hart (Keith Carradine) will be paid to create duplicates of three paintings (a Matisse, a Modigliani, and a Cézanne): the fakes will remain with the husband who has jilted her while she will take the genuine objects to America and the Museum of Modern Art. Nathalie's story is a subplot in an ensemble film that presents a wry view of a world in which art is commoditized; the various characterizations, including Kevin J. O'Connor as Ernest Hemingway and Elsa Raven as Gertrude Stein, tend more toward caricature than depth. Suitably, Chaplin's supporting performance for Rudolph in this film mostly eschews the discrete gestures and movements of *Welcome to L.A.* and *Remember My Name* in favor of a more broadly comical touch.

Her performance as Nathalie de Ville is especially vertiginous, for Nathalie is played by an actor who has more than once been the subject of the kinds of illustrations the Carradine character draws to earn money in the film. In his essay "On the Essence of Laughter," Charles Baudelaire identifies two overall types of caricature: one which relies on observation and amplification of detail for its often humorous effects, but which remains generally good-natured; and one which is more cutting and biting in its satire, often refiguring its subject in distorted or even cruel ways (he calls the former the "significant comic," and the later the "absolute comic"; see Baudelaire 1964: 158–9). In a pair of illustrations, signed by an artist named "J. Gen" and published in the 1960s in the French magazine *La vie Parisienne*, Geraldine Chaplin was subject to both kinds of illustrations. The first is evocative of the second type of caricature Baudelaire discusses, a rather grotesque rendition of Chaplin's features, overplaying the angularity of her face and amplifying the teardrop birthmarks under her eyes in what amounts to a rather cruel overall effect. The second (Figure 3.13) is an altogether more charming and good-natured illustration, and reminiscent of Baudelaire's "significative" effect: a drawing of Chaplin that flatters rather than exaggerates her features; that finds in the teardrop under her eyes beauty rather than strangeness; and discovers in her figure a gamine somewhat reminiscent of a female Pierrot clown or a playful street pantomime.

As these caricatures remind us, Nathalie de Ville in *The Moderns* is performed by a woman who herself had been subject to the varieties of withering cognoscenti judgment experienced by the characters in the film (the Nick Hart character is cut rather cruelly down to size by Gertrude Stein at a social event, and Stein herself is caricatured as rather vacuously witty by Elsa Raven in her performance in Rudolph's film). Appropriately, Chaplin's Nathalie de Ville is readable within the dialectic established by Baudelaire's discussion of caricature, that is, as both grotesque and charming, as both an exaggeration of a Parisian social type of the 1920s but also vulnerably, if rather comically, human.

Chaplin has one extended scene early in the film in which she establishes the tone of this performance. After leaving the Stein party, Nathalie motions for Nick to join her in her car. Carradine is about to speak but Chaplin, reaching her hand out of the window in silent gesture, hushes him: from here, the scene becomes mainly interesting for what is silently conveyed. Once Nathalie lures him back to her apartment (in her ongoing efforts to encourage Hart to forge the paintings for her), Chaplin has Nathalie communicate with a kind of pantomimic gesture (even when the two are speaking), delivering silent messages through gesture, poise, and touch. In this scene, paintings, and discussion of paintings, motivate Nathalie's every gesture, her movements timed, as if on a rehearsed beat in a stage play, to words about paintings, discussion about Hart's artistic reputation, or in response to the sensuous presence of paintings themselves. Nathalie asks Hart why he likes to paint, and as he explains (he likes the relative permanence of the art form, and the pleasure this brings him), she pours drinks and slinks over to where he sits on her couch. As he

**Figure 3.13** A caricature of Geraldine Chaplin, published in the 1960s in the French magazine *La vie Parisienne*. Author's collection

talks she begins to slowly unravel her head wrap, draping the black fabric over the edge of the couch, creating a kind of horizontal line in the film's own composition, connecting her and Carradine (Figure 3.14). Pressing him on the question of painting – which, a beat later, she connects to a

**Figure 3.14** Chaplin and Keith Carradine, flirting in *The Moderns*

discussion of "being in love" – she continues to fondle the black fabric, inching closer to Carradine. He talks of lost love and she suggests that in this sense "we might have a lot in common" – at which point Rudolph cuts, briefly, to a flashback image of Chaplin planting a kiss, at the Stein party, on Rachel Stone (Linda Fiorentino), Hart's former lover. The image is ambiguously perched between Nathalie's and Hart's subjectivities: is this Hart imagining Nathalie in love with Rachel, or Nathalie imagining all the various directions in which her desire might take her?

The brief cutaway is also the perfect complement to Chaplin's performance, which beautifully expresses Nathalie's desire for texture, fabric, frames, and canvas. It is her desire for these aesthetic objects that is most vividly expressed in the scene; any interest Carradine himself might hold is always placed by Nathalie in relation to the painting he might create for her. Appropriately, Nathalie directs the scene away from this romantic courtship and toward the paintings on her wall: her gesture cues three successive close-ups of the paintings themselves, images that fragment the paintings, emphasizing their textures, applications of color, contours of figures, and brushstrokes, rather than the subjects they ostensibly represent. This gesture also cues Carradine to move toward the paintings and share his childhood experience viewing a Cézanne painting with Nathalie. The moment, though, brings Chaplin closer to the paintings than to Carradine: with bound gestures that bring her hands to her chest, she speaks of why he might forge the paintings for her (not for reasons of love, she declares, but rather "life!") as Rudolph cuts

**Figure 3.15** A close-up of Chaplin with a portrait by Modigliani looming behind her, in *The Moderns*

to a close-up of Chaplin with a portrait by Modigliani looming behind her (Figure 3.15). The focus of the shot, which keeps both Chaplin and the portrait slightly out of focus (with neither given privilege in the film's imagery over the other) has the effect of figuring Chaplin very nearly *as* painting: her love for these objects has, visually, made Nathalie a part of them. (This close-up by Rudolph, a painter when he is not directing films, becomes its own kind of moving portrait of Chaplin, a beautiful equivalent of the Modigliani.) The corresponding reaction shot of Carradine, which clearly privileges his visual presence over the out-of-focus painting behind him, only throws into relief Nathalie's desire for this art form. As the scene continues, and as Hart gradually becomes convinced of Nathalie's scheme, he begins talking about the particular methods he'll need to employ in order to forge these objects. But Nathalie is uninterested in abstract discussions of technique: she is interested only in the sensuous presence of the objects themselves. She moves over to the other side of the room and caresses the frames encasing two Matisse works she particularly loves (Figure 3.16). A close-up of Chaplin's hand, stroking the side of one of the painting's frames, underscores her desire for these particular creations: Carradine himself is merely a vehicle that might preserve these objects and their sensuous presence in her life.

This performance as Nathalie for Rudolph bears traces of earlier performances for Altman; just as Opal badgers people for answers to her

**Figure 3.16** Chaplin as Nathalie de Ville, caressing the frames encasing two Matisse works she particularly loves, in *The Moderns*

silly questions, so too does Nathalie – who does not seem to know much about the technique or history of painting, concerned as she is only for her own palpable desires for these objects – press Hart for his insights about painting and love (for her, interrelated subjects). But her characterization of Nathalie, in the context of Rudolph's filmmaking approach, is altogether more intimate, as the close-ups of her gesturing hands in the sequence, which make palpable her love for painting, suggest. A viewer is free to laugh at Nathalie, of course, in the same way a caricature of any self-important individual might motivate laughter. But the character in *The Moderns* is closer, I think, to Baudelaire's "significative" type of caricature, which takes broad strokes in its representations of social personages but without the overt cruelty found in caricatures produced through an "absolute comic" sensibility. Just as the illustrations of Chaplin in *La vie Parisienne* – and the early discursive framings of Geraldine in journalistic reportage about her during her early career – hover between cruelty and charm, Chaplin's work for Altman and Rudolph straddles these divergent responses to performance. If we are sometimes persuaded to laugh at Chaplin's characters in the Altman films, Rudolph's work never finally detaches us from Chaplin's expressions of vulnerability and sensitivity. This is true of the way Rudolph films Chaplin even when she is playing characters like Nathalie de Ville, who offer clear opportunities for crueler forms of performative caricature. In *The Moderns* Nathalie's desire for painting, expressed by Chaplin through memorable forms of gesture and movement, only underscores the character's genuine and very human need for affection and love.

## The art of the self: *The House of Mirth*

In U.S. cinema, Altman and Rudolph are unique in their devotion of attention to Chaplin, and in this sense are more like Jacques Rivette and Carlos Saura than other American directors in their framing of her performances. But a rather obscure telefilm from the early eighties offers evidence that Chaplin could create similar kinds of characters in American cinema for other directors, even if she often did not get these opportunities in the Hollywood system. If in *The Moderns* Chaplin plays a character whose desires are expressed in part through fondling artworks, in her performance as Lily Bart in *The House of Mirth* Chaplin plays a character who yearns to turn her very self into a kind of artwork, honing a distinctive aesthetic sensibility that keeps her situated at a particular point in her social world even as economic machinations and emotional entanglements threaten to undo the very cultivated sense of self she has achieved.

This PBS television adaptation of *The House of Mirth* in 1981 was presented as part of the network's *Great Performances* series. Her performance as Lily is among the most notable of Chaplin's achievements. Unfortunately, this telefilm has been rarely screened since its initial broadcast in November of 1981 on various PBS stations in the United States. Directed by Adrian Hall, whose credits include earlier installments of the *Great Performances* series, the PBS film was produced by Jack Willis, an American documentary filmmaker whose career has also involved the production of public television programming centered around the fine arts. The 1981 adaptation of *The House of Mirth* was part of a trilogy of Wharton literary adaptations, entitled *The Life and Work of Edith Wharton*, that premiered on PBS during the same month, which also included an adaptation of *Summer* (directed and written by Charles Gaines) and a dramatized biography entitled *Edith Wharton: Looking Back* (written and directed by Steve Lawson). *The House of Mirth* was a project financed by the National Endowment for the Humanities and, apart from Chaplin and actor William Atherton (as Lawrence Selden), the cast comprised actors from Rhode Island's Trinity Square Repertory Company, a non-profit theater (see O'Connor 1981).

Chaplin's portrayal centers on one key aspect of Wharton's characterization of Lily Bart in the novel: the character's delicate and artistic cultivation of the self. A woman who lives above her means, Lily Bart's attempts to secure a place in the high society of New York City at the turn of the nineteenth into the twentieth century are made difficult by her numerous gambling debts, as well as other pleasures those in her society find unseemly in a woman, such as her enjoyment of cigarettes and the pleasure she takes in the company of married men. In the novel, Wharton describes the beautiful but unconventional Lily as one who cannot otherwise live except through this society, as it provides the necessary backdrop for her own carefully orchestrated performance of selfhood.

There is much evidence in the novel that Lily considers herself something of an artist in her performance of self, and this background offers context for understanding Chaplin's performance. In conversation with Lawrence Selden, her most sophisticated but least wealthy admirer, Lily discusses her social presentation of her personhood through metaphors of painting and frame:

> 'Your coat's a little shabby – but who cares? It doesn't keep people from asking you to dine. If I were shabby no one would have me: a woman is asked out as much for her clothes as for herself. The clothes are the background, the frame, if you like: they don't make success, but they are a part of it ...' (Wharton 1999: 12)

If clothing is the frame for Lily's performance of self, the canvas of her person becomes manifest through gesture and expression, and the way these interact with the largesse of the social backgrounds in which she seeks to secure her place. Wharton shifts quickly between descriptions of Lily's movement – "She began to saunter about the room, examining the book-shelves between the puffs of her cigarette-smoke" – and words dedicated to the effect this ambulation has on her potential male paramours: "She leaned forward, holding the tip of the cigarette to his. As she did so, he noted, with a purely impersonal enjoyment, how evenly the black lashes were set in her smooth white lids, and how the purplish shade beneath them melted into the pure pallor of the cheek" (Wharton 1999: 10). In this passage, Selden's admiration of Lily is described as one might describe the admiration of any painting or sculpture: a combination of intention and effect and, on Selden's part, a slight aesthetic detachment ("impersonal enjoyment") that keeps Lily at arm's length, an object to be admired.

Chaplin's performance in the PBS adaptation plays with these ideas from the novel about Lily's presentation of self. The first scene in the film shows Lily helping a married friend, Judy Trenor, into an uncomfortable corset; Chaplin's relatively unbound gestures and movements, and her casual smoking of a cigarette later in the scene, impresses upon us the more relaxed pleasures Lily takes in the company of women. In contrast, in subsequent scenes alongside male characters, such as Percy Gryce (Bradford Gottlin) and Selden, Chaplin's performance underscores Lily's ability to refine her self-presentation for the sake of the male gaze, using now a polite and feminine parasol in substitution of the cigarette and holding gestures and movements in reserve through relatively fixed and bound poses. However, at no point does Chaplin's performance suggest that Lily takes anything but pleasure in presenting herself to society in these ways, and the admiration of the men in the film – and the jealousy of several of the women, underscored in this telefilm by the use of expressionistic imagery which renders several of Lily's female competitors as bizarre grotesqueries – confirms her achievement of distinction and difference.

One of the contradictions of both the novel and Chaplin's turn as Lily in this film is that this performance for the gaze of certain men is nevertheless Lily's way of establishing a relative kind of autonomy, distinction, and agency. She cultivates, at least for a time, an identity and a personality that is enabled by, but not beholden to, the society of which she is a part. This idea is established in the telefilm's *tableaux vivants* sequence. In the novel, Lily's friend Carry Fisher organizes a social event wherein "a dozen fashionable women ... exhibit themselves in a series of pictures which, by a further miracle of persuasion, the distinguished portrait-painter, Paul Morpeth, had been prevailed upon to organize" (Wharton 1999: 129). Wharton describes Lily's inhabitation of one of these *tableaux* precisely as a dramatic performance:

> Lily was in her element on such occasions. Under Morpeth's guidance her vivid plastic sense, hitherto nurtured on no higher food than dress-making and upholstery, found eager expression in the disposal of draperies, the study of attitudes, the shifting of lights and shadows. Her dramatic instinct was roused by the choice of subjects, and the gorgeous reproductions of historic dress stirred an imagination which only visual impressions could reach. But keenest of all was the exhilaration of displaying her own beauty under a new aspect: of showing that her loveliness was no mere fixed quality, but an element shaping all emotions to fresh forms of grace. (1999: 130)

Wharton's description of Lily's inhabitation of the Joshua Reynolds painting *Mrs. Lloyd* (1775–6) is unforgettable:

> the unanimous 'Oh!' of the spectators was a tribute, not to the brushwork of Reynolds's 'Mrs. Lloyd' but to the flesh and blood loveliness of Lily Bart ... It was as though she had stepped, not out of, but into, Reynolds's canvas, banishing the phantom of his dead beauty by the beams of her living grace. (1999: 133)

If Lily steps into the Reynolds canvas, in the telefilm of *The House of Mirth* the effect is tripled: Geraldine Chaplin stepping into Lily Bart who steps into Mrs. Lloyd.

The film presents Chaplin's inhabitation of Mrs. Lloyd as beginning behind the scenes, cutting away from the chatter of the society people viewing preceding *tableaux* to a dressing room in which Chaplin's Lily prepares herself for performance. Powdering an exposed left shoulder and neck while facing a mirror (which lies offscreen left), Chaplin's beauty, and her character's preparation of beautiful effect, already strikes us, at this moment, before Lily has had any opportunity to dazzle the diegetic audience. When she does emerge on stage in the *tableau*, the film cuts to various members of the audience to underscore their amazement. But the film's presentation of Chaplin reminds us of the aesthetic detachment Lily achieves at this moment, even as she ostensibly offers herself up for admiration as object: a close-up on Lily at the end of the scene, prior to the falling of the curtain, abstracts Chaplin, the angles of her cheekbones and the soft amber halo of light surrounding her black hair thrown into relief against an entirely black backdrop bereft of any competing distraction (Figure 3.17).

At various other moments in the adaptation, Lily's cultivation of self is linked with the idea of haunting, of ghosts. In an earlier scene, Chaplin gazes at herself in a mirror, letting her hair fall to her shoulders by candlelight, before in the background two ghosts appear: Lily's mother and father, who speak to the camera about their difficulties with money (Figure 3.18). This is the telefilm's economic way of handling the backstory of Lily, and establishing her as nearly destitute, and it presents her mother and father as ghostly figures, inhabiting this space alongside her even though they are long dead. Later, there is yet another haunting. Before Lily makes the decision to kill herself by swallowing poison, she rifles through her clothing, drawing close to her person a white dress very much like the one she wore as Mrs. Lloyd. The film's presentation of Chaplin as Lily in this moment parallels the earlier presentation of her

**Figure 3.17** Chaplin as Lily Bart, creating a *tableau vivant* in *The House of Mirth*

**Figure 3.18** Chaplin's Lily Bart, haunted by ghostly figures in *The House of Mirth*

in the *tableau vivant*, with white fabric again set against an exposed left shoulder while the framing of the shot and the surrounding mise en scène abstracts her from any recognizable social space. In this moment, which precedes her suicide, Chaplin presents Lily as a kind of ghost of an earlier version of the character, as if Lily's final performance of selfhood were to enact again a performance in which she achieved the height of social acclaim. But Lily is now entirely alone, imagining and remembering her earlier inhabitation of the *tableau*, now apart from the eyes of society. The moment reminds us that, in Chaplin's hands, Lily's achievement of an artistically defined self finally requires no diegetic audience, even if it is precisely this same self which cannot survive in a social world that requires money in exchange for membership.

If these *tableaux vivants* both public and private alternately enchant Lily's viewers *in* the film and Chaplin's viewers *of* the film, Chaplin's achievement as an actor in this adaptation might be seen here, paraphrasing Wharton's own pictorial logic, as "banishing dead beauty by the beams of her living grace." This is because these striking close-ups of Chaplin evoke still other phantoms. At least one reviewer of this telefilm of *The House of Mirth*, upon its broadcast in 1981, commented on Chaplin's resemblance to her mother, Oona O'Neill, and the way in which O'Neill's spirit seemed to inflect her daughter's performance as Lily (see O'Connor, "The New York of Edith Wharton"). In this sense, Chaplin's performance in *The House of Mirth* is tethered to the past in more ways than one.

Like her other articulate, bright, dreaming characters in American cinema, Chaplin's characterization of Lily Bart is a vivid depiction of a particular woman and her uneasy place within male-controlled worlds of money, media, and social celebrity. She creates in Opal, Annie, Rita, Karen, Emily, Nathalie, and Lily women with lively, playful, ironic, creative, and dangerous subjectivities, whose ways of living onscreen move their viewers to thought.

# Chapter 4

# A Woman of Paris: Geraldine Chaplin across French cinema

The presence of *la fille du Charlot* in French cinema is slippery and protean. Geraldine Chaplin appears in many guises in her French films, on some occasions a comic figure, on others a melancholy, inscrutable one. She is cast in modernist films by auteurs of the French New Wave: in 1976, for Jacques Rivette – one of her father's most passionate critical admirers – she makes *Noroît* (*Une vengeance*), loosely adapted from the Jacobean play *The Revenger's Tragedy*, by Thomas Middleton; and again for Rivette, opposite Jane Birkin, *L'Amour par terre* (*Love on the Ground*), in 1984. These tantalizingly arcane films, which dispense with conventions of character interiority and psychology, often rely on the power of Chaplin's sheer presence, the figural authority of her gestures and movements. This is also partially true of the first of the two films she makes for Alain Resnais. In *La vie est un roman* (*Life is a Bed of Roses*, 1983), Chaplin embodies a disruptive, mischievous power channeling the anarchic energy some post-World War I French critics saw operating in her father's early work (see Wild 2015: 220). Her other performance for Resnais, a brief cameo in the bilingual comedy *I Want to Go Home* (1989), explores tensions between American popular culture – in this film, comic strips – and its reception among French intellectuals. Her character in the film – a playful reimagining of Opal from Altman's *Nashville* – is a member of the cognoscenti traveling through an exhibition of works by a popular American sketch artist. She is also seen, before the film is over, in gender-bending costume as Leon Mandrake, a character from the comic strip *Mandrake the Magician*, a hypnotist who uses his skills to trick his quarry (Figure 4.1).

An analysis of her performances for Rivette and Resnais, in particular *Noroît*, *L'Amour par terre*, and *La vie est un roman*, will concern the second half of this chapter's focus on Chaplin's presence in French cinema. But an important share of her work in French film goes beyond these two auteurs. Her first appearance in a feature film is in France: *Par un beau*

**Figure 4.1** Chaplin masquerading as Leon Mandrake in *I Want to Go Home*

*matin d'été* (*Crime on a Summer Morning*, Jacques Deray, 1965), discussed in the first chapter. She also has a small role in Robert Hossein's 1967 historical drama *J'ai tué Raspoutine* (*I Killed Rasputin*), an international co-production (France and Italy); and she takes on a comedic part as a daffy hitchhiker in the Louis de Funès comedy *Sur un arbre perché* (*Perched on a Tree*, 1971). Later, she plays a swinging tourist in *Le Mariage à la mode* (Michel Mardore, 1973; based on Mardore's novel); a rogue political activist in *Une page d'amour* (Maurice Rabinowicz, 1978); a painter, Catherine, who takes in a troubled teenager in *L'Adoption* (Marc Grunebaum, 1979); a filmmaker who creates videos for sociological research in *Mais où et donc Ornicar* (Bertrand Van Effenterre, 1979); a woman named Lucie, nostalgic for her youth in the lush *Le Voyage en douce* (Michel Deville, 1980); two characters in Claude Lelouch's epic musical *Les uns et les autres* (1981, released in truncated form in the U.S. as *Bolero*); and, later in her career, a role in a reunion with Jane Birkin, her co-star in Rivette's *L'Amour par terre*, in Birkin's own film as director, *Boxes* (a British–French film from 2007, discussed in the final chapter).

In many of these roles, Chaplin performs fascinating variations on the character type of the *Parisienne*, a liberated *flâneuse* whose journey through French cinema takes on various and striking incarnations. Not committed to any particular political project in these films – in contrast to her work with Carlos Saura in Spain – and no longer part of the large ensemble casts of the American films of Robert Altman and Alan Rudolph, Chaplin's playful presence in French cinema is alive to other possibilities. From the high modernism of Rivette all the way down to the broad comedy of Louis de Funès, she finds, again and again in these performances in France, opportunity to surprise her spectator.

## Chaplin's *Parisienne*

Chaplin's work for Jacques Rivette and Alain Resnais, explored in the second half of this chapter, places Chaplin at the modernist, esoteric margins of French cinema, and finds her eschewing conventional characterization in her performances. By contrast, some of Chaplin's performances in relatively more mainstream French films mark a return to the kind of work she does in U.S. and British cinema, where her often stylized and idiosyncratic approach to gesture, movement, and expression distinguishes her from other members of the cast. As in the Carlos Saura films, Chaplin constructs, in each particular film she makes in France, a kind of cosmopolitanism, her identity continually shifting across various cinematic projects. In many of her films in France, this cosmopolitan performative style can be understood via reference to a cultural type Chaplin performs variations upon in these films: *la Parisienne*.

La Parisienne is an iconic character type who appears across scores of films, including even Charlie Chaplin's own *A Woman of Paris* (1923), in which Edna Purviance incarnates the figure. In her study of *la Parisienne* in cinema, Felicity Chaplin suggests that this character's iconography – in some ways a female variation (the *flâneuse*) of the *flâneur*, a freely moving, independent bohemian whose lifestyle and mobility extends beyond the domestic and into the modern space of the European city – consists of the following qualities: "visibility and mobility (both social and spatial); style and fashionability, including self-fashioning; artist and muse; cosmopolitanism; prostitution; danger; consumption (the consumer and the consumed); and transformation" (2018: 15). In her various incarnations of *la Parisienne*, Geraldine's performances emphasize several of these aspects; her characterizations, of the concepts Felicity Chaplin cites here, especially prize cosmopolitanism, visibility and mobility, style, transformation, and fashionability, as well as self-fashioning and a sense of danger, depending on the film. Part of Geraldine's achievement in many of her performances in French cinema is to suggest the range of character interiority and psychological experience *la Parisienne* might hold, all the while showcasing memorable fashions routinely associated with chic or cosmopolitan women in French culture. (Here "fashion" can be understood as the wearing of stylized clothing exuding both distinction and personality, but also fashion in the sense of individualism, a fashionable or stylized way of inhabiting the world.) Although *la Parisienne* is an inherently public, even flamboyant iconographical type – defined by her clothing and stylization, her ways of seeing and of being seen – she is also an example, in a broader and more global way, of a modern woman whose subjectivity blurs the line between private and public spheres. As Rita Felski notes, modern, feminine forms of subjectivity remind us that the "so-called private sphere, often portrayed as a domain where natural and timeless emotions hold sway, is shown to be radically implicated in patterns of modernization and social change" (2009: 3). What Geraldine Chaplin especially underscores in her acting in French films are the mutable aspects of the *Parisienne* type, both in terms of her external and stylized presentation of self but also in the interiority projected in her characterizations. Geraldine's *Parisienne* is not one woman but several, defined not only by Chaplin's own inherently shifting, idiosyncratic screen personality – and by her cosmopolitanism, which inflects French femininity with her English accent – but also by the range of characters she plays across these films.

Even before Chaplin takes on the role of *la Parisienne* on French cinema screens, she is already characterized as fitting the type in French cultural discourse. As in the United States, Britain, and other countries during the 1960s, Chaplin is publicized as a socialite and celebrity in Paris before she emerges as an actor, and numerous magazine articles and profiles during the decade chart her attendance at elite social functions in France. Whether she is performing in dances (including the ballet *Cinderella*, discussed in the introduction), darting about Paris streets, or dining at trendy restaurants, these forms of social and cultural performance – pictorialized by paparazzi and narrated by journalists – serve, in tandem with her famous last name, as her first inhabitation of the *Parisienne* type. Discussions of her father still hover around Geraldine in such reportage, but the way in which this discourse understands Chaplin as *la Parisienne* ultimately serves to situate Geraldine in ways that go beyond Charlot.

In early French discussions about her celebrity, Chaplin inhabits contemporary, youthful social spheres in Paris that had little to do with Charlie, who in the early sixties had not released a film since 1957's *A King in New York* and was no longer at the center of French celebrity culture. One magazine profile, for example, featuring an image of Chaplin and her father taken by French-Swiss photographer Yves Debraine (Charlie Chaplin's official photographer after 1952), linked her with the cultural memory of her father's screen image, suggesting it was as if Charles Chaplin "had given to this young face the charm and poetry familiar from his legendary persona." Nevertheless, this same profile ultimately distinguishes "the beautiful Chaplin" – Geraldine – from the "comic Chaplin" – her father ("Chaplin beauté succède à Chaplin comique," c. 1964: 27–8). This perception of Chaplin's distinctive, feminine beauty as that which distinguishes her from her father, while at the same time signaling her social embodiment of *la Parisienne*, is linked to more risqué performance in another French magazine profile reporting on her role as a "Moulin Rouge girl" in a dance staged, in 1963, at Covent Garden in London's West End. The author of this piece cautiously notes that her father did not have to be embarrassed by Geraldine taking on this role, given that the performance is legitimated by the fact that it was held for charity at a respectable venue, with the Queen of England in attendance. The writer goes on to underscore how Geraldine's appearance in this production, styled on the paintings of Toulouse-Lautrec, convincingly "incarnates the 'happy *Parisienne*'" ("Son père ne s'est pas fâché," c. 1964: 66). The habit of associating Geraldine with this cultural type becomes a pattern across this discourse, as in a cover profile by Yves Salgues in the magazine *Jours de France*, which includes a picture of Geraldine, with two other socialites, at the trendy modern bistro Maxims, above the caption: "In less than a year, Geraldine ... has become one of the queens of *la vie Parisienne* [sic]" (Salgues 1964: 37). As these examples suggest, in the early 1960s, the cultural conversation about her in Paris has already christened Chaplin a *Parisienne*. While Parisian cosmopolitanism will be performed by Geraldine in her later films in France, this construction emerges first as a social performance in the early 1960s, even before she steps in front of a movie camera. The combination of her famous last name and her socializing in Parisian celebrity circles cement her reputation, and even distinguishes her from her father's legacy, prior to her appearance as an adult actor on a single French cinema screen.

More than in the American and Spanish conversations examined in previous chapters, once Geraldine begins appearing onscreen in France, her name appears in discussions that perceive inherent and cultural-shifting links between youth and cinema. As Richard Neupert has shown in his study of the French New Wave, cinema in this movement was closely tied to ideas about youth, with the new crop of films by young French directors in the late 1950s and early 1960s perceived largely as a break from, rather than a continuation of, earlier aesthetic modes (2002: 15). This cultural shift did not prevent French cinephiles from appreciating the films of the past (one of Geraldine's most important directors in France, Jacques Rivette, loved her father's films). But for Geraldine Chaplin, French postwar culture's tendency to prize youthfulness (often seen as part and parcel with the relatively young art of film) prepared French audiences to appreciate what was new about Geraldine's appearance in cinema, despite her cinematic pedigree. This discourse often links Geraldine's perceived "newness" and her youth directly to the cinema itself, as if she were one particularly distinctive manifestation of all the possibilities of a youthful, modern cinema. In one cover story for the magazine *Jeunesse Cinema* (Figure 4.2), an uncredited writer compares her to another performer who took some time longer to establish her reputation, finding in Geraldine not only a mix of youthfulness and ambiguous nationality, but also the kind of physical presence that seems ideally suited to the young art of the cinema:

> Sophia Loren, for example, has taken years to build herself up. Géraldine, at the age of twenty-one, has already become herself. Long-limbed, with a dancer's body, with a face that is half-Hindu and half-Saint-Germain-des-Prés, an extraordinary freshness, and a forehead that would capture the light of any *projecteurs*. It would be crazy for the cinema to let her escape to another path. ("Géraldine Chaplin," 1965: 6)

The writer's odd description of Geraldine's face as "half-Hindu" and "half-Saint-Germain-des-Prés" suggests the extent to which viewers in the 1960s were already prepared to see in Chaplin a cosmopolitan figure whose presence enables various kinds of border-crossing fantasies. Also found in this passage is a direct link between Chaplin's physical, performative comportment – the length of her dancer's body, and even the size of her forehead – as being somehow *essentially* cinematic, already ready for the *projecteurs* (the French word for "spotlight" which also evokes the whirl of a cinema projector) in the very fact and shape of her being. Those words, unusual though they may be, nevertheless suggest the extent to which French *cinéphiles*, even while still conscious of the legacy of her father, were also prepared to find in Geraldine a new, youthful, and essentially cinematic manifestation of *la Parisienne*.

**Figure 4.2** The *Jeunesse Cinema* cover girl. Author's collection

Also central to the modern depiction of the *Parisienne* type in the 1960s were outlets such as *Vogue* magazine, a periodical in which Geraldine appears several times in the 1960s (Figure 4.3). These photo spreads present Geraldine in various poses, her wearing of clothes promoting new trends in the seasonal cycle of fashion consumption. At the same time, they also emphasize, through her distinctive way of inhabiting the photographer's frame – her poise, her gesture, her glances – an individualized personality, the implication of a subjectivity lingering within the

**Figure 4.3** A 1960s photo spread for French *Vogue*. Author's collection

public performance of fashionable cosmopolitanism. The roles Geraldine plays in popular French cinema take this idea further, complicating the trendy self-presentation in the fashion of the day in a range of thoughtful and amusing characterizations. Geraldine's film performances work to provide knowing, ironic commentary on the way women are situated in this cultural discourse on *la Parisienne*, her way of moving onscreen serving as an implicit critique and thoughtful development of a character type that can easily veer into caricature and uncritical celebration of commodification. These performances, even when they appear to be building upon Geraldine's cinematic heritage, also underscore the extent to which she contributes something new to postwar French cinema culture. The next three parts of this chapter offer brief discussions of characters played by Chaplin in a handful of popular French films of the period, illustrating how she inhabited *la Parisienne* onscreen in different ways.

## Mademoiselle Muller in *Sur un arbre perché*

Chaplin's performance in the 1971 comedy *Sur un arbre perché* (*Perched on a Tree*) gives Chaplin opportunity to develop a comic character, a relatively rare type of characterization in her early career. French comic actor Louis de Funès – one of the most famous stars in France at the time of the film's release – plays a bumbling and corrupt businessman named Henri Roubier, who at the beginning of the film steals a design idea for a new superhighway that will connect France to other European countries. Roubier is on his way to Italy to implement his plans, but is impeded by a stifling traffic jam, caused by a worker's strike. Here he encounters two younger characters: an impudent hitchhiker (Olivier de Funès, son of the actor) and Chaplin's Mademoiselle Muller, a loquacious, flighty gambling addict stranded on her way to the casinos in Cassis. In this role, Chaplin's snazzy, stylish purple-and-black dress looks like precisely the sort of accouterment she might have modeled in French *Vogue* just a few years earlier (Figure 4.4). Along with the high-pitched barking of her yappy dog, it is Mademoiselle Muller's chattiness that distracts the clumsy Henri Roubier, sending the car over the edge of a cliff, below which the vehicle becomes improbably stuck atop a tree. There the three characters remain stranded for most of the duration of the film.

The premise of the narrative – which has all three actors trapped in the confines of an automobile for nearly all of the film's runtime – and the limitations of director Serge Korber's conventional, televisual style would not seem to form the most promising proscenium for an actor's work. Yet the satiric attitude of the film toward the automobile as an object in daily life provides a larger cultural context against which Chaplin's performance becomes meaningful. In her work on the function of cars

**Figure 4.4** As Mademoiselle Muller in *Sur un arbre perché* (*Perched on a Tree*)

and other modern technological objects in the cultural reordering of France after World War II, Kristin Ross notes that the rapidly increasing role of such objects in daily life "tended to dictate to people their gestures and movements – gestures that had not yet congealed into any degree of rote familiarity, and that for the most part had to be learned from watching American films" (1998: 5). This idea that the modern automobile in France prompts gestures that are in some ways unpredictable and not yet part of a society's norms, yet are also imitative of already existing (and American) cultural forms, is emblemized in one particularly funny moment in Chaplin's performance.

After awaking from being knocked unconscious by the car's fall over the edge of the cliff, Chaplin has Mademoiselle Muller react in terror to her discovery of the car's precarious situation, presented in the performance in a series of shrieking close-ups. Her efforts to prevent her dog from slipping off the edge of the car's hood send the automobile teetering to and fro. In an attempt to prevent her from rocking the car off the edge of the tree's splitting limbs and branches, Henri and the hitchhiker play classical music on the radio, the calming sounds of which eventually drift Mademoiselle back off to sleep. Inconveniently, though, the radio DJ fades out the gentle tickling of piano keys and cues the beats of a loud pop tune; a cut to a close-up of Chaplin, still sleepy, shows her comically bouncing her head and shoulders back and forth and up and down as if in unconscious, almost robotic imitation of the music, before eventually opening her eyes – which are fixed in a kind of hallucinatory gaze offscreen, as if she is reimagining the constricted space of this automobile as a disco club. "Disque chaud!" ("Hot record"!) Chaplin intones before leaping up to her feet and swinging her head and hair about in a goofy dance, as limbs and branches from the tree continue to crack off and fall to the bottom of the cliff. Henri shuts the music off and implores her to settle down. But Mademoiselle continues to behave as if she were at a night club, flirting with the hitchhiker and declaring a desire to fly (while outstretching her limbs like a bird in flight) when she sees the beautiful expanse of ocean and sky that lies before the precariously perched car. From this point forward, Mademoiselle Muller takes nothing but pleasure in this precarious situation. Chaplin's performance, in this way, is comically ironic, using free-flowing and unpredictable, unfixed gestures and expressions in a narrative context that would seem to call for only physically fixed, bound responses. Her *Parisienne* in this film, an early 1970s variation on the *flâneuse*, finds a distinctive way of moving and dancing in the least likely of places.

## Isabelle in *Mais où et donc Ornicar*

In 1979, Chaplin appears in Bertrand Van Effenterre's film *Mais où et donc Ornicar*. While Van Effenterre has had a long career as a director and writer in France, he is perhaps best known for his work as assistant director to Jean Eustache (*Mes petites amoureses*, 1974), Alain Tanner (*Le retour d'Afrique*, 1973) and Jacques Rivette (he was assistant director on Rivette's *Noroît*, made three years before *Mais où et donc Ornicar* and also starring Chaplin). The title of Van Effenterre's film, which does not sensibly translate to any corresponding phrase in English, refers to a linguistic mnemonic in French often spoken to schoolchildren to aid them in remembering various coordinating conjunctions. It is an appropriate title, for the theme of communication runs through the film.

Chaplin's character, Isabelle, is a filmmaker whose work focuses on the sociological study of women; in her present project, she is interviewing several French women who live in a high-rise in a Parisian suburb. Much of her work involves analyzing and compiling the resulting interview footage in the finished film. Although Isabelle's work as a filmmaker takes seriously the problems and issues faced by women in both the workplace and the home, Isabelle is shy to analyze her own complicated life through her filmmaker's methods. She is divorced, with a daughter, and she yearns to reunite with her ex-husband, but on her own terms, and in order to rediscover her original passion and zest for a sex life, which, as the film makes clear as it goes on, she finds missing from her world of adult work and responsibility. Isabelle, however, resists subjecting herself to her own sociological analysis as a means to think through her personal issues, until Chaplin's final scene in the film, in which we see Isabelle thinking about her own image via interview footage of herself, recorded at an earlier point in the preceding story.

On the face of it, Chaplin's Isabelle seems to have left a life as a *Parisienne* behind, committed to a life of professional and familial duty contrasting markedly with the fashionable, comic *flânerie* of Mademoiselle Muller in *Sur un arbre perché*. The film introduces the viewer to Isabelle in the context of her work as a filmmaker, which gives Chaplin's presence in the film a reflexive tinge. At the National Institute for Social Communications, where Isabelle works, Chaplin busily scribbles on a notepad, surveys interview footage, answers calls, observes various children at play in the room, and greets a male financial inspector to whom she explains the purpose of her project. "Look at them, listen to them," she says, when he asks why her project only focuses on the women living in the high-rise. "They don't even have their own language ... bit by bit they're discovering [it]. We should also listen to their silence." This moment does a good job of making clear the purpose of Isabelle's project: to give these women a voice. But it also demonstrates the presumptuous way in which Isabelle herself speaks of these women: when one older married woman breaks out into song during one of the interviews being recorded in the studio, Isabelle marvels at how a woman with kids, with a husband who "probably beats her," can possibly contain such poetry. If Isabelle's position of authority in the making of her video project, as well as her comfortably upper-middle-class existence, serve to distinguish her from the women who are the subjects of her documentary, her words in this scene nevertheless give the viewer of *Mais où et donc Ornicar* a kind of map through which to understand Chaplin's performance in the film. Isabelle is herself trying to develop her own voice, her own language in this film, one that is committed to a community of women but is nevertheless also staunchly individualistic and shaped not only by public duty but by her own personal desire. And as Isabelle remarks about her observations of her subjects, Chaplin's silent gestures and movements tell us as much about this language Isabelle seeks as does anything her character says.

The next time Chaplin appears in the film, it is when Isabelle, after a day of work, crashes a dinner party thrown by her ex-husband. Like the subjects whom Isabelle interviews, Michel (Jean-François Stévenin) lives in a high-rise on the outskirts of Paris. Here, Chaplin turns Isabelle into a stealth figure: she surreptitiously slips into his kitchen through the front door, stealing a cake from a windowsill and pouring herself a glass of wine in the kitchen while the party continues in the other room. If Isabelle's job as a filmmaker is to notice and observe with discipline the minute details of behavior of other women, she is herself a woman who prefers to go unobserved, and to define her desires on her own terms. Greeting Michel when he arrives in the kitchen, she haughtily observes his own failed domesticity (this kitchen is a mess, and Chaplin's facial expression, pitched at amused disgust, makes clear her feelings about it) while rejecting his invitation for her to join the party ("I want you, not them"). She guides her hands across his chest, claiming with outstretched palms what she wants (he is unable to respond with his own embrace, as his hands are full of dirty dishes) at the same moment as he notices the cake, the middle third of it eaten, on the table. In a comic gesture, she reassures him that it can be salvaged, as she presses the two sides of the cake together into a new whole. The setting of the scene suggests the domestic life together that Isabelle and Michel have apparently left behind, but Chaplin's sprightly way of sneaking into the apartment and stealing food and wine in the kitchen suggests a possible reconciliation between normative trappings and the contours of a more imaginatively nimble life. Michel returns to the party to reassure his current lover that everything is okay, while Chaplin, still desiring to go unseen by Michel's dinner guests, slips out of the kitchen through the balcony, and from there, across the chasm of the city streets below to an adjoining balcony connected to the other side of Michel's apartment. (This movement is only revealed as a risky and acrobatic one when, a beat later, we see Michel follow her along the same path, the camera now revealing that the actors are in fact several floors above the city streets.) While Michel tries to shoo his dinner guests away, Isabelle absconds into the bedroom to wait for him (a little comic business ensues in which Michel must keep his other lover, who has left behind her handbag in the bedroom, from discovering Isabelle's presence).

Chaplin, craftily weaving her way around the edges of the apartment, portrays Isabelle as plucky and mischievous. But as later moments in her characterization suggest, she is also thoughtful and reflective: after she and Michel have (offscreen) sex, the sequence ends with a shot of Isabelle, upright in bed, covered by sheets, smoking a cigarette while languorously contemplating the future of their relationship (Figure 4.5). "Maybe when we're old we'll live together again," she says ruefully, the evening's playful business done. Michel is there, listening, but the final impression is of

**Figure 4.5** Chaplin plays Isabelle in *Mais où et donc Ornicar*

a woman thinking to, and of, herself, as Chaplin gazes offscreen, more consumed with her thoughts, and her cigarette, than with the reality of the man of whom she thinks. In these scenes and others, Chaplin presents us with a characterization of Isabelle as *la Parisienne*, specifically as a woman desiring a balance between bohemian freedom and domesticated responsibility, a life in which she might balance social commitment and public responsibility with intimate partnership and private play.

## Lucie in *Le Voyage en douce*

Near the beginning of Michel Deville's 1980 drama *Le Voyage en douce*, Chaplin's character, Lucie, waits at the doorstep of her childhood friend Hélène, played by Dominique Sanda. Hélène arrives on this evening to find Lucie in tears. Lucie believes her husband is cheating on her, and has gone to Hélène's apartment (which Hélène shares with her husband) for solace. From here, the two friends reconnect, but also rekindle a potential erotic relationship: as still-frame flashbacks suggest throughout the film, theirs is an erotic bond that may have been cut short in their young adulthood, when young Lucie made the decision to marry her husband.

Once in Hélène's apartment, the two women begin to talk about their lives, their husbands, and their anxieties. More memorable than anything they say, though – and more pertinent to the film's theme of nascent desire – is the unspoken, expressive sensuality that flows between the two characters: the sharing and eating of fruit (a recurring motif in the film); Hélène's playful interaction with the statuette of a naked female figure, to which Lucie giggles in response; Hélène's offer of a shower, make-up, and clothing to Lucie, the first appearance of the repeated motifs of water and fabric in the film; and another recurring motif, mirrors, placed here throughout the apartment, in which both women see themselves reflected. These mirrors suggest the way in which the two characters are reflecting upon not only their own objectification (in their relationships with men) but also their future potential as erotic objects of fascination for one another, which in the context of *Le Voyage en douce* amounts to a discovery of a new subjectivity.

Chaplin portrays Lucie in these early stretches of the film as a modest and restrained woman, particularly in relation to Dominique Sanda's forward, headstrong Hélène, who eventually persuades Lucie to forget about her husband and join her on a brief vacation to the French countryside. But Chaplin's performance gradually begins to shift as the relationship between the two women develops, opening up new emotional dimensions and desires in Lucie. From here, Chaplin's gestures become relatively unbound and expressive, suggesting a nascent ability in Lucie to explore other ways of being in the world. The first of these relatively liberating gestures is glimpsed, appropriately, in Hélène's closet, in which we see Sanda pull various outfits off their hangers, clothing Chaplin's character intends to borrow for their journey to the countryside. Spying lingerie, Chaplin asks to try it out, which she does. As Chris Straayer remarks, "Hélène pampers and grooms Lucie, appreciates her visually, and verbally reassures her about her beauty and desirability" (Straayer 1990). In this scene, it is clear through Sanda's performance that she takes Chaplin's Lucie as an object of desire, taking pleasure in dressing her and convincing her again of her beauty. But it is also notable that it is Chaplin's performance expressing, here, for the first time in the film, an active subjectivity in Lucie – the pleasure *she* takes in this garment, and in wearing it for Hélène's eyes. This pleasure is most convincingly conveyed not through dialogue, but through gesture: after removing her bra from under the lingerie, Lucie places it between her teeth, her swaying body mimicking a striptease; and then, as she plays the role of a department store customer who has agreed to purchase this garment, she raises her hand and mimics pulling back an invisible curtain to an imaginary dressing room (Figure 4.6).

**Figure 4.6** Chaplin raises her hand and mimics pulling back an invisible curtain to an imaginary dressing room, in *Le Voyage en douce*

These moments in the closet, as generated by Chaplin's performance, are contradictory. They suggest both Lucie's playful gesturing toward a different set of erotic possibilities, a potential discovered with the encouragement of Hélène. They also connote shyness, as Lucie uses her hands to pantomime the pulling back of a curtain, keeping whatever new desires are being discovered here private. But this moment is just the first of several in which Lucie begins to gesture toward another possible identity; and as in her performance in Carlos Saura's *La madriguera*, discussed in the second chapter, fabric, clothing, and make-up become important throughout the rest of Chaplin's performance in this film. In *Le Voyage en douce*, clothing and fabric are used by Chaplin as part of a slow striptease, a further sign of Lucie's new – if still somewhat shyly expressed – willingness to perform as object of desire for Hélène's gaze. This striptease – which in Chaplin's performance is conveyed as the gradual revelation of new shades of personality – is dispersed across several scenes in the last hour of the film, in which Lucie and Hélène make their journey to the French countryside for a vacation.

Upon finding accommodations, the pair order breakfast, and linger together in bed for its delivery to their room. Chaplin is splayed across the bed, joking that she hopes room service is delivered by "a shy, handsome, young man ... who'd shoot glances at my plunging neckline." With this line of dialogue she pulls her white shirt down below her neck and playfully stretches out a limb, fashioning herself into an awkward and humorous display, before retreating to shyness by comically hiding herself under the blanket when room service knocks on the door. And who should enter but precisely this "shy, handsome, young man" Lucie described in words a moment before. From here Hélène cajoles Lucie to once again make herself available in an erotic display, now for this handsome young man, who has just entered the room, whom Hélène also urges to perform a kiss upon her friend. As the boy approaches the bed and leans over Lucie, Chaplin's performance makes clear that Lucie's gestures are now under the spell of Hélène's words: she moves her head and her lips to and from the boy's face, expressing desire but then just as quickly withholding it, a to and fro of erotic play that comically swoons along to the rhythm and the content of Hélène's sensually, slowly spoken words: "The lady, becoming responsive, slightly parts her lips – I said 'slightly,' Lucie!" The kiss, despite Lucie's exuberance, does not go any further; the scene ends with the skittish boy darting out of the room after the two women begin giggling at him at the end of this little play. But a kind of psychological striptease has nevertheless occurred, with Lucie unveiling a sharply subjective willingness to perform as erotic object – for both her own pleasure, and for the pleasure of Hélène.

Only near the end of their journey through the countryside does Chaplin's performance become a literal striptease, as Hélène begins taking photographs of Lucie outside the hotel, and as Lucie, with Hélène's sly encouragement, begins to slowly reveal her body to her friend's camera. But even in these scenes, which threaten to take this gently erotic art film nearer to the edge separating it from softcore titillation, Chaplin's characterization of Lucie remains flirtatious and reserved in equal measure. Even as she begins to reveal more of herself – physically, emotionally, and psychologically – she also remains the shy and slightly submissive object of desire whom Sanda's Hélène refashions into the beautiful woman her camera's eye desires. Chaplin's characterization here is of a woman whose submissiveness and hesitancy are part of a vibrant subjectivity and attractively eccentric personality, her Lucie's modesty and reserve never depicted as at odds with the growth and development of new erotic possibilities. Chaplin's performance in these stripteasing scenes, suitably for this characterization, suggests a mixture of willing objectification and playful subjectivity. Even as her Lucie agrees to display herself for Hélène's camera, she is never quite still; she twirls about and playfully tosses her hair to the side, removing her shirt a moment later but coquettishly covering her breasts with her hands after doing so: this striptease for Hélène is a performance that stops short of full revelation (Figure 4.7). Notably, Chaplin's gestures suggest that for Lucie this exposure of her

**Figure 4.7** A striptease that stops short of full revelation in *Le Voyage en douce*

body – and perhaps of a new self – is still pretend, a kind of pantomime: as Lucie intermittently removes her hands from her chest in order to give Hélène's camera lens a peek, she mimics with her voice the lurid music one might hear accompany a striptease in a seedy nightclub. She is at once fulfilling her role as erotic display – for Hélène and also for the viewers of Deville's film – and at the very same time poking fun at the very idea of displaying herself in this way.

The French *Parisienne*, like her male *flâneur* counterpart, is usually framed in scholarship as an individualistic figure, flitting through new worlds of consumption, communication, transportation, and visuality in order to carve out her own playful, affective realism. However, Chaplin's performance in *Le Voyage en douce* – in tandem with Dominique Sanda, with whom Chaplin performs a friendly duet – takes us beyond these individualistic conceptions. She creates in Lucie a character who initially seems to be the very opposite of the *flâneuse*: she is skittish, submissive, and frequently poses as a willing erotic object for Hélène, a headstrong and confident character who projects her own desires upon Lucie. And yet Lucie is never only a figure of desire: her playful movements and gestures, at once revealing and reserved, convey an active subjectivity even as she plays with the idea of satisfying another woman's yearning. By the end of the film, Chaplin has created in Lucie a character who desires, and is expressive of, a new emotional reality. As she performs for Hélène's gaze, Chaplin's Lucie actively discovers an ability to perform, to pantomime another selfhood, albeit one that retains a slight shyness and that is tantalizingly unfinished at the end of the film. This lack of final realization or confirmation of a lesbian relationship in *Le Voyage en douce*, perceived by some scholars as part of the film's ultimate capitulation to heterosexual norms (see Straayer 1990), might be more optimistically read as a gesture toward future potential (one more fully explored in a later performance in Chaplin's career, the 2014 Dominican film *Sand Dollars*, discussed in the final chapter). Regardless of its interpretation, her characterization of Lucie remains one of Chaplin's memorable performances, a highlight of her work in French cinema.

## Framing Geraldine in modernist cinema: Jacques Rivette's writing on "Charlot"

If her characterizations of Mademoiselle Muller, Isabelle, Lucie, and other characters in mainstream French cinema find Chaplin performing cosmopolitan variations of *la Parisienne*, her work for Jacques Rivette and

Alain Resnais sees her creatively collaborating with auteurs immersed in more cinephilic and philosophical strands of French film culture. Her work for Rivette, in particular, builds in a distinctive and creative way upon the memory of her father, given Rivette's status as one of the major New Wave *cinéphiles*, and within that group, one of the passionate admirers of Charlie Chaplin's films. An important aspect of her performances for Rivette is that in working with this filmmaker, Geraldine finds herself at play – "play" being perhaps the key word for understanding Rivette's cinema – with a director who has spent more than a little time thinking about the meaning and significance of her father's work. In her collaboration with Rivette, Geraldine Chaplin is paired with an auteur whose fascination and appreciation for *le père Charlot* is discursive – inscribed in the film criticism he writes before becoming a filmmaker – as well as generative, an influence, among the many cinematic influences that besot Rivette, that drives the creation of his own cinema. Before turning to a close look at Geraldine's performances for Rivette, it is worth looking briefly at his writings on Charlie Chaplin – in tandem with the writings of Rivette's New Wave compatriot Éric Rohmer, whose ideas about Chaplin complement those of his colleague's. These writings offer insights for thinking about the kind of aesthetic frame Rivette and Geraldine Chaplin create together in their two films, *Noroît* and *L'Amour par terre*.

The texts on Charlie Chaplin by Rivette and Rohmer develop an understanding of Chaplin as an auteur, a filmmaker whose chief contribution to the art of the cinema goes beyond his creation of the Little Tramp character to include, particularly in his later films, a careful and economical deployment of mise en scène as a kind of material, authorial inscription or mark. Rivette and Rohmer develop these notions in articles on two of Chaplin's late films – *A Countess from Hong Kong* and *Monsieur Verdoux* – and in terms that characterize these films as nearly modernist works. For Rohmer, it is the absence of the mythological "Tramp" character in both films – in particular, in *A Countess from Hong Kong*, in which Chaplin appears only briefly, in a cameo role – which enables the cinephile to pay close attention to the filmmaker's mise en scène. Rohmer, responding to the negative critical reception of *A Countess from Hong Kong*, prizes the film's play with the aesthetics of cinema:

> At any rate it would render [Chaplin] a disservice to keep seeing in him the superstar that he became under the internal influence of his myth. Let's thank him for helping us out and for presenting himself for the last time under the furtive and good-natured persona

of a steward [Chaplin's cameo role in *A Countess from Hong Kong*]. Since he finally gives us his pure *mise-en-scène*, previously lost in the fogginess of a message, let's take advantage of the opportunity instead of being picky. (1985: 80)

Rivette, meanwhile, writing about Monsieur Verdoux, valued in Chaplin "an economical style that can pass, and often does pass, for an impoverished style," an ostensibly modest mise en scène that, when held under the close critical scrutiny of the cinephile's eye, reveals a richness in framing, staging, and gesture. In his writing on Monsieur Verdoux, Rivette is particularly fascinated by the way Chaplin begins with a scheme or premise – in Verdoux, the transformation of his former screen persona as the endearing "Charlot" into a character who murders women for money – only to then use this framework as a means to contemplate more abstract, philosophical ideas. Chaplin, for Rivette,

> often seem[s] to start with an idea, or schema (and the start of his films, the first five or ten minutes, are often arid, and without sparkle), gradually recovering the real: it is because their schema are not skeletons but rather dynamic figures ... the internal dialectic [of the films] gradually recreates, before our eyes, a concrete world. (1963: 43)

For Rivette, plot and theme are, in Charlie Chaplin's films, frames for dynamic performance: acting, but also the performance of the director, whose orchestration of framing and staging might also be understood as a kind of gesture.

Rivette's and Rohmer's writings suggest something important about the evolution of Charlot's reception in French film culture. If Charlie Chaplin's Little Tramp character, as discussed in the first chapter of this book, is often understood as a symbol of universal humanity which could transcend its historical moment and remain meaningful for later generations, Chaplin's characters in his postwar films have personalities that are by contrast historically contingent, their ways of being in the world inextricable from the ways that world changes after the devastation of World War II. This is particularly true of Monsieur Verdoux, in which Chaplin's title character – a startlingly alienating incarnation in comparison to the Little Tramp – swindles and then murders women of means in order to secure the finances necessary to support his disabled wife and their young son. The character performs these activities in ways that are inextricably tied to the film's sense that moral certainties have diminished in the wake of mechanized, twentieth-century devastation. When we first glimpse him in the film, Verdoux is tending to his rose garden, politely, discreetly, privately the picture of a perfect *bourgeois* – but behind him, as a leftward pan of the camera will momentarily reveal, is an incinerator, in which, we learn, Verdoux's most recent victim is currently burning (Figure 4.8).

Such an image underscores not only a certain irony in Chaplin's performance – a distance between the self as presented in performance and another, perhaps more dangerous self inscribed in clues of the surrounding mise en scène – but also something crucial about Chaplin's performance of subjectivity in *Verdoux*. In *Monsieur Verdoux* the personality of Verdoux is inextricable from the morally compromised world which surrounds him, and which Chaplin the director organizes in his mise en scène. Verdoux is not "contained," in terms of either subjectivity or personality, solely in the body of Chaplin's performance as actor; as a psychological entity, Verdoux is dispersed across Chaplin's frame, no longer a figure in tension with a mechanized world – as the Little Tramp was in *Modern Times* (1936) and other earlier Chaplin films – but a figure who is now a product and a consequence of that world, and

**Figure 4.8** Charlie Chaplin, lingering offscreen in the dispersive mise en scène of *Monsieur Verdoux*

whose own moral compromises are inextricable from the failings of the world surrounding him. This might be an example of the kind of "internal dialectic" Rivette found in *Verdoux*, wherein the subjectivity of the title character does not merely come into contact with a world but is rather produced through a connection to a world with its own moral tensions and contradictions.

This productive tension which Rivette glimpses in Chaplin's films, between concept and incarnation, between abstract idea and the inscription of a gestural reality in the mise en scène, obliquely informs the performances Geraldine Chaplin gives for Rivette. In both *Noroît (Une vengeance)* and *L'Amour par terre*, Chaplin's gestures, movements, and expressions are not directed toward the revelation of an interiority or psychology "contained" in the character. If in Carlos Saura's early films, for example, Chaplin was playing women whose interiority and subjectivity came into conflict with the often brutally circumscribed, patriarchal worlds of Franco-era Spain, in her films for Rivette the boundary separating the skin of her characters from the texture of the director's experimental worlds is not quite so clear or constant. Her physical achievements in Rivette's films are inscribed in an aesthetic frame that is itself mobilized by an abstract, conceptual consideration of both art and cinema; here, "performance" is understood as a collaboration between actors and the other dynamic and contingent elements of the filmmaker's mise en scène and the auteur's various literary and cinematic influences. As Mary Wiles has discussed in her work on Rivette, *Noroît* in particular draws upon a rich array of artistic, literary, and cinematic references: the play *The Revenger's Tragedy* (1607); Fritz Lang's *Moonfleet* (1955); George Stevens's *Shane* (1953); Gérard de Nerval's *The Daughters of Fire* (1854); Celtic symbolism, particularly as utilized in Maurice Maeterlinck's play *Pelléas et Mélisande* (1893); Jean Cocteau and Debussy, both of whom staged productions of the Maeterlinck play; as well as opera and music, in particular the choreography of American dancer Carolyn Carson (2012: 66–71). *Noroît* was part of an intended cycle of four films that Rivette called "Les Filles de Feu" (in homage to the Nerval text), wherein, as Richard I. Suchenski writes, Rivette intended to stage "exercises in purely elemental cinema . . . a pure choreography of filmic space centered on the physical actions and corporeality of the performers . . . rather than the psychological states they project" (2016: 127).

Rivette's *L'Amour par terre*, meanwhile, takes its title from a Paul Verlaine poem, and is reflexively about performance: Geraldine is cast as Charlotte, one of two actresses who rehearse a new play in the world of the film. But this rich play of artistic signifiers – among which Chaplin's performance is central – does not simply result in reflexive pastiche. As Douglas Morrey and Alison Smith suggest, Rivette's method of filmmaking generates a form in which the most theatrical, non-realistic manifestations of cinema can give rise to uniquely palpable and grounded experiences of both the seriousness of death and the lively release of play:

> In fact, paradoxically, it is the non-illusionistic, theatrical presentation … which gives [the performance of death] a significant reality … When [*Noroît*] evokes cinema, on the other hand, it is to offer the audience a defusion of tension, a space for doubt and distance through the possibility of a playful image. (2015: 160)

Chaplin's performances are key to the theatrical tension, in both of her films for Rivette, between the dark and despairing threat of death and the relieving, playful incarnation of artistic, performative life. When Chaplin acts for Rivette, her performance does not work to create a subjectivity that in turn encounters the world, as she was doing in the Saura films, where her characters' interiorities brush up against social situations with which they must contend. Instead, the meanings of Chaplin's performances for Rivette are at play in the pure, economical, and vivid trace of gesture, and the way in which her gestures and movements engage with, and become inextricable from, both the surrounding and equally creative mise en scène of the film, as well as the larger history of cinema into which Rivette's films reflexively and self-consciously project themselves.

## Chaplin and Rivette, Part I: the revenger in *Noroît*

Chaplin's first appearance in *Noroît* is startlingly abstract and mysterious. The shot begins with a vista of the sea, across which the camera tracks to reveal a rocky beach with the sun on the horizon line. Eventually, this shot reveals Chaplin herself, her face resting on the back and arms of a prostrate male figure at whom she clutches. She looks away, her eyes invoking offscreen mystery, her palms and fingers now slipping into a more intimate caress of the male figure's thighs, buttocks, and torso. "Shane! Mon frère!" ("Shane! My brother!") Chaplin sighs, these first words signaling one of Rivette's obsessive intertextual references (here, the American Western *Shane*) while also generating incestual overtones in relation to Chaplin's touch of this figure's body (Figure 4.9). "I found you," Chaplin now says

**Figure 4.9** Invoking *Shane* and other intertextual references in *Noroît*

(again, for this stretch of the dialogue, in French), her left arm continuing to massage the arm of Shane while her right continues its clutch of his leg. "On the rocks . . . tattered," she says, in incantatory monotone, describing the lost figure of Shane she has found in this landscape while also trying, with her gestures, to physically hold the remains of this body together. Now, though, the performance draws our attention away from the man's body to Chaplin's own: although her words – "my breath, with my hands, I put you together again, like this, your body, like before" – remain ostensibly fixated on the dead figure of her brother, our attention is to the slow development of Chaplin's movements, as she sits upright and begins to guide her hand – first gently, then with increasing tension – through Shane's hair. She then moves her head to look at something behind her, a slight shift in position which motivates a cut to a reverse-angle. Rivette's camera remains fixed on Chaplin's intense, invocative eyes, as she gazes beyond the edges of the frame toward the castle (Figure 4.10), which belongs to her character's enemy – Giulia (incarnated later in the film by Bernadette Lafont), the Goddess of the Sun.

Much of this first moment grounds Chaplin's performance in concrete, material gestures. In particular, she draws her viewer's attention to her hands, which at first seem to gather up the dead Shane as she evokes his memory in her words, and then remain fixed solidly on the surface of the beach as she turns her steady gaze toward the horizon beyond which she will find the castle of the Goddess of the Sun, responsible for her brother's

**Figure 4.10** Chaplin's intense, invocative eyes, gazing beyond the edges of the frame in *Noroît*

death. "You left us both finished, when you left him for dead," Chaplin says (again in French), gazing offscreen at the castle, her words abstractly referring to a past moment in *Noroît*'s story world (in Rivette's cinema, the past is always a kind of ghost, conjured only in the present moment of mise en scène, and in the various resonances of such moments). Here, Chaplin's words and gestures work to imagine, as actors are often called upon to do in Rivette's cinema, what that story might be or become through her words, and through her way of looking and moving. Even as the bandages wrapped around Chaplin's wrists, here and throughout the film, spark questions about her character's "past" (a suicide attempt?), they also serve to cleave the viewer from her character's interiority, as if the bandages were not so much a clue to an emotional reality lying on the "inside" of the character but rather a material reminder that a search for meaning in this film should remain fixed on Chaplin's physicality and her graceful, dance-like movements and gestures. In this way, Chaplin's performative work in the film does not illustrate a pre-existing, scripted text, but instead generates a present-tense inscription of meaning in an undulating mise en scène, her gestures and movements becoming a vivid cinematic writing. As Douglas Morrey and Alison Smith write of Rivette's cinema, his films "abrogate to themselves, through the mediation of their explorer-protagonists, the power to locate suitable points and to confer significance upon them" (2015: 60). And so Chaplin in these shots becomes a performative mediator, the various other aspects of

Rivette's film – the sound of the sea's eternal waves, the fast whip-pan of the camera as it suddenly spies the castle lying beyond the beach's rocks – all filtered through her, like a sieve, and translated into vocalizations and movements that generate narrative and, ultimately and more importantly, cinema.

It is worth remembering that Chaplin, in *Noroît*, is a goddess. She will give herself the name Morag in a subsequent sequence, but Morag is also known in the film as "The Goddess of the Moon," an idea that becomes important to Chaplin's performance. In this opening sequence, Chaplin's status as a goddess is already implied, given the powers her performance confers upon the character she is playing: as she turns her attention away from the castle on the horizon and back toward her dead brother, her hands positioned, in the frame, behind his body, the viewer perhaps notices that Shane is now, mysteriously, breathing. This is less a mistake on the part of the actor playing the dead character – the breathing is quite noticeable in the frame and the body is placed by Rivette in the foreground of the mise en scène – than a suggestion that Chaplin has invested her screen goddess with the power, here, to bring the dead magically back to life (in Rivette's framing, only the bandages around her wrists are visible, her hands placed as they are behind the body of Shane). This idea is reinforced by a later sequence in the film in which Shane again comes magically – if only momentarily, through the body of another character – back to life while again in Chaplin's presence.

Chaplin's performative conjuring of a goddess also involves her character's powers to magically invoke and incarnate references to literature and cinema, as already glimpsed in this opening sequence's reference to *Shane*. Rivette's intertextual citations pass bodily through, and are mediated by, Chaplin's performance, particularly in those stretches of dialogue in which her character intones words from *The Revenger's Tragedy*, the play upon which the film is very loosely based. As in her films for Carlos Saura in Spain, Chaplin's performance in *Noroît* is bilingual, and she will sometimes shift her speaking in this film from French to English, during moments in which her words are taken directly from the English play. "Here," Morrey and Smith remind us,

> Rivette makes use of language as sound, exploiting the foreignness of his text ... in ways which were also typical of certain currents of the avant-garde. The English text has a meaning – and is subtitled for French audiences – but it is obscure and allusive, and most of all separate from all other exchanges, doubly theatrical and potentially magical. (2015: 160)

Spoken words are able to come to the forefront here as theatrical and magical precisely because it is Chaplin speaking them, her inflection of voice and her status as a cosmopolitan *flâneuse* in French cinema giving her performance of English in *Noroît* its own particular and enchanting cadence.

Here are the words from the play (in *The Revenger's Tragedy*, they are spoken by the character Vindice, Chaplin's equivalent in the text), as spoken by Chaplin in English, with some variations and departures from the original text, in this opening sequence from the film:

> Oh, thou goddess of the palace, mistress of mistresses
> To whom the costly perfumed people pray
> Strike thou my forehead into daunted marble
> Mine eyes into steady sapphires
> Turn my visage and if I must needs glow
> Let me blush inward

In her speech, Chaplin chooses "daunted" rather than "dauntless" (the latter word is what appears in the text of the play; see Tourneur 1966), a figure of speech that adds an extra layer of vulnerability to her character, despite her desire, with these words, to turn her eyes and body into "steady sapphires" and cold marble that might help cloak her emotions and allow her to slip stealthily into the palace to avenge her brother's death. After speaking these words Chaplin gazes downward and puts her head in her hands, ending the sequence. Her frozen positioning here, at the end of the opening of *Noroît*, is part of the larger punctuation of the sequence created by her invocatory words, in which she bids mysterious spirits to confer upon her the power to remain emotionless, so as to strategically cloak her intentions to seek vengeance from the Goddess of the Sun.

This dialectic between the concrete and conceptual – the gestural and the magical – continues after Chaplin's character (who has, at this point, christened herself "Morag") begins her plan to infiltrate the sun goddess's castle. With the help of Erika (Kika Markham), her secret confidant inside Giulia's fortress, Morag stages a fictional twilight assassination attempt upon Bernadette Lafont's sun goddess, near the castle's front lawn: Chaplin darts in front of the "assailant," her outstretched arm and lithe dancer's movements saving the sun goddess from the end of a dagger. This action wins Morag the sun goddess's trust, granting her access to the grounds, even though Rivette's staging and cutting link Chaplin to that which opposes the sun as day turns into night: the moon. Chaplin's appearance and movements in this sequence are bracketed by two shots of Earth's satellite, its illuminated surface thrown into relief against the nighttime sky just as Chaplin's visage, in this sequence, stands out against the frame of her black hair, and the surrounding darkness.

After Morag successfully infiltrates the sun goddess's castle, Chaplin's performance, initially isolated from most of the other players in the film in the opening beach sequences, is placed into counterpoint with the movements and gestures of other actors. In the castle scenes staged by Rivette, Chaplin's movements and expressions become part of a larger theatrical ensemble, inscribed within Rivette's collective orchestration of mise en scène and serving, through her own occasional performative pauses, to open up spaces for other actors to work. These scenes are among the most radical assemblages in Chaplin's acting career. Rivette's stated intentions in directing the performances in *Noroît* (and the other three films he intended to make during this period of the career, referred to as part of his "Les Filles de Feu" cycle) make clear the singularity of his method:

> during shooting, each "unit" (each block-sequence) will be subjected to a method designed to break down not only conventional dramatic techniques but also the more recent conventions of improvisations with all the prolixities and clichés it entails (hesitations, provocations, etc. ...), and to establish an *ecriture* based on actions, movements, attitudes, the actor's "gestural", in other words. The ambition of these films is to discover a new approach to acting in the cinema, where speech, reduced to essential phrases, to precise formulas, would play a role of "poetic" punctuation. Not a return to the silent cinema, neither pantomime nor choreography: something else, where the movement of bodies, their counterpoint, their inscription within the screen space, would be the basis of the mise en scène. (Rivette 1977)

Rivette's emphasis on the "movement of bodies" and "their inscription in the screen space" means, as Sam Rohdie observes, that "The writing of a Rivette film does not precede it, but is simultaneous with it" (2016: 55). And as Rohdie writes elsewhere,

> Nothing pre-exists [Rivette's] film: no script, no narrative, no plot, no *découpage*, nor do the actors mimic a preconceived character... The film is made at the moment of its making as are the performances and the characters ... The film is itself, not a representation of something else that precedes it. (2006: 106)

*Noroît*'s viewer has already seen, in the beach sequence, how Chaplin's speaking of dialogue in English (from the play *The Revenger's Tragedy*) functions as a kind of poetic punctuation of the mysterious opening scene. In the castle sequences, her movements and positionings are now placed into counterpoint with other kinds of movements (the other actors; the musicians, themselves performing in *Noroît*, improvising the score to the film – at times visibly so, in front of the camera – in conjunction with the actors' movements; the movements of Rivette's camera and his various choices in cinematography), and are a generative source of meaning in the film's mise en scène. Rather than the castle itself serving as the basis, or container, of the film's action, the performances of the actors, as Rivette's words about his strategies suggest, work to "author" the sequences in conjunction with other elements of cinematic composition.

Given this, Rivette's film might seem like an abstract, aridly modernist exercise, were it not for performers like Chaplin, who, alongside Lafont, Markham, and the others in the cast, invest the conceptual frame of *Noroît* with beguiling life. Chaplin's performance, throughout the middle stretch of *Noroît*, repeatedly establishes Morag – a character with relatively clear narrative motivations, but with no legible, biographical past – as a figure always just on the threshold of an act of violence, expressed in the film as a gesture or movement held or suspended in a momentary tableau that keeps the film, and Chaplin's performance, on the edge of bloodshed. This idea is often underscored by the fact that Chaplin frequently places herself, in the architecture of Rivette's screen space, near doorways, staircases, and other passages or liminal thresholds, positions which occasionally offer Morag an opportunity to survey bodies lying just around the corner, but which also sometimes threaten to limit or obstruct her view. During Morag's first morning in the castle, for example, the sun goddess guides her to a room in which various pirates practice swashbuckling. Still only tentatively a part of this band of violent outlaws, Chaplin stands, alongside Lafont, under the stone arch of an entryway, the movements of the pirates visible in the background as Morag, in the foreground, continues to assure the sun goddess of her loyalty. From this point forward, Chaplin's gradual procession toward the band of pirates is marked by a series of performative pauses: a slight, nervous movement of her head, when the sun goddess first bids Morag to move closer; Morag's stopping her walk toward the pirates, and raising her knee on a bench and her arm over her knee, in contemplative stillness as she assumes the position of a spectator watching the group's rehearsal (Chaplin here also finds herself on the threshold of Rivette's frame, as the camera first frames her on the right edge of the shot, before tracking past her); Morag's look of laughing disbelief, as she walks toward one of the pirates who, standing now in front of her, evokes the appearance of her dead brother, Shane; and her frozen gesture of holding a dagger near the neck of another pirate who, feigning an attack on the sun goddess, again tests Morag's loyalty. These moments all have possible psychological connotations: they can be read as legible "signs" of Morag's hesitation, her careful tentativeness as she prepares to infiltrate this motley, mysterious group. But they serve more substantially as physical counterpoints to other actors in the ensemble, Chaplin's tendency in this film to occasionally suspend certain gestures in space generating momentary opportunities for other performers to throw themselves into relief against her stillness.

In *Noroît*, Chaplin's most important screen partner is ultimately Rivette's camera, and his other various – and often abstract – strategies of mise en scène. And it is crucial that this be so, since for much of the film Chaplin's Morag – the character whose lines of dialogue from *The Revenger's Tragedy* gives her a goal and a purpose – grounds this tantalizingly oblique film in something resembling plausible narrative motivation. Throughout *Noroît*, Rivette's strategies of framing repeatedly "catch" Chaplin's graceful comportment; in no other film has her dancer's physicality, as well as her ability to position herself, during moments of necessary stillness, in intriguing ways in the film frame, been so thoroughly engaged. At the same time, the film still occasionally underscores Morag's goals and intentions. In this way, Chaplin's performance balances narrative legibility (Morag's desire for revenge) with abstract, balletic energy. Shortly after successfully infiltrating Giulia's band of pirates, Morag returns, exhausted and momentarily relieved, to her bedroom quarters, where Erika waits for her near a bed. Clutching their hands in unison as if clinging for life, Chaplin and Markham walk over to the fireplace, in front of which Chaplin lies down. The camera, tracking backward from the door of the room to the other side of the bed, rests on a shot of Chaplin lying on the floor, her positioning in the frame relative to the position of the camera rendering her upside-down, and strangely foreshortened (Figure 4.11). Morag is presented here as an exhausted figure. However, from offscreen, two other elements of cinematic composition work to return Morag, and Chaplin, back to fascinating movement: first, a single held musical note – presumably played just offscreen by the same on-set musical accompaniment put into play by Rivette for other scenes – and then, the gradual

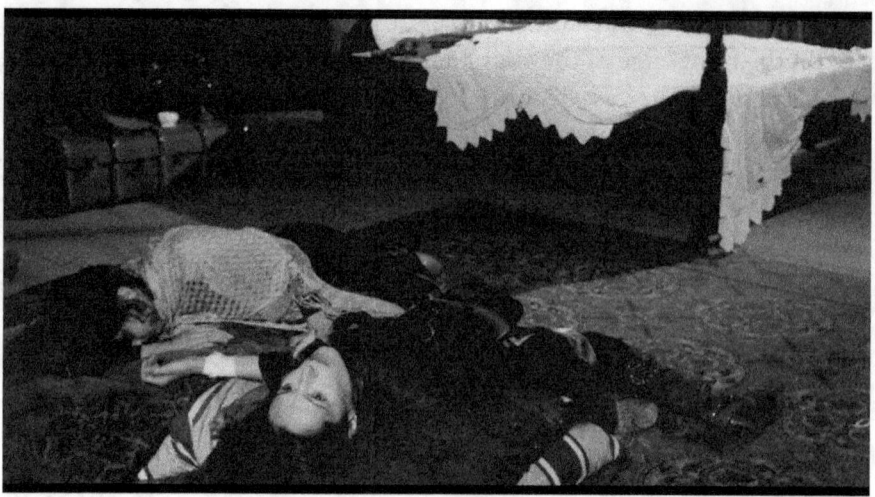

Figure 4.11 Chaplin, as a foreshortened Morag in *Noroît*

raising of a single fill light, which works, in conjunction with the red rug upon which Chaplin is splayed, to generate warmth and life in the image. These two aesthetic conceits work in concert with Chaplin's gestures to animate Morag once again: raised to her feet, she guides Markham, now also back standing, over to the bed, once more speaking lines from *The Revenger's Tragedy*. Here, she affirms her important partnership with Erika, who, with Markham speaking these lines alongside Chaplin, is once more positioned as Morag's most important confidante inside the castle.

Rivette's camera will continue to follow Chaplin's Morag carefully and patiently throughout much of this middle section of *Noroît*, as Morag continues to wait for openings to enact her revenge, giving the film's modernist play with image, sound, and editing concrete figuration. But even as this careful filming of Chaplin remains somewhat narratively motivated, Rivette's direction of Chaplin is never merely functional. As Chaplin told Jonathan Rosenbaum in an interview on the set of the film, every moment of performance in *Noroît* is the product of weighing various possibilities in gesture and movement, sets of options which become the burden of Rivette's performers to invent:

> Rivette is very positive that he doesn't know what he wants. But he knows what he *doesn't* want – and he's very particular, too. He's very tough. You have to invent thirty-five different ideas and show them to him like you were selling carpets, and then he says, 'Okay, do that.' But it's exhausting. (quoted in Rosenbaum and Adair, "Les filles du feu, Part Two").

While this on-set dialectic between actor and director remains unseen by Noroît's viewer, who only witness the final, edited results of Chaplin's "exhausting" creative partnership with her director, knowledge of these working methods does amplify strange tensions at play in even the film's relatively conventional scenes. In a later sequence, Morag encounters Jacob, one of Giulia's dashing pirates, on a hillside outside the castle. Convinced that Jacob is the risen image of her dead brother, Shane (Rivette casts the same actor, Humbert Balsan, in both roles), Chaplin guides her hands over Jacob's face, and falls to the ground with him in a caress. Despite the incestual – and ghostly – undertones of this sequence, it plays like a moment of melodrama from an adaptation of *Wuthering Heights* (see also Rosenbaum and Adair for this comparison), a novel Rivette would, a few years later, adapt to the screen. But a performative choice Chaplin makes near the end of the sequence – shrieking out the name "Shane!" with a stridency as sharp as *Noroît*'s unpredictable editing patterns – reminds us that this film is grounded in something other than normative conventions. Chaplin's desperate cry punctuates an ostensibly "digestible" narrative sequence with estranging, piercing vocality, a choice in keeping with the overall tonality of *Noroît*.

These kinds of raw, unbridled expressions at times work to transform *Noroît* into a kind of extraterrestrial, avant-garde ballet. This alluring strangeness is especially palpable in two moments near the end of the film. In the first, Giulia arranges for Jacob and Ludovico to stage a sword fight on the castle's battlements, in order to convince Erika (who is in love with Jacob) that the fight is real, and in doing so win Erika, Morag's only confidante, back over to Giulia's side. When Giulia brings Morag to the battlements to witness this display, Morag is blindfolded, and Chaplin's movements across the side of the castle's precipice – at various moments Chaplin herself seems nearly to fall over the edge – invest the sequence with danger and energy. But as Rosenbaum reveals in his writing on his visit to the set of the film, Chaplin could see through her blindfold – meaning that these movements and gestures are in fact a conjuring trick not unlike the one Giulia stages for Erika (once we are aware that Chaplin can see through her blindfold, the sequence plays less like an enactment of real danger and more like a carefully patterned dance). Later, during the final battle between Morag and Giulia – in which Morag achieves her goal of vanquishing the sun goddess, a victory presented as less a fulfillment of narrative and more an achievement of abstract dance and play with cinematic reflexivity – Rivette films Chaplin, in occasional close-up, through grainy, black-and-white lens filters, amplifying our sense of

Morag as a ghost but also displacing a substantial share of Chaplin's performative agency onto the film stock itself.

Finally, though, what most lingers after viewing Chaplin's performance in *Noroît* are not so much these angular orchestrations of movements and gesture but rather those moments in which she is given the space and time to incarnate Morag as precisely what she is: a goddess, whose striking visage alone authorizes her purpose. The most vivid example of this arrives during the battlements sequence. As Jacob and Ludovico's staging of swordplay begins, Rivette briefly cuts to a shot of a blindfolded Chaplin, looking up at the heavens: despite our knowledge that Chaplin can see through this mask, she convincingly embodies Morag here as an otherworldly figure on the edge of emotional disaster – the character is about to lose her only confidante in the castle, her only connection to earthly reality. But it is perhaps only through this loss that Morag will become completely what she is: a powerful figure whose authority – in Rivette, this is always a performative authority – comes not through her connection to another figure in the frame, but solely through the artistic command of the actor playing her. After Erika's capitulation to Giulia, Morag removes her blindfold (Figure 4.12), and Rivette cuts to an extended, medium shot of Chaplin, staring at these events as she stands against the side of the battlements. Against the purple-pinkish haze of the horizon line and washed-out blue of the sea, Morag remains suspended between fulfillment and disaster. But Chaplin here remains confidently

**Figure 4.12** Blindfolded in *Noroît*

**Figure 4.13** Chaplin, confidently poised as a performer in *Noroît*

poised as a performer, sublimely incarnating Rivette's frame in such a way as to make the narrative palimpsest of *Noroît* at least momentarily moot (Figure 4.13). If the modernist abstraction of Rivette's film ultimately works to distance its viewer, emotionally, from the goals and desires of the characters (and often from Morag herself, even as she remains the most psychologically legible character in the film), it is in frames like these that the film's strategies enable more mysterious enchantments. Chaplin, in this frame incarnating the goddess of the moon who eclipses our view of the sun against this horizon line, has never been more entrancing: here in her eyes seems to lie the unspoken, intangible secret of the film. *Noroît*'s viewer, never grasping that secret in words, may only serve to witness that Chaplin's eyes possess it.

## Chaplin and Rivette, Part II: Charlotte in *L'Amour par terre*

In her next film for Rivette, Chaplin is cast as Charlotte, an actor living in Paris, one of two performers we follow throughout the narrative; the other is Emily, played by Jane Birkin. The names of the two female leads in this film are another of Rivette's allusions, suggesting that, in *L'Amour par terre*, Rivette's actors again incarnate abstract, metaliterary conceits: the film, as already noted, takes its title (and one of its key scenes) from a Paul Verlaine poem, and Chaplin, as Charlotte, embodies a character whose very name is a playful allusion to the French nickname for her father, "Charlot." The fact that Jane Birkin's character is named Emily also likens the names of both female characters to the Brontë sisters. This idea of past figures haunting actors becomes a key theme in the narrative of Rivette's film.

When we first meet them, Charlotte and Emily are acting in an experimental play staged not in a conventional venue but in an apartment in Paris. In the opening scenes on the city streets, the camera follows an audience, gathering together for a performance in the apartment of Silvano (Facundo Bo), an alcoholic actor who has recruited Charlotte and Emily for an unauthorized staging of a play by the dramatist Clément Roquemaure (Jean-Pierre Kalfon). Rather than gazing upon actors placed under a traditional proscenium arch, the diegetic audience in the first sequence of *L'Amour par terre* follow and look at Chaplin, Birkin, and Bo through doorways and around corners, in an avant-garde production that evokes Rivette's own unconventional methods in cinema. During the performance of the play (a light comic melodrama about a love affair), Silvano slowly drinks himself into a stupor, resulting in a soused invention of new lines of dialogue, which the audience receives as an intentional improvisation. After the show, Charlotte and Emily, frustrated with Silvano's unexpected, inebriated variations on the script, take up the offer of Roquemaure (who is in attendance at this performance) to star in his latest production. This play, too, will take place within the confines of a house: Roquemaure's elegant estate in St. Cloud, at the villa Gounod (something of a palatial French cinematic landmark: as Mary Wiles reminds us, this residence also features centrally in Alain Robbe-Grillet's 1983 film *La belle captive*; Wiles 2012: 112).

As Charlotte and Emily, Geraldine Chaplin and Jane Birkin perform a kind of duet in *L'Amour par terre*, their characterizations relying on the audience's ability to "read" each performance in relation to the other, and in light of certain biographical parallels between Chaplin and Birkin. Both are French- and English-speaking actors of partial British extraction, and each emerged in cinema during roughly the same moment in the 1960s: Birkin in an early role in Michelangelo Antonioni's *Blowup* (1966) and then, after the making of the film *Slogan* (1969), in a highly publicized romance and professional partnership with French singer Serge Gainsbourg. Nevertheless, it is Chaplin's character in *L'Amour par terre* who strikes the viewer as more of a foreigner in France, as Chaplin occasionally slips into a British-inflected English (for which she is teased, in the film, by Birkin's character; Birkin herself is here the relatively more "French" of the two performers, a quality amplified through the viewer's knowledge of her presence in French pop music and culture in the preceding two decades). Other elements of Chaplin's and Birkin's contrasting characterizations are more subtle, and emerge through careful attention to the way their performances play with and against one another onscreen. Chaplin's Charlotte is the first to arrive at Roquemaure's villa: her first steps into the empty estate are hesitant and cautious. This arrival is in contrast to the way in which Birkin's Emily will later rush into the house, spilling the contents of her purse all over the floor. Charlotte is also the first to glimpse herself in one of the house's many reflective surfaces: when she meets Paul (André Dussollier) – a magician, and one of Roquemaure's collaborators – he grasps her hand, sparking a doubled vision of Chaplin, with Charlotte now glimpsing another version of herself on the other side of the room. In this sudden mirage, Chaplin is sitting down, cross-legged, sipping a drink – a position and a gesture Charlotte will, mysteriously, find herself unconsciously performing in the subsequent scene in Roquemaure's office, when he delivers the two actors the first draft of the play. The moment suggests that who has control over Charlotte's diegetic performance (both of her own self, and of the character she is to assume in Roquemaure's play) is an open question: does she have performative agency or is she a marionette manipulated unconsciously by the "magic" enabled by the male *metteurs en scène* in the film? These unexpected moments of mirrored imagery imply that Charlotte is herself struggling with achieving control over her life and her performance (which, in Rivette's cinema, amount to the same thing). Birkin's Emily will not glimpse similar visions of herself until halfway through the film, suggesting, in contrast to Charlotte, the emotional and psychic distance Emily initially erects between her personal life and the mounting of this play. Momentarily startled by her magical vision, Charlotte's caution and hesitation is balanced by her enthusiasm for the play, and her desire to win the part of Barbara, a character based on the lover who jilted Roquemaure at some point prior to the beginning of *L'Amour par terre*.

As Douglas Morrey and Alison Smith discuss in their book on Rivette, *L'Amour par terre* is a film about love and jealousy, and, like many of the director's films, about the way in which life imitates art (2015: 211). The theme of love involves the Chaplin character's romantic past. Initially resistant to offer details of her personal biography to either of the male "directors" (Roquemaure and Paul), Chaplin, in a scene in which Charlotte is besotted by drink, eventually reveals her character's past, which involves a love affair with an American playwright named David who wanted to write her the perfect part, but who was so in love with her that he ultimately could not bear to see her perform for other eyes. This revelation, to some extent, is part and parcel with one of the central motifs of the film, which involves male authors using the theatre to reflect upon their obsession with "la nostalgie d'une femme idéale" ("a nostalgia for an ideal woman"). In her alternately bemused and anguished revelation of her own romantic past to Paul, however, Chaplin's Charlotte challenges the way in which the male authors in the film torture themselves over poetic visions "d'une femme idéale" through her very existence as a woman whose emotional reality is not a romantic fantasy of the past but instead part of a more complicated present moment.

In the scene in which her character reveals her love affair to Paul, Chaplin, rather than assuming the stilled pose of an idealized figure, moves about the room as she tells her story, variously positioning herself in order to embody certain details and emotional realities of the personal history she is relating. Her lover, David, had vertigo, and suffered from alcoholism; as she tells Paul about their move from a second-floor apartment to the ground floor (in part to assuage David's fear of heights), Chaplin positions herself on the top edge of a couch before moving down to the floor, reenacting the move to a lower floor in a building. As her account begins to reveal more aspects of Charlotte's relationship with David, including his refusal to write a part for her, preferring that she instead suffer for his art in private, the camera moves gradually closer to Chaplin's face as she and Paul embrace. But as Chaplin's account of her relationship with David becomes more emotionally vexed – she reveals that David loved her "for my tears," rather than for the skill she might have offered to an artistic collaboration – she moves away from Paul and back over to the couch, this time on the side closest to the camera, framed now in a medium close-up. As she concludes her story, Paul moves over to the couch, again to console her. Chaplin breaks free of his grasp ("My life doesn't revolve around men!," she exclaims, in French), now moving over to an adjacent room, where she curls up on a bed, facing the camera and away from Paul. This moment of performance by Chaplin rejects the attempt of the male authors in the narrative to idealize or "fix" feminine subjectivity. Instead, Chaplin presents Charlotte as an individual with a complex relationship to her emotional past, a past which cannot be fixed by another author but remains contingently alive in Charlotte's experience, and in Chaplin's performance.

If Chaplin's work here suggests her character's resistance to the romantic idealizations of the male authors in the film, many of her scenes with Birkin foreground the importance of female camaraderie, an alternative formation. Charlotte's and Emily's friendship to some extent also counters the way in which Birkin's and Chaplin's on-set relationship was characterized in publicity for the film. In one interview, for example, Birkin revealed that she was jealous of the attention Rivette was lavishing upon Chaplin in his direction of *L'Amour par terre*, perhaps another case of life imitating art in Rivette's cinema (see Morrey and Smith 2015: 209). Admittedly, there is at times a tension between Charlotte and Emily in the film: in one scene, Charlotte calls Emily a "bitch" after Emily teases her about the rather unfashionable jumpsuit Charlotte wears during rehearsals for the play. But these moments of tension are almost always playful and benign, and the viewer is ultimately left, when attention is paid to the way Chaplin and Birkin work onscreen together, with a much stronger sense of the bond between the two women.

This camaraderie is particularly evident in scenes in which Charlotte and Emily are alone with one another. Early in the film, for example, after first arriving at Roquemare's villa and receiving a copy of the play they are to perform on the estate, Charlotte and Emily, alone in Charlotte's room, commiserate about the strangeness of the situation and the oddness of both Roquemare and Paul. Initially, Chaplin presents Charlotte, curled up on the bed in a tightly bound position, as the more stable and emotionally contained of the two, in contrast to Birkin who, annoyed in particular with the magic acts of Paul (in an earlier scene, he has conjured a dove from behind the folds of her scarf), darts around the bed in nervous agitation. After Emily sits down on the bed, she encourages Charlotte to be optimistic about her chances of winning the part of Barbara, as Chaplin now extends her arms and legs outward as the camera begins to track in slightly closer toward the pair. Both the gradually unfolding positioning of the two actors as well as the dialogue – which emphasizes the non-competitive friendship of the two characters, who both assure the other that they are better for the part of Barbara – illustrate that they are very different people who are nevertheless able to maintain a close bond. This friendship is further underscored a moment later when Emily, again standing, listens with bemusement to Charlotte's revelation that she may be romantically interested in Roquemare. After listening

**Figure 4.14** A moment of companionship between Chaplin and Jane Birkin in *L'Amour par terre*

to Charlotte speak, Birkin returns to the bed, now sitting back-to-back with Chaplin, the two joined together in a shared position emblemizing the characters' friendship. Moments of companionship and commiseration like this one occur throughout the film, functioning as performative parentheticals that to some extent throw the scenes between Charlotte, Emily, and the more aggressive, nostalgic male characters in the film into relief (Figure 4.14).

If *L'Amour par terre* functions to some extent as a Chaplin–Birkin duet, Chaplin's most memorable moment in the film is nevertheless a solo performance. Charlotte, frustrated with both the rehearsals and her ambiguous dalliance with Roquemare, returns to the villa under a twilight sky after spending the evening alone in a bar. Chaplin's gestures and movements convey Charlotte's tipsiness, her outstretched arms providing balance as she ambles down the steps to the lower part of a garden bordering the house. She arrives soon at a gazebo, held up by six Roman columns, in the middle of which is perched a statue of Cupid. Chaplin, her hand lightly caressing the first column she meets, performs a series of half-circles around each of the columns (and traces the entirety of a circle around the whole of the gazebo), musing with ambivalence about her once and future loves, speaking a different fragmentary phrase for each column upon which she alights: "I love him – a little – a lot – passionately – not at all – a little – anyway, love bores me!" Arriving at the column with which she began, she turns around and faces the house: "Love bugs me! Shush!" she cries, a play on words in French that couples her irritation with the men in her life to the sound of the cicadas and crickets chirping around her in the garden. Walking away from the gazebo, Chaplin steps toward the camera, placing herself in a medium long shot, continuing to reflect upon her frustrations in love as she mimes affectionate gestures, raising her hands in the air in an embrace of an invisible partner – "you feel for his hand . . . come affection . . . a last kiss" – before comically dropping them to her side – "he's snoring!". She keeps her hands partially outstretched, as if remaining open to a potential lover, a continuing expression of her ambivalence. Returning to the columns, she repeats her circle around the gazebo, now wondering if her potential paramour snores, and if so, how much – "a little, a lot, passionately, or not at all – They all do" – snorting loudly and mockingly for each column she touches. Arriving, in the center, at Cupid, she tickles the toes of the statue. Rivette cuts to a closer medium shot as Chaplin climbs the half-column upon which Cupid is perched, comically pinching its buttocks while bringing her face close to the statue's in a kiss (Figure 4.15). Alternating between expressions of affection and disgust as she brings her lips to Cupid's, after a moment she knocks down the statue, watching it shatter. Climbing to the top of the half-column, Chaplin now stands in place of Cupid, but only momentarily. "I hate children," she muses wryly, looking down at Cupid's broken shell. She darts away from the cracked pieces of the statue and, gathering her shoes,

**Figure 4.15** Chaplin encounters Cupid in *L'Amour par terre*

returns to the house. In this scene in the gazebo, Charlotte is a figure of movement who is alive to her own skill in playful, light gesture, responsive to but also questioning of love, refusing finally to give in to the magical, but also oddly static, idealizations of the male authors in the film, figured here by Cupid's statue. As performed by Chaplin, Charlotte embodies the feminine subjectivity at work in *L'Amour par terre*, creating a character who becomes something more, and more memorable, than the sum of Rivette's references and authorial obsessions.

## Chaplin and Resnais: *La vie est un roman*

Chaplin's work for Jacques Rivette finds her experimenting with the various possibilities of screen space, guided by the idea of mise en scène as a present-tense inscription to which the performer contributes at the moment of filming. In contrast, in her films for Alain Resnais, she works for an auteur whose major subjects are time and memory, and whose primary aesthetic conceit involves unconventional editing strategies. While her parts for Rivette place Chaplin in lead roles in which she commands substantial stretches of screen duration, her presence in two films for Resnais takes the form of supporting work: in 1983's *La vie est un roman* (translated, in its English-subtitled release, as *Life is a Bed of Roses*) and in Resnais's bilingual 1989 film *I Want to Go Home* (her part in *I Want to Go Home*, as mentioned previously, amounts to just slightly more than a cameo). Her brief moments in *La vie est un roman* suggest the skill with which Chaplin is able to adapt to various aesthetic strategies at play in French art cinema.

Gilles Deleuze, a major commentator on Resnais's films, offers a useful context for understanding the adjustments Chaplin makes in her work for Resnais. Deleuze considers Resnais one of the major practitioners of the "time-image," a cinematic approach which questions the causal agency of protagonists in classical "movement-image" cinema (see Deleuze on Resnais; 1989: 116–25). Time and duration are key to Resnais's films: no longer is duration "filled up" by the heroic acts of central characters (who would otherwise conform to norms of adult subjectivity and hold that normative world together through their actions and behavior). Instead, time in Resnais becomes a space for play and invention, with characters now unsure how to act in a destabilized situation. Some characters, however, rather than simply suffering under the pressures of time, work to invest the world with further disruption, opening up new ways of being and acting. This is the philosophy governing the world in which Chaplin's mischievous character in *La vie est un roman* lives.

The film focuses on a group of teachers who gather at an elegant palace, ostensibly to discuss new ideas in education. The major conflict in these scenes is between two different groups of teachers: those who prefer "policing" child behavior, and those who see value in productive, organized chaos, free of unnecessarily repressive structures. Chaplin's character, not surprisingly, prefers the imaginative approach of the second group. Resnais combines these contemporary scenes with sequences set on the same stretch of land on which the castle is constructed, flashback sequences set in various time periods. These sudden irruptions of memory, which seem to belong to the landscape itself rather than any one character, mainly occur in the years surrounding World War I, the period in which the castle was built as a kind of retreat in which adults desensitized by mechanized modernity might escape into restorative reverie. Resnais also includes stylized sequences set during the medieval period, and layers elements of these different temporal landscapes in single shots, indicative of the way history becomes like a palimpsest in human memory.

In *La vie est un roman*, Resnais's interests in temporality enable Chaplin to generate moments of performance that are economical and broadly comical, establishing her character as a privileged, impishly disruptive figure. Her performance for Resnais, as is suitable for a filmmaker interested in questions of time, also suggests that her character is in a thoughtful state of becoming, untethered to any stable understanding of interiority or already-articulated subjectivity, and able to comment ironically on past forms of subjectivity she has inhabited. As Elena del Río writes of performance in "time-image" films, "the moving body is not an a priori entity undergoing a series of static poses, the reconstruction of which into a continuous flow would only reaffirm the body's stability and unity" (2008: 12). Instead, "moving and gesturing processes" in Resnais generate affect (and are themselves affected), creating bodies and characters undergoing uncertain "lines of flight." In this respect, each moment of performance in Chaplin's work for Resnais suggests a different wrinkle in her character's becoming, each gesture or expression conveying not so much interiority or psychology but rather an emerging possibility for her character to explore.

Chaplin plays Nora Winkle, a cosmopolitan, gender-bending teacher whose work has taken her around the world: before arriving at the conference it is revealed that she traveled to Canada and disguised herself as a man, in order to carry out an academic study on masculine labor. Chaplin's characterization makes clear her character's androgynous sensibility: dressed throughout in masculine shirts and slacks, and with her hair cut boyishly short, Chaplin's self-stylization complements Resnais's ambiguous temporal structure with an equally indefinite presentation of gender (Figure 4.16). There is also a subtle queer undertone to much of her performance: while it initially appears Nora has ostensibly returned to the conference to see her former lover, the conference's keynote speaker Walter Guarini (Vittorio Gassman, the other major transnational actor in the cast), her comments about men in the film are caustic and ironic, and she spends most of her time with other women. (In this Nora is something of a sister to Lucie in *Le Voyage en douce*, as well as to Rita, who near the end of Robert Altman's *A Wedding* expresses a desire for the bride played by Amy Stryker.) Nora is also ambivalent about children, a striking trait in a film about teachers: in her first scene, flustered by a car stranded just on the outskirts of the palace, Nora leaves her daughter behind at a garbage dump; and unlike the other characters in the film, who endlessly debate pedagogical strategies, Nora is more interested in intervening in the romantic dalliances of other women, as in the scenes in which she attempts to bring together the disruptive, boisterous teacher Robert (Pierre Arditi) with his opposite, the mousy, shy Élisabeth (Sabine Azéma).

**Figure 4.16** Chaplin as Nora Winkle in *La vie est un roman*

When Nora Winkle arrives at the palace, she is late, and the conference is underway: Walter Guarini has already started pontificating about pedagogy in a speech to the other teachers. Chaplin sits down to rest for a moment, as the viewer hears from offscreen, in the other room, Guarini's words extolling the virtues of "undisciplined" pedagogical forms. Recognizing the voice, Nora stands up and begins repeating, verbatim, the words of the male speaker. As Chaplin moves to the conference room, her performance not only continues to experiment with gender as she mimics the words and gestures of the offscreen male orator, but she also underscores the hypocrisy of the speaker's message: Walter, whose words emphasize the importance of undisciplined, improvisatory teaching, is nevertheless so predictable in what he is saying that Chaplin is able to anticipate and silently mouth each word as the speech unfolds.

Chaplin's performance presents Nora as someone who will disrupt proceedings: arriving late, parodying the keynote speaker, and showing up not so much to debate pedagogical strategies but to experiment with amorous relationships and formations. Up to this point Nora is presented as a solitary creature. But in the next scene Nora becomes, like Charlotte in Rivette's *L'Amour par terre*, a character for whom camaraderie is important; and she expresses her philosophy of friendship not through a lecture but through her way of living, her performance. Once she is inside the conference room, Chaplin has Nora linger in the doorway, observing the end of Walter's speech as well as the beginning of the first debate between the teachers in the film. A few moments later, Nora quietly slips into the room to greet Guarini, but is soon noticed by her friend Claudine (Martine Kelly), who begins to shout a loud greeting. Chaplin's Nora begins to perform an impromptu dance with Claudine, interrupting the proceedings. This irruption gains the attention of the conference organizer, who, far from being displeased, greets Nora like a celebrity performer, guiding her to the center of the room – which is elevated like a theater-in-the-round – and introducing her to the rest of the participants. This position distinguishes Nora, and Chaplin, from the other performers in the room, but a beat later she effaces this personal and social distance, descending from the stage to plant kisses on the lips of several men and women gathered around to see her. The moment establishes Nora as an energetic, unpredictable, and sexually ambiguous figure in this otherwise unsurprising world of buttoned-up pedagogy.

If, in this sequence, Chaplin presents Nora as a radical, androgynous academic equally at home with men and with women, and even momentarily forgetful of her normative, familial responsibilities (she has, after all, left her daughter behind to fend for herself before arriving at the palace), in later scenes the film tends to associate her with her small group of female friends. At the end of the conference day, she gathers in a room with Élisabeth and Claudine, enjoying drinks. Élisabeth is complaining about the boorish behavior of some of the men at the conference. Nora, a more experienced academic, assures Élisabeth her best option is not to sulk but rather to engage in an alternative, feminine form of "tribal" behavior. (Unlike the other two women, however, it is possible to imagine the androgynous Nora enjoying both masculine and feminine forms of camaraderie.) As notable in this sequence than anything Chaplin does or says is how she is dressed: all in black, as if her character were a stagehand at a theatrical show. And from this point forward, this is largely how Chaplin characterizes Nora: as something of a puckish, diegetic *metteur en scène*, who spends the rest of *La vie est un roman* hovering at the edge of the frame, inhabiting the margins of Resnais's unstable time-images in order to draw Élisabeth into the romantic circle of the other academics, attempting to set her up with a teacher whose philosophy of pedagogy, if not his personality, most matches hers. In this sense, Nora functions as something of a gatekeeper to the professional world in *La vie est un roman*, her sprightly and undisciplined behavior in her first sequence in the film reflective of Nora's social privilege, her success and status already established.

There is also a reflexive element to this performance. In *La vie est un roman*, the slightly older, wiser, and more privileged woman, Nora, is played by Chaplin, while the young, inexperienced, and wary Élisabeth is played by Sabine Azéma, a new actor in the first of what will be several roles for Resnais. *La vie est un roman* was negatively received upon its initial release in France, with the exception of the performance of Azéma which, as Emma Wilson discusses in her study of Resnais (2009: 157–8), was celebrated by critics as the work of a promising young ingénue. In this respect, the making of this Resnais film, which tells the story of Chaplin's character initiating Azéma into a world of academics, to some extent mirrors the way in which Chaplin herself gives way, in French cinema, to the arrival of yet one more new *Parisienne*. But most notably, the moment also enables Chaplin, with nearly two decades' distance at the time of making *La vie est un roman* in the early eighties, to wryly and ironically comment on her own former status as the new starlet in Paris, the earnest young *Parisienne*. At one point in the film, Élisabeth bursts suddenly into song, singing of her desire for true love and earnest romance. In contrast to this, Chaplin, viewing the awkward performance in reaction shot, has Nora offer wry and ironic commentary on Élisabeth's earnest paean to love:

> Romantic love, my dear, is culturally quite recent ... Blinded by romantic illusions ... It can strike you suddenly, and be gone as fast. Depending on the circumstances, the lighting, the packaging, like in a supermarket: why favor one brand of detergent soap over another?

These lines, spoken by a character who is a cultural anthropologist, can also be taken as a critique of the packaging of young actresses themselves in swooning and romantic film narratives, including the publicization of Chaplin herself as a new star in marketing materials for *Doctor Zhivago*. In this way, Resnais's cinema, which relies upon the disjunction of images and perspectives rather than their fluid continuity, enables Chaplin not only to ironically comment upon the earnest, romantic yearnings of Azéma's character, but also to implicitly critique the very idea of the star system through her experience of having inhabited the *Parisienne* type.

Eventually, Nora settles into the shadows of *La vie est un roman*, to some extent becoming a propmaster and stagehand working to slyly orchestrate and direct Élisabeth's professional and personal life. In this way, so too does Chaplin step aside for the emergence of another star in French cinema. Nevertheless, her ironic counterpoint to Élisabeth's attitude toward love suggests an awareness, in this film, of this inherent sexism in film culture (French and otherwise), which demands that one former starlet, and a former new *Parisienne*, step aside for the arrival of another one. Chaplin offers a wry commentary on these machinations, and to the film's credit, this irony is presented in the film as part of a professional and personal discourse conducted between the Chaplin character and the other women in the film. Even if *La vie est un roman* in this respect marks something of an end to Chaplin's career as a young *Parisienne*, Chaplin's own journey through world cinema does not, of course, end here. Her career in cinema, French and otherwise, continues without rest well into the twenty-first century, resulting in a prolific and ongoingly cosmopolitan body of work that continues to transgress boundaries and conventions.

# Chapter 5

# Modern Times: Geraldine Chaplin across contemporary cinema

To begin, two shots. In each, a Chaplin alternately reveals and withholds a self:

The first is the final close-up of the Little Tramp in Charlie Chaplin's masterpiece, *City Lights* (1931). Here (Figure 5.1) he is frozen in his final gesture, a moment shimmering with uncertainty. Chaplin holds a flower in his hand and lets slip the faintest trace of a smile, as the Tramp looks upon the blind flower girl (Virginia Cherrill) with whom he is smitten. The Little Tramp, having gently tricked this lovely girl into believing him a handsome and wealthy benefactor, in the final sequence of the film meets her again in her flower shop, her sight freshly restored via surgery through his efforts (earlier, having come briefly into money, he has paid for the operation which restores her sight). In this close-up, she sees him stripped of the pretense with which he adorned himself when she was sightless: no longer the dashing, wealthy figure she mistook him for in her mind's eye, he is now nothing other than the man he appears to be. Who that precisely is, however, remains a question as the shot fades to black and the film ends.

In her study of Chaplin as director, Donna Kornhaber describes *City Lights* as a film "about uncertainty: of relationships, of status, of the body, of love itself" (2014: 198). Her words serve as suitable descriptors of the final gesture in the film. William Rothman, however, in an essay that also lingers with this final shot, contends that Chaplin achieves in his cumulative moment of performance in *City Lights* nothing less than a disclosure of self, a revelation of humanity stripped from all performance, pretense, and distance. "In describing this last moment," Rothman writes,

> I am no longer willing to refer to this human figure as "the Tramp." It is *Chaplin*, this human being of flesh and blood, who stands exposed in this frame, revealed in his mortality and his desperate longing to be loved. (1988: 52–3)

**Figure 5.1** Charlie Chaplin in the final frames of *City Lights*

**Figure 5.2** Geraldine Chaplin as her grandmother Hannah in *Chaplin*

George Toles, in an essay on the film which cites Rothman's reading, questions the extent to which Chaplin reveals a self fully and intimately available to viewers. "I would prefer to regard Chaplin as simultaneously knowing and not knowing where he stands in relation to the Tramp at the end of *City Lights*," Toles writes; "Why could he not be unsure what his look is finally releasing *and* hiding *and* in need of?" (2011: 104). To contemplate this question, Toles recounts a possibly apocryphal childhood anecdote from John McCabe's 1978 biography of Chaplin. In it, Chaplin's mother visits young Charlie in a workhouse, where the child is said to have been "ashamed to greet her because he was filthy, lice-ridden, and his head was shaved" (Toles 2011: 104). According to this account, Chaplin's mother, in response to her son's anxiety over his appearance, cradles his face in her hands and says, simply: "With all thy dirt, I love thee still" (McCabe 1978: 11). Chaplin's mother's gesture, as described, and at the same time mythologized, in McCabe's book, is itself a kind of close-up, in which Charlie's mother brings his face to hers to reassure him of her love. For Toles, the final frames of *City Lights* – in which the close-up of Charlie would seem to ask for, but not immediately confirm, love's acknowledgment – does not bring the "real" Chaplin any closer, at least not unambiguously. Our view of Charlie's face in this moment is not free of conundrums. As Toles writes,

> To what extent does [the film's] final shot draw on such memories and memory-fictions, driving Chaplin back to a place where he still does not know how to protect himself, nor how to appear, nor what he is seeking in the way of love or recompense? (2011: 104)

The closer the viewer gets to Charlie, the more puzzling – and tantalizing, in its ongoing promise of a human meaning – Chaplin's face becomes.

The second shot I draw attention to here is of Geraldine Chaplin (Figure 5.2), in Richard Attenborough's biopic about her father, *Chaplin* (1992). The film offers the opportunity to see Chaplin play Hannah Chaplin, her grandmother. Although only a supporting role, her performance is nevertheless the most remarkable aspect of the film, which presents Charlie's mother with the kind of loving – if ambiguous – intimacy the final shot of Charlie in *City Lights* would seem to want to find again, or restore. When Geraldine Chaplin occupies the screen as Hannah Chaplin in this film, Hannah becomes a moving figure in a screen biography that seeks to make a contribution to the mythology of Charlie Chaplin's life and work.

In terms of the perceived spatial distance created by the placement of the camera, we never get quite as close to Hannah Chaplin in these early scenes of *Chaplin* as we do to Charlie's Little Tramp at the end of *City Lights*. Nevertheless, this shot of Geraldine Chaplin in a film about her father's life generates its own emotional perplexities. In her performance, Geraldine portrays Hannah as someone with a love for entertaining others (and a desire to eke out a living doing so in vaudeville). But because of the economic conditions surrounding her, as well as Hannah's schizophrenia (a condition supported by the biographical record on Chaplin's life and made palpable in Geraldine's characterization), she is unable to achieve her theatrical ambitions.

This shot I have selected here is a remarkable moment appearing early in *Chaplin*, a fleeting moment of intimacy between mother and son. Rather than frame Geraldine from a slight distance, as he does in most of *Chaplin*, Attenborough here places the camera in a relatively intimate medium shot, at an angle slightly above her, underscoring Hannah's vulnerability. Hannah is huddled in the corner of a room, near a coal stove. She nervously kneads between the palms of both hands a lump of coal, Chaplin's gestures suggesting that Hannah has taken the unpliable black lump for soft bread. Charlie, at the age of fourteen in this scene – he is played here by Thomas Bradford – moves close to Hannah; Bradford joins the shot as the camera begins to move closer to Geraldine, taking the lump of coal in his own hands before cradling his arm around Hannah. The moment unambiguously conveys Charlie's love and care for his mother, and as such is a kind of inverse of the gesture described in McCabe's biography of Chaplin. There, a mother receives a scraggly son with fulsome love and acceptance, unconditionally; here, a son receives a bedraggled mother with total affection. Further, young Charlie's own handling of the coal in this scene suggests a willingness to acknowledge the legitimacy of her way of seeing the world – coal for bread – even as it is colored by a mental illness that renders her unable to be fully a part of his.

This is a quietly remarkable moment of performance created between Chaplin and Bradford. The shot here of Geraldine – a relatively close one, as *Chaplin* elsewhere presents Hannah Chaplin in long and medium shots – also poses puzzles of performance akin to those generated by Charlie Chaplin's final close-up in *City Lights*. How fully can Hannah accept or even understand this love offered by her son, given her own fragile – by the moment of the above shot, shattered – mental state? How fully can Geraldine herself understand her own grandmother, given that here she is incarnating a character whose life she characterizes from a distance (Hannah Chaplin died in a mental institution in 1928, sixteen years before Geraldine was born)? I, for one, am certainly moved by the *fact* of watching Geraldine play her own grandmother in this film; the beauty of the performance is located in Geraldine's ability to conjure, with convincing emotion and startling presence, a blood relation she never met in life. Here she is not writing a biography but incarnating one: contributing to the mythology of her father's life, but also underscoring in her performance the emotional and economic reality in which her grandmother was fated to live. The effectiveness of the performance – and of the tenderness of this scene, in which young Charlie embraces his mother with love – works to convey the emotions shared between Charlie and his mother. But the film nevertheless keeps us at a slight, respectful remove, painting a picture of the tragic circumstances of Hannah's life. *Chaplin* positions us not only to empathetically connect to Geraldine's characterization of her own grandmother but also to appreciate the difficult economic reality in which Hannah remained submerged, a situation kept in view through the film's insistence on a medium shot distance, even during this tender moment of affection, in its framing of Chaplin's performance.

This juxtaposition of two moments of intimacy in *City Lights* and *Chaplin*, the encounter staged here between Charlie's and Geraldine's performances in these films, underscores the inherently familial nature of Geraldine Chaplin's work in *Chaplin* and its possible resonances with her father's own disclosures of self in cinema. This encounter also helps frame the discussion of Geraldine's performances in the final stretch of this book. This last chapter does not attempt a complete discussion of the dozens of films Geraldine has made outside of the contexts of the 1960s, 1970s, and early 1980s art cinemas, films that have been my main point of interest in the earlier chapters. Instead, in the following pages I try to understand selected moments from Geraldine's work, across her long and prolific career, in other kinds of films, using the intimate close-up as a motif for analysis. A "close-up," here, does not refer necessarily to the specific kind of shot distance defined in film studies textbooks as a "close-up" (although, in certain cases, it may take that form). My own use of the term is, rather, informed by something Charlie Chaplin himself said about the close-up as a device: "there is no set rule that a close-up gives more emphasis than a long shot" (quoted in Mast 1992: 117). Chaplin's words imply that closeness may be at play in shots of relatively longer spatial distance, an intimacy achieved through performance (and not only through the spatial proximity of the camera), a gesture toward the revelation of emotion in the context of a network of other gestures in a given film. Any moment of close intimacy inaugurated by a gesture or movement potentially creates its own context for a back and forth between intimate disclosure and a private withholding of a character's (and a performer's) self. Further, across the moments I will look at here, Geraldine's performances, while still occasionally citing her father, begin, especially in the later years of her career, to refer more and more to her own body of work in cinema, which is ongoing and prolific. At the same time, each of these performative moments continues to ask questions not unlike those generated by her father's final, magisterial close-up at the end of *City Lights*: to what does this intimacy with a character created by an actor amount? Do moments of performative intimacy transcend uncertainty? In what ways does Geraldine Chaplin "reveal" a humanity onscreen in these late films?

This emphasis on gestures of closeness – including moments when Chaplin's face becomes her most salient performative resource – to some extent works as a counterpoint to the preceding pages in this book. Earlier chapters have privileged Chaplin's remarkable achievements for directors such as David Lean, Carlos Saura, Robert Altman, Alan Rudolph, Jacques Rivette, and Alain Resnais. Several of these filmmakers employ art cinema narrative strategies. In such arrangements, Chaplin is either placed in a networked ensemble (as in the cinemas of Altman and Rudolph) or in a series of images in which her gestures and expressions express psychological interiority (or, at other times, conjure ambiguities that prevent us from fully knowing her character's interior state of mind). I have focused primarily on these performances in the earlier chapters because I believe they are Chaplin's most remarkable screen achievements, a body of work belonging to a particularly eccentric art cinema, performances that this book understands as one the most beguiling contributions Geraldine Chaplin has made to cinema as a performative, thoughtful art.

My fascination with her art continues here, but now seeks to extend itself beyond the framework of the earlier chapters, and as it does so becomes interested in the legacy Chaplin is herself leaving behind, relatively autonomously of her father's iconicity in cinema. The performances discussed in this chapter are also different from the films studied in the earlier chapters of this book. Chaplin has, throughout her career, appeared in a variety of films: a popular cinema, from the 1960s until the present day, that stands apart from the aforementioned art cinemas, much closer in spirit to *City Lights*, which seeks a connection to a larger audience; and also more recent forms of art cinema and independent cinema, such as her films for auteurs Pedro Almodóvar and Guy Maddin, work that sometimes refers to and plays with Chaplin's own legacy. In the films discussed in this chapter, however, Chaplin infrequently enjoys the same pride of place she held in the works of Saura, Altman, Rudolph, and Rivette. She is instead frequently cast as a supporting performer, her gestures accentuating a larger narrative frame. Chaplin's work in these films, nevertheless, is fascinating; perhaps because she appears as a marginal figure in many of them, her performances often suggest ideas and thoughts that stand in contrast to the narrative machinations surrounding her characterizations.

To draw the reader close to her achievements in these films, in this final chapter I am interested in moments of performance in which her face becomes a crucial, if at times also ephemeral and ethereal, performative resource. The luminosity, resonance, and expressivity conveyed by Chaplin's eyes and expressions in these films stand apart from and at times momentarily transcend the narrative preoccupations of their directors. As these various films move toward moments of close intimacy – either through the proximity of the frame or through the way in which Geraldine's performance draws us closer, or both – it is more often than not in her face, and in her eyes, that Geraldine's viewer finds a thoughtful and complex humanity, and a suggestion of other kinds of stories that otherwise often lie dormant in these films.

## Carol in *Z.P.G. (Zero Population Growth)*

The dystopic narrative of the 1972 British film *Z.P.G. (Zero Population Growth)* imagines an early twenty-first century in which childbirth, owing to severe overpopulation and environmental devastation, is banned for a stretch of thirty years. The film begins with the delivery of this dictatorial edict to a population already living under stringent social norms. The film follows the story of Carol (Chaplin) and her husband, Russ (Oliver Reed), as they attempt to circumvent their society's rules and have a child. Z.P.G. was the subject of some controversy upon its release in 1972, when an environmental activist group – also called ZPG – objected to the film's distortion of its message of "population stabilization," which for the group involved only a kind of responsible family planning, encouraging couples to have no more than the two children necessary to replace them upon their death (see Olszynko-Gryn and Ellis 2018: 56–7). Likewise, some critics have fretted that, "in forcing us to invest sympathy in characters exercising their right to procreate, the film bears interpretation as a pro-life (or perhaps free love) parable, and maybe as a reactionary lament for the decline of the traditional family" (Leggott 2010: 337).

To the film's credit, however, the first act of *Z.P.G.* primarily focuses on Geraldine Chaplin and her character's anguished decision to flout the law of society and procreate. These scenes focus on her character's internal deliberation over this matter and in doing so enable an alternative interpretation of this stretch of the film. (This is in contrast to the second hour of the film, which focuses mainly on the efforts of Oliver Reed's character to protect his wife from social surveillance, which will sentence both of them to death should the pregnancy be discovered.) Chaplin's performance during the early sequences in the film is enlisted not so much to sway us one way or another in a moral debate over the topic of abortion (with which *Z.P.G.* is, ultimately, not very concerned) but rather to persuade us of the ongoing importance of individuality and expressivity in a repressive and excessively normative social context. But even this rather obvious message is itself less interesting than the way in which it is expressed: through close-ups, sometimes startlingly close, of Chaplin, whose visage during fleeting moments obstructs – on occasion, entirely – our view of the studio-bound, dystopic mise en scène. In such fleeting moments Chaplin's face becomes the film's very "proof" of individuality, in contrast to a backdrop of social repression.

An especially striking close-up of Chaplin appears in a sequence in the film's first act in which Carol reveals to her doctor her desire to have a baby. The inhuman, administrative nature of this encounter is underscored by the fact that this conversation with her doctor takes place entirely through a telescreen, through which the characters communicate, and see one other, from within separate spaces. As the doctor reminds Chaplin of the harsh punishment waiting for couples who violate the reproduction law, the film cuts to an extreme close-up of Chaplin's eyes (Figure 5.3). This close-up of Chaplin momentarily draws our attention away from the surrounding mise en scène and, in fixing our eyes exclusively on hers, from all of Chaplin's other gestural resources. What Chaplin's Carol is expressing here in this frame – against her doctor's demands for mere obedience – is earnest, individual desire, which for the film is expressed in Chaplin's eyes, markers of uniqueness that stand ineluctably against stringency.

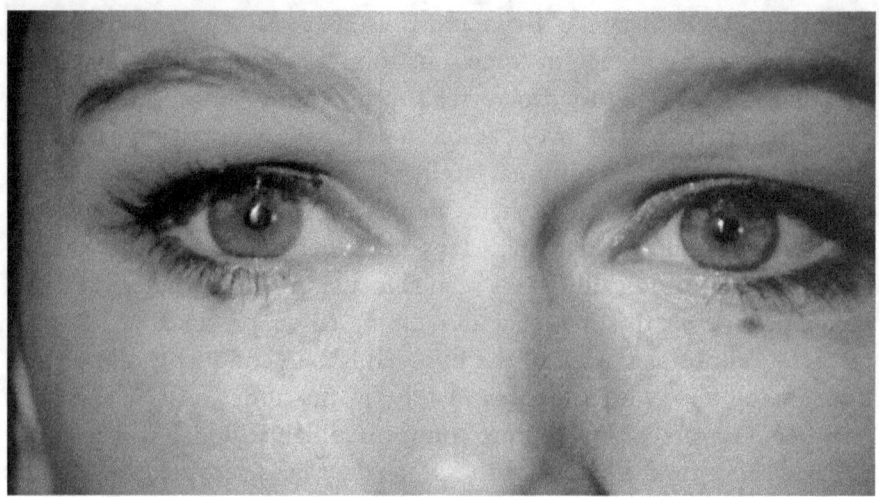

**Figure 5.3** An extreme close-up of Chaplin's eyes in *Z.P.G.: Zero Population Growth*

The most fascinating close-up of Chaplin in the film arrives shortly after this discussion with the doctor. Carol is sorting through dusty old belongings – books, a framed picture of a child, a plush toy tiger, blankets, a music box. Chaplin opens the toy box and a song twinkles out of it. The film cuts from the music box to an extreme close-up of Chaplin's eyes, similar to the close shot described previously. But rather than cutting from this shot of Chaplin's eyes to another figure in the frame (as in the earlier sequence), the camera instead zooms out from Chaplin's eyes to a close-up of her entire face (Figure 5.4). Her face is here stoic and inexpressive, even though our movement toward it might have suggested a revelation of psychological plenitude. As we zoom out from her eyes to this close-up of her face, Chaplin and the camera, both apparently fixed on a rotating device, begin to spin around the room; Chaplin keeps her eyes cast beyond the bottom left corner of the frame, as if the notes from the music box were prompting her to imagine an alternate reality. Remarkably, this moving close-up of Chaplin reshapes the mise en scène surrounding her: as she spins, the background subtly shifts from the utilitarian set design of the film's future world to what appears to be a child's bedroom with a window and yellow curtains. In its play with shot distance and the transformation of space, in concert with Chaplin's stone-faced expression, the shot brings us intimately close to Carol even as it displaces any kind of deep psychological meaning onto her social surround, the source of

**Figure 5.4** Chaplin, in close-up in *Z.P.G.: Zero Population Growth*

the repression preventing her expression of personal meaning. As the last notes of the music box decay (and as the background set design reverts back to a familiar, neutral, brutalist gray and white), the camera zooms back toward Chaplin's face, re-locating the source of this temporary fantasy in her eyes. In this sequence, Chaplin's face is presented as a sign of individuality, but the meaning lingering behind her eyes is nevertheless ambiguous, an index of the kind of distinction and singularity ultimately held in a kind of repressive, psychological straitjacket in the world of this dystopic film.

## Queen Anne in *The Three Musketeers*

Anne of Austria, Queen of France, is described by Alexandre Dumas upon her first appearance in his novel *The Three Musketeers* (1844) in this way:

> Anne of Austria, then twenty-six or twenty-seven years of age, was at the height of her beauty. Her bearing was that of a queen or a goddess; her eyes, sparkling like emeralds, were of matchless splendor yet filled with sweetness and majesty. Her mouth was small and rosy, and though her under-lip, like that of all the princes of the House of Austria, protruded slightly, it was eminently gracious in her smile and profoundly haughty in her scorn. Her skin was much admired for its velvety softness; her hands and arms, surprisingly

> white and delicate of texture, were celebrated by all the poets of the age. And her hair, very blond in her youth, had turned to a warm chestnut; curled very simply and amply powdered, it framed her face so admirably that the most rigid critic could only have desired a little more rouge and the most exacting sculptor a nose somewhat more delicately chiseled. (Dumas 2001: 116–17)

Dumas places this paragraph-length description of Anne in-between two shorter paragraphs in which the Duke of Buckingham, her secret paramour, marvels helplessly at the queen's radiance (from the duke's perspective, she is described as an awe-inducing "apparition," an appreciation that eschews the flaws Dumas includes in those passages that convey a relatively more sober, objective description of the character). The placement of this descriptive paragraph humanizes the queen even as it suggests the remarkable effect her presence has on her subjects, all of whom tend to view her as more celestial than human.

In Richard Lester's 1973 adaptation of *The Three Musketeers*, Chaplin plays Queen Anne, as she does in Lester's two sequels to the film, *The Four Musketeers* (1974) and *The Return of the Musketeers* (1989). Her appearance in the first film is particularly notable, given that much of the plot revolves around her character (in some parts of the world, the film was known as *The Three Musketeers: The Queen's Diamonds* upon release). In the film's version of the story, the Duke of Buckingham, in love with the queen, asks for a memento he might remember her by, given that their love must hide away in secret and that they must remain, for long stretches, apart; she gives the duke her necklace, upon which are lavished twelve jewels. In turn, Cardinal Richelieu (Charlton Heston) devises a plan to steal two of these jewels from the duke while the necklace is in his possession, enabling a political scheme whereby the queen will be publicly embarrassed once it is discovered she has given her now-purloined necklace to another man. But the duke replaces the two jewels, gives (with the help of the Musketeers) the object back to Anne, and the queen is able to keep up appearances.

Nearly every scene in Lester's *The Three Musketeers* is riven with some narrative machination or another; the film is a relatively faithful adaptation of the Dumas novel, and as such is burdened with plot. It is striking, however, that the queen is herself mostly oblivious to all this intrigue swirling about her. The film differs from the novel in the way it introduces Anne to us, and does so in ways that underscore the queen's happy oblivion: while in the novel she is introduced as a beautiful object for the duke's gaze, in the film she is first seen immersed in her own pleasures, child-like, enjoying a rotating swing in her courtyard while commanding her servants to rotate it faster and faster. The novel's slightly ironic description of the queen – emphasizing her otherworldly beauty, only to undercut it with words reminding us of her humanity – is echoed in the film. As Roger Ebert writes in his review of the sequel, it is certainly true that Chaplin (like Faye Dunaway and Raquel Welch, two of her co-stars in *The Three Musketeers*) appears as if "made into [an] exquisite china doll" (Ebert 1975). Nevertheless, Chaplin's characterization of Anne – Neil Sinyard, in his study of Lester's work, has described her performance as "generously unflattering" (2010: 90) – makes clear the daffiness that lies within her character's outwardly aristocratic appearance. In this first scene, while Richelieu, visiting the court, begins his scheme to manipulate the king, Chaplin's Queen Anne twirls round and round on her swing, eyes closed, blissfully and childishly ignorant, her privilege for a time protecting her from the twists of plot that eventually engulf her.

Later in the film, once Anne's eyes are open to the cardinal's devious plan, Lester will include a striking close-up of Chaplin and her eyes, rhymed to an image of the two jewels swiped from Anne's necklace (Figure 5.5). The two jewels are briefly superimposed over Chaplin's eyes in a dissolve connecting two sequences. The image is a cinematic transliteration of words describing the queen from the Dumas text ("her eyes, sparkling like emeralds"). Even so, the image gradually draws us, across the dissolving superimposition, away from any preceding text and closer to Chaplin's eyes, and to their unique surrounding features: the little teardrop birthmarks below her eyelids are complemented by the circular chain links at the bottom of each emerald, Lester's placement of the jewels in the first shot harmoniously matching the most particular features of Chaplin's face in the next. It is remarkable that the daughter of Charlie Chaplin should be positioned – here, through the device of the superimposition – as an aristocratic, irreplaceable jewel, of the type that the Little Tramp could himself never afford to even catch a glimpse of, let alone possess; and yet her performance as Queen Anne reinforces throughout the character's simplicity, her basic humanness, and her child-like whimsy, all traits that link her more closely, in terms of behavior if not appearance, to her father's signature character. This arresting, bejeweled close-up of Chaplin brings us close to Anne even as it reasserts the aristocratic lavishness of the distant, detached queen.

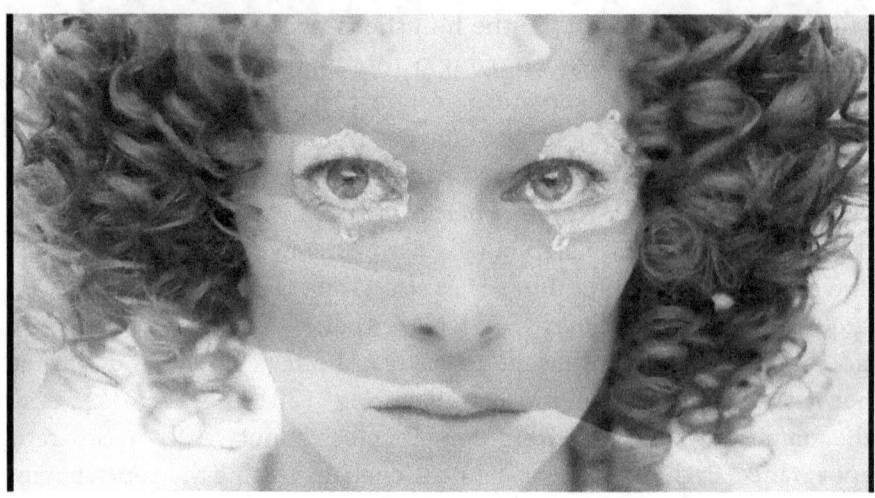

**Figure 5.5** A striking close-up of Chaplin and her eyes, rhymed to an image of the two jewels stolen from Queen Anne's necklace, from *The Three Musketeers*

## Marilyn in *Roseland*

> Interviewer: What's impressive in Geraldine Chaplin's performance [in *Roseland*] is how sharply she suffers. In a striking moment the camera trains on her face and then moves forward for an even closer view, which it holds for another five or six seconds. Her needle-sharp wounding is immediately apparent in her eyes. Tell me if I'm wrong, but don't those dark, glinting eyes remind you a little of her father, Charlie Chaplin?
>
> James Ivory: I felt that they did. (Long 2006: 138)

"It wasn't only father who was an artist," Geraldine Chaplin comments in a 1964 interview, when the subject turns to Oona O'Neill; "mother also wanted to be an actress" (Fallaci 1967: 173). Chaplin is fond of remarking, as she does in the same interview, that she has "mother's face from my forehead to my nose, and father's from my nose to my chin" (168), even though the idea that her face carries marks of familial inheritance infrequently plays an explicit role in the narratives of Chaplin's films. One exception to this tendency is the Merchant-Ivory production *Roseland* (1977), a feature comprising three short stories all set in the New York City ballroom of the film's title. In the second of these three narratives, "The Hustle," Chaplin's character, Marilyn, is said to resemble a mother figure. But in the film, this mother figure does not belong to the character Chaplin plays; instead, the unseen mother belongs to a man named Russell, played by Christopher Walken. Russell is a former dancer-turned-gigolo who now spends his days attending to the various needs of his benefactor, Pauline (Joan Copeland), while enjoying mild flirtations from his former dance partner, Cleo (Helen Gallagher), who would like to see Russell return to competitive ballroom dance. It is with these two older women that Chaplin's Marilyn competes for Russell's affections. While Russell is himself romantically interested in Marilyn, he does not have the wherewithal or motivation to extricate himself from the life of relative ease afforded him through his relationship with the wealthy paramours upon whom he is dependent.

In one of the few scenes in the film that takes place outside of the Roseland ballroom in New York City – a celebrated New York City venue that existed from 1922 until its closure in 2014, and the space around which the lives of all of the characters in the film converge – Walken brings Chaplin to a bar for a drink, having met her in an earlier scene in the ballroom. Here, Russell explains to Marilyn why Pauline introduced the two of them: the older woman wanted Russell to look after the younger, whose husband has walked out on her. Marilyn, perhaps owing to the fresh wounds from her failed marriage – and likely also because of Russell's status as Pauline's "kept man" – is approaching Russell with caution, a state of mind expressed here in Chaplin's performance through the way she guards her mouth with her hands (Figure 5.6). This gesture momentarily masks the part of Chaplin's face which she took to most resemble her father, and in doing so draws attention to the top half of her face she has suggested most resembles her mother. Marilyn's attempt to remain reserved fails, for Russell reads in her eyes a look of worry that reminds him of his mother, who, he reveals, would take him out for elegant dinners upon receiving her alimony payment, and who was the one who taught him to dance. In a later scene, Russell will comment to Cleo, after a dance practice session, that Marilyn reminds him not so much of his mother as she was but how his mother would have liked to be seen, particularly in the way Marilyn dresses, speaks, and holds herself. In reflecting upon *Roseland*, the director James Ivory, in the quote preceding this section, imagines a cinematic genealogy lingering behind Chaplin's eyes as she suffers, in a later scene, the eventual rejection from the dashing Russell. But where Ivory sees only a paternal lineage in Chaplin's eyes, Walken's character in the film finds – in her eyes, and her way of speaking and dressing – a lingering matrilineality, which reminds him of

**Figure 5.6** Chaplin as Marilyn in *Roseland*, guarding her mouth with her hands

a lost mother and recalls for the film's viewer the lingering memory of Oona, a figure herself mythologized as a woman with her own unfulfilled aspirations (see Scovell 2009, especially pages 103–4, for a discussion of O'Neill's early ambitions for a movie career).

The connection Ivory draws here between Chaplin's eyes and her father's, admittedly, is colored mostly by the broader humanism Charlie Chaplin's Little Tramp character is often said to represent. In characterizing the eyes of both father and daughter Chaplin as expressing the inherent humanity of sorrow and suffering, Ivory leaps over some of the more specific struggles conveyed through Chaplin's characterization of Marilyn in *Roseland*, which have less to do with tropes of essential humanity and more to do with female desire and anxieties over class status. Where the Little Tramp struggles for his next meal, Marilyn does not have this worry: although she has been left on her own after her husband's abandonment, she has no problem getting a job and her own apartment. In fact, it's the money from this job and the habitat of this apartment that Marilyn offers to Russell as a means of supporting him (she would like to see him return to competitive dance with Cleo, but wants to pay Cleo for her effort, so as to extricate Russell from any obligation he might have to his former dance partner). Further, where the Little Tramp often looks toward a young gamine with affectionate desire – Edna Purviance in the short films, Virginia Cherrill in *City Lights*, Paulette Goddard in

*Modern Times* and *The Great Dictator* – it is the elegantly, handsomely dandyish Christopher Walken that all the women in *Roseland* gaze upon, Chaplin most especially. In this respect, her gesture of guarding her mouth with her hands also functions as a means for Chaplin to direct her viewer toward her eyes, which here signal a subjectivity, a longing, that takes Walken as an object of affection. This desire reminds us less of the universal humanism Ivory reads into her eyes, and more specifically, of her character's own hunger for Walken's Russell, who represents a chance for her to be the autonomous provider and caregiver, an independent woman looking after a "kept," dependent man.

What is also striking about Chaplin's performance in *Roseland* – and another aspect of her characterization that distances her from, rather than connects her to, her father's memory and lineage – is that, for a film set nearly entirely inside a dance ballroom, Chaplin does not dance very much. I have already mentioned in this book her father's own predilection for dance, Geraldine's early career efforts at ballet, and her characters' tendencies to dance (to an ecstatic pop song in *Peppermint Frappé*, at an aristocratic ball in *Doctor Zhivago*, in a flirtatious dance in *Los ojos vendados*, and, as we'll see later in this chapter, in her role as a ballet instructor in Almodóvar's *Talk to Her*). But a common trope in Chaplin's performance in *Roseland* is her character's efforts to guide Walken's Russell *away* from the ballroom, to another space – a practice room, a coat check, outside the Roseland – apart from the dancing that connects him to the two other women who compete for his affections. In one of the more memorable shots of the film, Chaplin speaks to Walken, in a practice space away from the ballroom, of her character's desires to look after him so he may return to competitive dance. Ivory frames the image to ensure that Chaplin's visage is reflected in a mirror, a common trope in cinema to convey a divided state of mind (Figure 5.7). Here, Chaplin's Marilyn seems divided between two different paths her future might take – a life with Russell orbiting Roseland, or some other existence entirely. But the ultimate effect of the mirror-image close shot in a sequence that otherwise takes place largely in the context of a famous dance ballroom is to redirect us away from the dancer we know from other films, as her eyes again direct us toward something else. It is her object of desire she moves us toward; she wants to look and appreciate a man who can dance, rather than dance for us. Chaplin's performance in *Roseland* is notably reserved, as befits the caution and hesitancy Marilyn takes as she approaches the possibility of a new kind of life with another man.

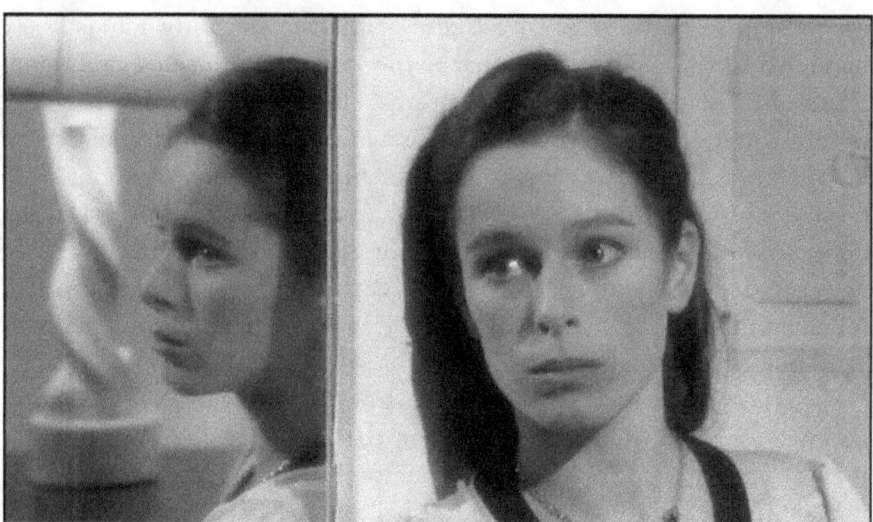

**Figure 5.7** Chaplin's Marilyn in *Roseland*, in mirror reflection

The desire for this possibility is something very specific conveyed here by Chaplin, escaping the totalizing tendencies of a transcendent humanism in favor of something particular and local.

## Katerina Bilova in *Talk to Her*

Geraldine Chaplin's presence in Pedro Almodóvar's 2002 film *Hable con ella* (hereafter referred to by its English title, *Talk to Her*) might be taken as a kind of homage to her legacy in Spanish cinema, particularly its art cinema, of which Almodóvar is the central contemporary figure. (Almodóvar's film is an even more moving acknowledgment of Chaplin's importance to Spanish cinema than the Goya Award she received for her performance in the Spanish thriller *La ciudad sin límites*, released the same year as Almodóvar's film.) Her first appearance in *Talk to Her* takes the form of a framed photograph, placed on the hospital bedside of the comatose Alicia (Leonor Watling). Almodóvar's camera pans across a series of objects belonging to Alicia, mementos of a performative career that hangs in the balance after a devastating traffic accident, which include this bejeweled portrait of her beloved ballet teacher (Figure 5.8), Katerina Bilova, played by Chaplin. In casting Chaplin as a ballet dancer and instructor, Almodóvar's film refers to a key aspect of Chaplin's early

**Figure 5.8** Chaplin's first appearance in *Talk to Her* takes the form of a framed photograph

career, her attempt to become a ballet dancer, and in the last name of her character – "Bilova," a vaguely Russian surname – to the transnationalism of her screen persona. (Elsewhere in the film, which takes place mainly in Madrid, Katerina – who slips between English and Spanish as she speaks – talks of her plans for a ballet in Geneva, amplifying the idea that her character in the narrative is a border-transgressing figure, much like Chaplin herself.) But what is most moving about Chaplin's performance in *Talk to Her* is that Katerina is a character who works to pass along knowledge – embodied knowledge – to another woman.

Like her student, Katerina is a performer, and she lives a theatrical life on and off the stage. In the sequences presented to us in flashback, before Alicia's injury, Chaplin's Katerina mentors the younger pupil on gesture and movement, conveying knowledge of dance through passionate, embodied instruction. Elsewhere, she also attempts to pass along knowledge to Alicia through words, spoken powers of description that work alongside gesture. In her first appearance as a moving figure in Almodóvar's film – the first time we see her after glimpsing the still portrait of Chaplin in the photograph by Alicia's bed – Katerina is seated on a balcony patio outside a hospital room, alongside Alicia, whom she visits as nurse Beningo (Javier Cámara) looks on. She is here describing to Alicia (and also to befuddled Beningo, who listens to her ideas with a mix of curiosity and incomprehension) her design for a ballet about World War I she plans to call "Trenches." In doing so she uses words the sleeping Alicia *might* be able to hear but also employs gestures only

Beningo, and the viewer of *Talk to Her*, can see. Her description of her concept for *Trenches* –

> Problem. You need lots of male dancers, because in the war, sorry, there are lots of soldiers. But in Geneva everyone dances. It's wonderful. There are also ballerinas because in the ballet, when a soldier dies, from his body emerges his soul, his ghost, and that's a ballerina. Long tutu, white like the "willis" in *Giselle*, classical, but with blood stain, red ... From death emerges life. From the male, emerges the female.

– is accompanied by a series of hand gestures that Chaplin uses to bring this description of a prospective ballet to bodily life: a lateral movement of her right hand, like a camera panning across a battlefield, as she speaks of the death of soldiers; the gradual unfolding of a clenched fist into expanding fingers and palm as she describes the emergence of a soul from a dead soldier's body; and a sweeping, downward movement of the hand as she imagines the tutu her dancer will be wearing, a description of soul through fabric and costume and embodied here by Chaplin through this gesture (Figure 5.9). Not all of these gestures are glimpsed, or at least not completely, because Almodóvar has framed this moment as a medium-close two-shot of Katerina and Alicia (keeping Beningo, for most of the description of the ballet, offscreen); the closer shot distance reveals, in Chaplin's performance, the thought she conveys as she describes her ballet in words, with the viewer only partially seeing

**Figure 5.9** Chaplin's Katerina describes her vision for a new ballet in *Talk to Her*: "The ethereal, the impalpable, the ghostly"

the gestures of body she uses to provisionally incarnate it. Near the end of her description of the ballet, she gestures upward with her outstretched palm, as if pantomiming a seed sprouting from the earth; she attempts to pair this movement of her hand with the appropriate accompanying words. "From the earth emerges . . ." She pauses, at a loss; Beningo's literal suggestions ("a tree?") are not helpful. Finally, she hits on the right words to accompany her gestures: "The ethereal, the impalpable, the ghostly."

Throughout this book I have suggested that Chaplin's very presence in cinema functions as a kind of citation of her father's memory, as if Charlie Chaplin were at times haunting our engagement with Geraldine's work in cinema. In this sequence from *Talk to Her*, as Chaplin's Katerina describes her prospective World War I ballet, Chaplin gives us a description of a female spirit emerging from deceased men, something that not only serves to blur the distinction between genders but also works as an uncanny echo of the way Chaplin herself often reminds her viewer of her father's past image. But in this sequence and through his casting of Chaplin in this part in *Talk to Her*, Almodóvar pays even more substantial and reflexive tribute to Chaplin's own distinctive ethereality, a key motif of her achievements in Spanish cinema, a cinema which more than any other part of her career distinctively stands apart from her father's legacy. In *Talk to Her*, which involves a plot primarily focused on viewings of female suffering, Chaplin underscores the tendency of women to survive as memories, as ghosts. In the second chapter of this book, which focuses on her work with Carlos Saura, I describe the ways in which, in *Cría cuervos*, Geraldine Chaplin plays a suffering woman – the mother, María – who is in some sense also a memory, a ghost. Throughout her career, Geraldine plays figures who are ethereal, ghost-like: in her films for Spanish writer and director Enrique Brasó, for example – *In Memoriam* (1977), *En la ciudad sin límites* (2002), and *Oculto* (2005) – Chaplin frequently plays characters who are either deceased or are the stuff of the past, of memory; in Saura's *Mamá cumple 100 años*, as discussed in the second chapter, Chaplin's character Ana, murdered in an earlier film, is resurrected; in the Spanish horror film *The Orphanage* (2007), she plays a medium, channeling the past through seance; and in surreal films by Canadian auteur Guy Maddin (discussed later in this chapter), Chaplin collaborates in cinematic projects concerned with the way cinema's past continues to haunt the present. *Talk to Her* is the most powerful of these later incarnations of ethereality by Chaplin; the aforementioned sequence gives her time and space to describe – through word and gesture, using her character's prospective ballet as a narrative pretext – the very quality of her performative ghostliness, a legacy of past cinema incarnate in her gestures. And in the narrative of *Talk to Her*, Chaplin passes this knowledge down to another woman. If Chaplin's screen presence so often evokes memories of her father, and of the past cinema of which he is a part, in many of her late performances – and no more than in her performance in this remarkable Almodóvar film – she ultimately pays tribute to nothing other than the legacy of her own presence on the cinema screen.

## Maman in *Boxes*

*Boxes* (2007) reunites Jane Birkin (the director of the film, and its lead player) with Chaplin; the two of them previously worked together on Jacques Rivette's film *L'Amour par terre*, discussed in the fourth chapter. Like the Rivette film, *Boxes* is a playful work of fiction that weaves together themes of theatricality, memory, and jealousy. Birkin's film is loosely based on aspects of her own life, telling a story about her character's relationships with three different men and the three daughters these bonds produced. (In real life, Birkin had daughters with John Barry, Jacques Doillon, and Serge Gainsbourg; in *Boxes*, playing the eldest daughter, Lou Doillon is cast as a version of herself, while the other two daughters are played by actors.) The story unfolds in one sprawling estate bordering the water in southern Brittany, and involves the flood of memories confronting Birkin's character as she unpacks boxes and looks at the various photographs stored within them. Lingering in these memories are not only Anna's former paramours but also her mother, played by Chaplin, and her father, played by Michel Piccoli. Near the end of the film, Birkin's Anna sits among these boxes and a pile of old photographs that includes photos taken around the late 1960s and early 1970s of both Chaplin and Piccoli. These images provide a kind of retrospective frame around which the preceding film can be understood. *Boxes* is in part a work of remembrance (the film never reveals if Anna's mother and father are living or dead, although their embodiment by Chaplin and Piccoli give them a palpable presence), and one of self-reflexivity (the pictures of Chaplin and Piccoli recall earlier moments in the lives of both actors, each of whom, like Birkin, are luminaries in an earlier art cinema tradition).

*Boxes* is another film in which Chaplin plays a ghost-like, ethereal figure. Birkin's original intention was for Chaplin to have played Anna, the character loosely based on Birkin herself. Chaplin, feeling that she was too old to play the character (at the time Chaplin made the film, she was in her early sixties; the character of Anna is in her forties), opted instead to play the mother of Anna. While this choice produces its own interesting effects in the finished film – Chaplin and Birkin have a tender rapport onscreen that conveys the mother–daughter bond required by the fiction, and that to some extent also quashes any suggestion of lingering resentments that resulted from the earlier filming of *L'Amour par terre* – her casting as the mother nevertheless creates its own odd resonances. One of these is that although Chaplin is playing Birkin's mother, Chaplin herself is only two years older than Birkin (and almost twenty years younger than Michel Piccoli). But because Chaplin's character in *Boxes* exists not only as a remembered figure but also as one who lingers – occasionally palpably, at other times invisibly – in the space of a house that is itself a storehouse for vague and possibly misremembered recollections, the various discrepancies in age at play in the film arguably heighten the film's surrealist and dreamlike qualities.

Given that *Boxes* is concerned with personal memory – and that the visions we see in the film are all more or less filtered through Jane Birkin's Anna – the backstory of Chaplin's mother figure is left foggy. Nevertheless, there are details in the character that suggest the film's ostensibly autobiographical aspects belong not only to Birkin, but extend also to Chaplin herself. The mother character repeatedly refers to an earlier, frustrated life, spent raising Anna, in which she desired to become a dancer, and attend performances at the theatre and go to the cinema; but she gave up these cultural pursuits to tend to her family on their relatively isolated European estate. This narrative of a talented but ultimately self-sacrificing young woman echoes biographical details of the life of Chaplin's own mother, Oona O'Neill. Late in the film, when Anna begins talking to her mother about her own regrets and mistakes in life, Chaplin's character advises her to "smile" – so that "the world smiles with you," a familiar saying that also evokes words from the song "Smile," written by John Turner and Geoffrey Parsons as lyrical accompaniment to a musical theme Charlie Chaplin wrote for his 1936 film *Modern Times*. Given these resonances within Geraldine's own biography and her father's mythology, when the mother appears in *Boxes* we are invited to read Chaplin's performance in the film not only for what it says about the film's ostensible auteur, Birkin, but also for its resonances in Chaplin's own life and career.

Appropriately in a film about memory and its relationship to both the tangible and the intangible, Chaplin's performance as the mother in *Boxes* flits between impalpable ethereality and concrete embodiment. The film's title refers to the various "boxes" – a metaphor occasionally mixed in the film's imagery to include also "compartments" and "rooms" – in which Birkin stores her memories. In the film, Chaplin's mother figure persuades Birkin to open up these boxes and traverse previously closed doors, rather than keep memories of different parts of her life compartmentalized. For much of the first stretch of the film Chaplin's voice is heard offscreen, lightly admonishing the daughter character played by Birkin and only appearing, initially, to greet Piccoli with a kiss before disappearing offscreen again. Here Chaplin not only fulfills her by-now expected function in much art cinema as a kind of "ghostly," ethereal figure, but also characterizes Anna's mother as something of a remembered object "kept" in its place, called up occasionally as therapeutic memory but lingering offscreen when Birkin's Anna is distracted by something else. During this first stretch of the film, the mother is not fully a part of Birkin's interactions with the father character played by Piccoli, whom Birkin would prefer to remember as an isolated figure.

As the film goes on, however, Chaplin's character works to break down some of these boundaries, working to intervene in the way Birkin's character remembers her father. In her first substantial sequence of the film, Chaplin journeys with Birkin and Piccoli to the father's island off the coast of Brittany. Here, we see Chaplin and Piccoli walk hand in hand across the lush vegetation and trees of the countryside surrounding the estate, with Piccoli eventually sweeping Chaplin up in his arms in an attempt to carry her to the boat (Figure 5.10). For any lover of 1960s and 1970s art cinema, the sight of one of the luminaries of French cinema gathering up the daughter of Charlot in his arms is endearing. Within the narrative of *Boxes*, Piccoli's tender gesture – performed outside of the view of Birkin, who is not in this scene, and all the more moving given that the aged Piccoli, unable to carry her very far, must eventually put Chaplin back on the ground again – suggests an emotional bond between the characters that goes beyond the memory of what Anna can remember of them. The moment also implies a path not taken in earlier French art cinema, which failed to cast Piccoli and Chaplin onscreen together during the height of their careers; they are two stars whose endearing and cerebral eccentricities have the capacity to generate, as this (unfortunately short) scene in *Boxes* attests, unconventional charm. "This is better than the war, Michel,"

**Figure 5.10** Michel Piccoli eventually sweeps Chaplin up in his arms in an attempt to carry her to a boat, in *Boxes*

Chaplin says, as Piccoli (whose character shares a first name with the actor playing him) carries her on his back for the final stretch of the walk. This brief but memorable moment suggests the extent to which Chaplin's character works to redirect the memories of Piccoli (which hover around his character's World War II experience) and Birkin (whose character remains narcissistically obsessed with her own emotions throughout the film, positing *Boxes* as something of an autocritique by its auteur) away from obsessive fixations and toward emotions and relationships the two of them have forgotten.

This tender moment might suggest that close-ups of Chaplin's face in *Boxes* register as a storehouse of forgotten memories and past possibilities, a plenitude of meaning that lies in wait – like the old photographs in Birkin's boxes – to counsel Anna, who is struggling with her relationships with her daughters and her own anxiety about her future. And yet Chaplin's face in *Boxes* ultimately works to redirect Anna – and the viewer – away from direct access to her character's interiority, again and again insisting on the expressiveness of her face not as an immediately readable expression of either psychological interiority or legible historical meaning, but as an exterior skin that insists on autonomy, privacy, and playful irony. A glimpse of this idea is evident during the scene on the boat, after Chaplin and Birkin drop off Piccoli on another island. Anna tells her mother that she is uneasy because she believes she is entering menopause, and anxiously wants to know when her mother began to cease menstruation. To this, Chaplin insists she cannot remember, a fact that Birkin's Anna finds incredible but that Chaplin insists is the truth. The close-ups of Chaplin with Birkin in this boat sequence, and throughout the entire film, situate her as a playful – but also terse and at times impatient – conversational counterpart; she expresses a willingness to indulge these anxieties and obsessions but is ultimately unwilling to provide access to a full account of her personal past which, in any event, she may not fully remember.

These close shots of Chaplin (Figure 5.11) in the boat sequence and elsewhere in the film insist on the autonomy of the character's memory, which may be lost to history and, in any event, which she has no desire to recount. In *Boxes*, Chaplin's face does not serve to convey fully accessible autobiographical meaning (an ironic gesture, given that *Boxes* is intended as a cinematic memoir). Instead, Chaplin expresses her character's desire to live in the present moment, rather than in the past (even as the past is invoked in her presence in Birkin's boxed photographs). This is no more true than when, near the end of this sequence, she stumbles off the boat and falls into the water after it catches a rough wave, a moment during which Birkin, as director, keeps Chaplin in swaying close-up

**Figure 5.11** In *Boxes*, Chaplin expresses her character's desire to live in the present moment, rather than in the past

as the waves carry her alongside the boat; she is shortly rescued by a handsome boatman, with whom she then flirts in a gentle riposte to her daughter's insistence that she deliver a precise narrative of mature, "past" womanhood. Chaplin's mother in *Boxes* drifts our attention away from the narcissistic Anna, enjoying a playfully alive, smartly ironic, and – most importantly – ongoing life. Her performance in *Boxes* flits between earnest conversation with Birkin's character and playful irony, falling back on the expressions of the face to alternately reveal and conceal a range of possible meanings. In a film shaped by autobiography and remembrance, Chaplin's presence cites and confirms the ongoing presence of the past even as she insists on the perpetuity of a playful existence.

## Anne in *Dólares de arena* (*Sand Dollars*, 2014)

More than any other of her late films, Chaplin's close-ups in *Dólares de arena* (referred to hereafter by its English title, *Sand Dollars*), an international co-production between the Dominican Republic, Mexico, and Argentina, evoke a similar kind of uncertainty and vulnerability as that glimpsed in her father's visage at the end of *City Lights*. But where the Little Tramp's plea for love and acceptance culminates in a single shot at the end of the film, Chaplin's vulnerable gaze offscreen in her close-ups in *Sand Dollars* are a recurring motif throughout her performance. The desire and vulnerability Chaplin expresses in her character never culminates in a single moment, but rather disperses, at the end of the film, into the energy of the surrounding space; the final shot of the film shows us Chaplin dancing in a nightclub, uncertain of her future after a failed love affair but open to the next connection. In this film, Chaplin plays Anne, a wealthy tourist in the Dominican Republic, who has been in a relationship with the much younger Noeli (Yanet Mojica) for three years. She wants to bring Noeli to France, to make the relationship permanent. Noeli is a domestic worker and escort in the Dominican Republic; at the beginning of the film she accompanies an older man alongside a beach, exchanging her time and affection in exchange for money and other trinkets (she is given a necklace by one of her clients). Her relationship with Anne has a similar transactional quality; throughout the film she asks Anne for money, and Anne lavishes gifts upon her young lover. But in contrast to the time she spends with older men, Noeli has, at least intermittently, something closer to genuine affection for Anne. Chaplin's and Mojica's work together conveys the emotional ties shared between their characters: in her first appearance in the film, Chaplin holds Mojica's hand tightly as the two of them slip into a lake for a swim, a gesture of closeness that throws into relief the less personal bonds Noeli has with her older, male companions. (In one shot early in the film, Mojica holds the hand of one of these men, but in a loose and noncommittal way, in contrast to the much firmer grip she has, in the aforementioned shot by the water, with Chaplin.)

What is expressed in many of Chaplin's close-ups in this film is Anne's implicit plea for tender and earnest love and affection from Noeli. Anne's gaze is charged with vulnerability and uncertainty precisely because Noeli at times seems to value her relationship with Anne purely for its economic benefits. Early in the film, after a swim, Anne stares at Noeli, Chaplin's eyes registering both affection and uncertainty in relation to her character's lover (Figure 5.12). Just at the edge of the screen, Noeli is gazing down at her phone, only intermittently glancing up during this conversation to look at Anne. The viewer assumes it might be another lover Noeli is texting; Noeli reassures Chaplin that it is her brother, who has been in an accident. The fact that no brother belonging to Noeli appears at any point in the film increases the possibility that the affection Chaplin implicitly yearns for here is being met with lies and deception, underscoring the vulnerability of Chaplin's character. Later, these deceptions are confirmed. Midway through the film, Anne and Noeli go to a nightclub to dance, enjoying their time together until Noeli spies her boyfriend Yeremi (Ricardo Ariel Toribio) flirting with another woman. Noeli slips away to admonish Yeremi while Anne takes a break from dancing. When Anne returns to the dancefloor, several shots show her looking for Noeli, with one close-up capturing the play of the nightclub's flashing, pink and green neon lights across her face (Figure 5.13) as her eyes eventually land on Noeli quarreling with Yeremi on the opposite side of the dancefloor. The look offscreen for acceptance is here met with an implicit rejection in the discovery of Noeli's boyfriend, the pulsating rhythm of the disco lights serving as a counterpoint to Chaplin's steady – but disappointed – gaze.

A plea for unconditional love and acceptance – beyond all transactional or economic concerns – inflects Chaplin's performance as Anne, recalling the similar emotional yearning for authentic connection at the end of her father's *City Lights* (in which the Little Tramp also faces the possibility that his love for the blind flower girl will be treated by her,

**Figure 5.12** In *Sand Dollars*, Chaplin's eyes register both affection and uncertainty

**Figure 5.13** The play of the nightclub's flashing pink and green neon lights across Chaplin's face, in *Sand Dollars*

upon her discovery of his real and lowly status and after she has already received the gifts of restored sight and financial security, as nothing more than monetary in nature). But *Sand Dollars* also functions powerfully as a virtual anthology of themes and motifs that have appeared throughout Geraldine Chaplin's own body of work, serving as another example of a late performance in which Chaplin's characterization cites her own past in cinema. The role of Anne finds Chaplin returning to the kinds of tourist characters she played in her early films for Carlos Saura; Anne could indeed be an older and wiser sister to Elena in *Peppermint Frappé* or Ana in *Ana y los lobos*, as she is also a cosmopolitan woman of ambiguous origin (Anne is heard to speak both French and English in the film, and although she speaks of bringing Noeli to France, in other scenes she mentions the idea of returning, more broadly, "to Europe"). As with her earlier cosmopolitan characters, Anne is visiting a Spanish-speaking country in a bid to reimagine or reconstruct her own identity. What is different in *Sand Dollars* is that Chaplin's tourist character is now wealthy, experienced, and independent, no longer spending her time with the professional men with whom Chaplin's characters are linked in the Saura films. Her relationships are now not with older men who represent a bygone tradition, but with a much younger and relatively inexperienced woman who is hustling her way through an uncertain economic reality, and who does not have the socioeconomic privilege to transcend cultural borders the way Anne does. (In her offer to bring her to France, Anne is trying to give Noeli a gift that might bridge socioeconomic distance; this can be seen as a parallel to the situation in the Saura films, particularly *Peppermint Frappé*, in which Chaplin's women were often dependent upon the financial resources of men.) There is also, in *Sand Dollars*, the obsessive repetition of pop songs that score the central romantic relationship, recalling a similar device used in the Chaplin–Saura films, including *Peppermint Frappé* and *Cría cuervos*. The film begins and ends with a public performance of music, and throughout the film Anne's relationship with Noeli is scored by the repetition of love songs that give Anne's fixation upon Noeli a recursive, obsessive quality (something of the reverse of the narrative situation in the early Chaplin–Saura films, in which Chaplin is herself frequently the object of another's obsession). Further, the relationship between Anne and Noeli, although sexual in nature, also has overtones of a mother–daughter bond, a key aspect to one of Chaplin's earlier, celebrated performances, in *Cría cuervos*. Both characters have experienced estranged relationships – Anne, with her son, with whom she has not spoken in years; and Noeli, with her mother, whom she has not seen in as long – so to some extent their relationship is framed by the film as a means to compensate for these lost figures in their lives. Finally, the queer romance between Anne and Noeli suggests a consummated (and more economically complicated) variation on the flirtation between Chaplin's Lucie and Dominique Sanda's Hélène in the earlier *Le Voyage en douce*.

What is different from all these earlier roles is that Chaplin's performance as Anne in *Sand Dollars* also expresses her character's frustrations with aging. Many shots in the film emphasize the movement of Chaplin's body, giving Chaplin opportunities to express Anne's frustrations at her occasional inability to move as fluidly and as freely as she might like. These moments often throw Chaplin's experienced presence into relief against the physicality of Yanet Mojica, a non-professional actor whose twenty years of age at the time of filming *Sand Dollars* cannot help but create a contrast with Chaplin's seven decades. In this film, Chaplin stumbles, trips, falls: getting up after sitting on a deck chair and soaking in sun, she plummets onto the ground, and must be helped up by hotel staff. And in a shot of Chaplin and Mojica in bed, the legs and feet of both women teasingly push and pull against one another, young and old coming together in a moment of erotic and physical contact, but with the texture of the visible years marking a temporal distance between them. In the many shots of the film taken in and under water, however, Chaplin's Anne regains movement and fluidity, her being melding with the waves and in doing so momentarily escaping the fact of time and age. *Sand Dollars* is a film in which the vulnerabilities of the face are amplified and set against the fragility inherent in growing older, a clear-eyed and grounded love story told from the perspective of a wise and experienced woman, and one that resonates meaningfully within its central star's screen persona.

## Performative reincarnations in the films of Karl Lagerfeld and Guy Maddin

As my discussions of *Talk to Her*, *Boxes*, and *Sand Dollars* suggest, the various films in which Geraldine Chaplin appears in the later stages of her career frequently cite and play with ideas from her earlier films. Her late performances for fashion magnate Karl Lagerfeld and Canadian auteur Guy Maddin continue to present Chaplin in similar ways. When we see Chaplin in these films, as in the films for Birkin and Almodóvar, her presence continues to function partially as a citation of her last name and the twentieth-century cinema it represents. But her work in these films also offers the opportunity for inventive forms of engaging with the past, reminding us also that Chaplin's performances, throughout her career, have in part represented the potential for understanding the inherited past as a creative resource, rather than as a burden or stringent tradition. For Lagerfeld and Maddin – both filmmakers who, in different ways, are preoccupied with the past – Chaplin's presence not only inscribes the personality of an individual who has lived through and helped shape a wide swath of late-twentieth century cinematic history, a fact that becomes all the more salient when Chaplin is seen in relation to the younger and relatively inexperienced characters and actors in these late films. Chaplin's is also a face that Lagerfeld and Maddin project *onto* the past, casting her in roles that find her creatively reincarnating lost figures of cinema. Chaplin's presence in these films not only signals a kind of wisdom and experience that exists in the present, but also a kind of intelligence that we might imagine having existed in the past, now a part of the textures woven by Lagerfeld and Maddin in their idiosyncratic and distinctive films.

In most respects, the cinematic sensibilities of Lagerfeld and Maddin could not be more different. Nevertheless, a discussion of Chaplin's performances for these two directors offers a fitting end to this book. Lagerfeld, a fashion designer and creative director of the Chanel fashion house (from 1983 until his death in 2019), understands "the past" in the two short films he makes with Chaplin as something that might be creatively reimagined via details of fabric and texture. Such materials are, for Lagerfeld, kinds of secret totems that reveal the work and labor of fashion as it has existed historically. In these films, Chaplin plays a historically existing figure, fashion designer Gabrielle "Coco" Chanel (in the first of these films, she plays Chanel at a very specific moment in the designer's life, during her "comeback" in the 1950s, when her fashions became popular in the United States). Maddin's recouping of the past, by contrast, sees the past as itself a kind of cinematic fabric or material: in his work, Maddin often signals his creative engagement with the past through the tactility of cinema itself, the very textures of "old" films – the splices, faded color, and scratches of film prints registering as surreal and resonant marks of time that Maddin uses as a poetic resource. In Maddin's *The Forbidden Room* (2015) Chaplin appears onscreen as another ghostly spirit, something like a background character from a lost silent film brought back to life in Maddin's wry blend of surrealism, comedy, and Gothic horror.

While their sensibilities are different, where Lagerfeld and Maddin are broadly similar is in their understanding of cinema as a kind of machine of desire. These two auteurs are not traditional storytellers; they are less interested in using the frame as a vehicle for narrative information and more with the possibility that specific filmic fetishes might in turn generate new experiences of cinema. Chaplin's performances for both directors serve to ground these obsessions in concrete, performative ways, making them part of the lives and real histories of the characters she plays.

The two short films Lagerfeld made with Chaplin, "The Return" (2013) and "Once and Forever" (2015), evince – as one might expect in a film made by a leading fashion designer – an interest in fabric and texture. Chaplin's performance in "The Return" finds her playing Chanel at an uncertain moment in the fashion designer's career, during the 1950s, when Chanel attempted to stage a "comeback" after more than a decade of being out of the fashion spotlight. Lagerfeld's dialogue in these short films often takes on a purely expositional role, signaling to the viewer prevailing cultural attitudes about Chanel's fashions at a given moment in history (in the film, a French designer played by Arielle Dombasle pointedly criticizes Chanel's latest designs, while an interviewer, speaking with Chanel later in the film, reminds her that her new designs have become quite popular in America). Chaplin's performance, in this context, serves to bring Chanel to life as someone who was not simply subject to whims or trends, but who laboriously worked to create her designs, reminding us that without this labor with fabric, there could be no critical reception at all. In this sense, the images in "The Return" are driven less by a point-by-point recapitulation of a certain stretch of Chanel's life, and more by the gestures and movements Chaplin uses to express Chanel as she might have lived and worked: nervously but intendedly pulling, stretching, and examining fabric and clothes as she hangs them on her fashion models (with whom "The Return" imagines Chanel as having warm and friendly relationships); patiently but pointedly answering the questions of an interviewer later in the film, for whom she states her philosophy of style and beauty ("style is the conquest of the mind over the senses"); and repeatedly bringing to and from her lips a cigarette, an expression of the kind of repetitive – but always distinctively performed – gestures that bring both Chanel's fashions and "The Return" to vibrant life. Nevertheless, Chaplin's presence in the film is bounded by Lagerfeld's insistence that the character be presented as a kind of caricature: Chaplin's expressivity in this film, although frequently shot in close-up, is partially obscured by Chanel's hat, her large glasses, and the cigarette she repeatedly brings to her lips (Figure 5.14). These accouterments convey the idea of the character in a few quick, broad strokes, but at the same time keep something of the "real" Chanel cloaked in privacy.

The second film Chaplin makes for Lagerfeld, "Once and Forever," is something of a self-reflexive deconstruction of "The Return." This film is not directly about Chanel herself, but instead focuses on a filmmaker

**Figure 5.14** Chaplin's expressivity in "The Return" is partially obscured by a hat, large glasses, and the cigarette she repeatedly brings to her lips

(Jérémie Elkaïm) who is working to make a short film about Chanel as an older woman looking back on her youth. Chaplin plays an actor cast as the older Chanel, while Kristen Stewart plays the young actor who is to incarnate Chanel as a young woman. There is a reflexive quality to Chaplin's casting in the film: here, she is very nearly playing a version of herself who made a film with Lagerfeld three years previously. In this, "Once and Forever" is somewhat like her performance for Carlos Saura in *Mamá cumple 100 años*, with Chaplin again creating another iteration of an earlier character. Throughout much of "Once and Forever" Chaplin often simply watches the behavior of others, sitting in repose and observing as Stewart and her director work to create a character Chaplin has already played, at a different stage in Chanel's life, in an earlier film. Further, most of Stewart's scenes in the film do not present her as Chanel at all, but as a rather contentious young actor who spends most of the film arguing with her director and her producer, all the while struggling with how precisely to play Chanel in front of the camera. The ease and effortlessness with which Chaplin inhabits Lagerfeld's images in "Once and Forever" – and in her role in the narrative as an experienced, wise witness to a younger actor's strident, and hardly self-assured, labor – becomes nothing short of authoritative and magisterial. While Stewart's actor character complains and fusses with her director about how to make the film, Chaplin – whose final line in the film is, simply and confidently,

"I am Coco Chanel!" – embodies a kind of performative authority beyond the grasp of youth's impatient, insolent brashness. In this, the film reminds us that Geraldine Chaplin is now the one passing down gifts, the more experienced actor perhaps teaching a kind of implicit lesson to the relatively less experienced – although still performatively impressive – Stewart (who, through the strength of her own strong performance in Lagerfeld's film, is surely nothing like the character she plays in "Once and Forever"). In the final shot in the film, Stewart – her character appearing to have finally arrived at a kind of breakthrough or moment of self-reflection – walks into Chaplin's dressing room and gives her a hug, the only moment in "Once and Forever" in which the Stewart character's defenses break down and she engages in a real moment of affection and camaraderie with a co-star (Figure 5.15). This moment tells us something about the relationship between these fictional actors but also is a sign of a kind of shared tenderness between Chaplin and Stewart themselves, indicative perhaps of the thoughtful gift – here, of her experience and her time – that the older actor is sharing with the younger one.

Chaplin's work for Guy Maddin, even as it seeks to evoke an idea of the past as in her films for Lagerfeld, is pitched at a different register. In Maddin's cinema, the star "performance" is often given not by a person but by the materials of cinema, in particular materials fashioned so as to

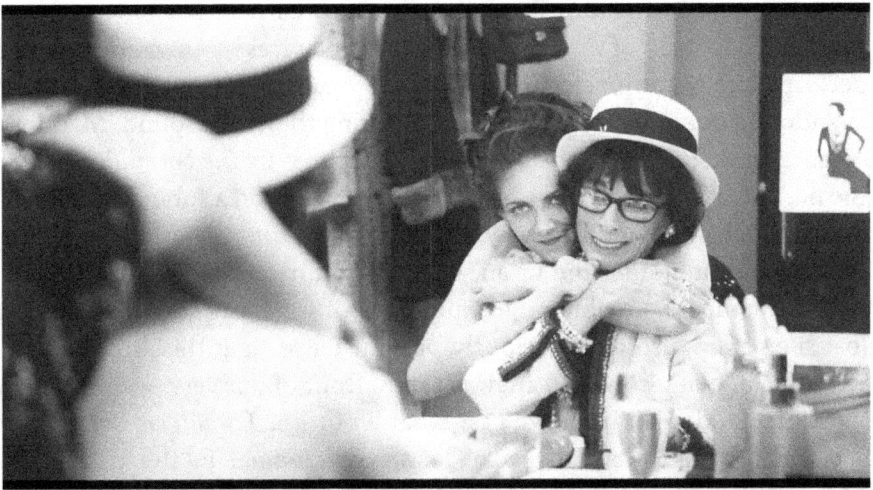

**Figure 5.15** A shared moment of tenderness between Chaplin and Kristen Stewart in "Once and Forever"

appear "rescued" from the drift of bygone, silent-era cinema. "All of his films," Dana Cooley writes of Maddin,

> show a patina of wear that evokes early film. Marked with scratches that would indicate repeated projections (and presumably much attention, possibly even love), the intertitles which Maddin often employs jitter (spelled out in letters that appear fuzzy around the edges, ostensibly because they have become blurred over time), as if the sprockets of the film have been worn and no longer run smoothly through the projector. (2009: 174)

In Maddin's surreal reincarnation of silent film aesthetics, whatever exists of plot ripples within a dreamy flow of silent-film imagery that demands an affectionate engagement on the viewer's part not only with actors playing characters but also, and often more, with the very tactile qualities of celluloid itself.

Maddin's film *The Forbidden Room* is a surreal project that reimagines the possible form and content of a number of lost films from early cinema (Maddin's primary fascination is with silent melodramas and Gothic horror). Taking his cue from a list of titles or fragmentary footage from "lost films," in *The Forbidden Room* Maddin recreates a sense of this lostness using contemporary actors and technologies, generating the ambience of a cinematic seance in which fragments of cinematic history are brought back to life. But Maddin conjures these fragments not in the spirit of reflexive, ironic play. *The Forbidden Room*, like many of Maddin's earlier projects, instead evinces the director's earnest desire to explore the poetic power of "residual" cinematic devices – intertitles, silent performative gesture, rejection of narrative realism or causation – largely abandoned in mainstream filmmaking during the era of sound. Maddin's cinema, to that end, only ostensibly tells stories – in *The Forbidden Room*, the narrative circles around several crew members on a submarine slowly and gradually making their way to the room of the title. But this plot is only a kind of clothesline upon which Maddin can hang other surreal, wacky fragments, in which the experience of watching something like a lost silent film also feels curiously present-tense, as if this "lost" object were in fact being conjured anew for us in front of our very eyes.

That Maddin should have cast Chaplin in *The Forbidden Room* only accentuates this intent to evoke lost, past cinema; in the context of Maddin's idiosyncratic project, Chaplin's presence works more than ever to function as a kind of poetic citation of a cinematic legacy. But what is remarkable about her presence in *The Forbidden Room* is her uncanny *presentness*: Chaplin here is not so much legible as a "lost figure" of cinema but rather a mysteriously alive presence from the past driving forward our curiosity and passion for understanding and experiencing the ongoing power of supposedly "outmoded" cinematic techniques, forms and styles still alive to our viewing (rather than archival and distant). In this sense, *The Forbidden Room* shares, in a broad way, the sensibility of the Charlie Chaplin who made *City Lights*, *Modern Times*, and *The Great Dictator*, works of a filmmaker who refused to abandon the marvelous potential of silent gesture during an era of sound.

Geraldine Chaplin appears twice in *The Forbidden Room*, during two fragmentary, short sequences that delightfully interrupt the submarine narrative. Both of her appearances are framed by Maddin through intertitle character cards styled as fragments from fictional, "lost" silent films. In the second of these sequences, she appears alongside fellow contemporary art cinema luminary Mathieu Amalric, haunting Amalric (Chaplin's "character" in this sequence is known only as the "nursemaid" in the official credits) in a short sequence that takes on the appearance of something plucked from a silent Gothic melodrama, looking on with haunting, blank eyes as the Amalric character devolves into a kind of frenzied insanity.

But it is her first appearance in *The Forbidden Room* that is more memorable, and also very funny. In this section of the film, which appears during the first half-hour, Chaplin plays a figure known only to us as "The Master Passion," as a stylized silent-film character card introduces us to her at the beginning of this sequence (Figure 5.16). As this portion of the film unfolds, it becomes clear enough that Chaplin, whose appearance is accompanied by the recurring crack of a whip (a sound accompanied in turn by her occasional witch-like cackle), is playing a kind of haunting, quasi-embodied incarnation of the obsessive drive of another figure, an older man who, as a dialogue intertitle tells us, is "plagued by bottoms." (As accompanying images of the man flesh out, he has an insatiable fetish for the rear ends of women.) In one startling and hilarious close-up of Chaplin in this surrealistic chain of nutty images, she appears dressed in top hat and whipping incessantly as if the man whose brain she plagues were in fact a horse driving a deliriously out-of-control carriage. All the while Chaplin does this, repeatedly cracking her whip, she smiles a devilish grin – that same luminous grin, so reminiscent elsewhere throughout this book of her father, but now for Maddin doing the devil's naughty work. Her visage has never been more wonderfully evil onscreen

**Figure 5.16** Chaplin appears in a stylized silent-film intertitle card in *The Forbidden Room*, playing a figure known only to us as "The Master Passion"

(in this her "haunting" of *The Forbidden Room* is the most memorable of her many appearances in Gothic horror films in her late films), her gestures and movements working to convey an eternity of endlessly repeating, mad desire. Of course, what Chaplin is seen to be doing here, in Maddin's singular vision, is ultimately inseparable from the tactile screen upon which the filmmaker captures and inscribes her image: her devilish grin combines with the grainy, red-tinted celluloid image to create an altogether uncanny and cheekily haunting cinematic figure, as if obsession and desire decided to up and become a person.

The man Chaplin haunts in this sequence of *The Forbidden Room* eventually sees a therapist and is "cured" of his psychic derangement, and her ghostly, delightfully demented visage as "The Master Passion" is expunged from the film. But in just fleeting moments in this sequence, Chaplin has effectively inscribed something essential that complements not only Maddin's approach to cinema, but that also implies something about her own presence and performances in film across nearly seven decades of work. As "The Master Passion," Chaplin's gestures send us on a surreal to-and-fro journey, her visage appearing to emerge from out of the emulsion of a lost silent film even as her gesture of cracking the whip compels us on and on, repeatedly, into more and more images, more and future cinema. Geraldine's gestures crackle here with unhinged, insatiable life, and at the same time are inflected by that aforementioned "patina of wear" touching all the figures inscribed in Maddin's movie. Chaplin in *The Forbidden Room* is glimpsed through the marks and scratches that, taken together, function as a kind of palpable trace of the passage of time upon the surface of the screen, her performance new and startling even as it bears traces of earlier cinema.

* * *

A thoughtful engagement with Geraldine Chaplin's performances, in a context of the larger cinematic history she inherits and of which she is a part, works in a similar way. Her very presence resonates with and cites past cinema – signified by that inescapable last name, Chaplin. At the same time, the new, bold performances she creates for us – those gestures that belong only to Geraldine – work to create characters of her own, and take us into worlds of which her father, being a man of a different historical era and temperament, could not have imagined. Her performative art in cinema is a beguiling achievement and in its combination of the new and the old, the familiar and the yet-to-be-discovered, Chaplin moves her viewer creatively and imaginatively back toward the luminous cinematic past from which she was born, and forward through the dizzying array of screen characterizations to which she has given life.

## Notes

1. Sydney Chaplin, in this letter, also reveals Geraldine's desire as a child to someday become a painter.
2. The decision to create this second "society girl" character appears to have been made rather late by Chaplin, since Geraldine's character does not appear in the shooting script or earlier script drafts for the film in the Chaplin Archives at Cineteca di Bologna; see Chaplin, *A Countess from Hong Kong*, shooting script, 73–4.
3. Many years later, in 1996, Faithfull and Chaplin would both appear in the British thriller *Crimetime*, although they do not share a scene together in the film.
4. Chaplin's voice is dubbed by another actor in her role as the "future Ana" in *Cría cuervos*, during the flash-forwards in which we see Chaplin play the future version of the child played elsewhere by Ana Torrent, in order to better match the dialect a Spanish viewer might expect of Torrent as an adult.
5. Rudolph's 1977 shooting script for the film literalizes Emily's fantasizing somewhat: in two sequences she imagines other women joining her in her apartment. The first one is cryptically named Marlene (perhaps the woman with whom Neil was having an affair who was killed by involuntary manslaughter in the car accident that, we soon

learn, sent Emily to prison); the second, "Butterfly," is Emily's caustic nickname for Barbara, Neil's new lover. The film itself excises these explicit dream sequences, although, in a later scene, Emily does coo words of vengeance to a "Butterfly" as she drifts off to sleep.

# References

*Abbreviations*
BOL    Charlie Chaplin Archives at Cineteca Bologna, Bologna, Italy
HER    Margaret Herrick Library, Academy of Motion Picture Arts and Sciences, Beverly Hills
RAA    Robert Altman Archives, University of Michigan Library
*Translations of magazine articles from France and Spain are my own, unless otherwise noted.*

Barthes, Roland (2010), *Camera Lucida: Reflections on Photography*, New York: Hill and Wang.
Baudelaire, Charles (1964), *The Painter of Modern Life and Other Essays*, ed. and trans. Jonathan Mayne, Greenwich, CT: Phaidon.
Bazin, André (1985), "If Charlot Hadn't Died," in *Essays on Chaplin*, ed. and trans. Jean Bodon, West Haven, CT: University of New Haven Press, pp. 51–8.
Brasó, Enrique (2003), "Interview with Carlos Saura on *Cría cuervos* [Raise Ravens] and *Elisa, vida mía* [Elisa, My Life]," in Linda M. Willem (ed.), *Carlos Saura: Interviews*, Jackson: University Press of Mississippi, pp. 42–51.
Brownlow, Kevin (1997), *David Lean: A Biography*, London: Faber.
Buszek, Maria Elena (2006), *Pin-up Grrrls: Feminism, Sexuality, Popular Culture*, Durham, NC: Duke University Press.
Cabrera Infante, G. (1991), *A Twentieth Century Job*, trans. Kenneth Hall and Cabrera Infante, London: Faber and Faber.
Castro, Antonio (2003), "Interview with Carlos Saura," in Linda M. Willem (ed.), *Carlos Saura: Interviews*, Jackson: University Press of Mississippi, pp. 52–64.
"Chaplin beauté succède à Chaplin comique" (c. 1964), undated French magazine clipping, author's collection.
Chaplin, Charles (1951), *Limelight*, October 1951 screenplay draft, 10: BOL.
Chaplin, Charles (1966), *A Countess from Hong Kong*, shooting script, January 24, 1966 draft, BOL.
Chaplin, Charles ([1964] 1992), *My Autobiography*, New York: Plume.
Chaplin, Charles and David Robinson (2014), *Footlights/The World of Limelight*, Bologna: Cineteca di Bologna.

Chaplin, Felicity (2018), *La Parisienne in Cinema: Between Art and Life*, Manchester: Manchester University Press.

Chaplin, Sydney (1956), "Letter to Geraldine" from Gypsy [Henriette] Chaplin and Sydney Chaplin, March 12, 1956, BOL.

"Charlie's Girl Tries Television" (1967), *TV Guide*, September, n.p.

Chion, Michel (1999), *The Voice in Cinema*, trans. Claudia Gorbman, New York: Columbia University Press.

Clowes, Edith W. (1990), "Characterization in *Doktor Živago*: Lara and Tonja," *Slavic and East European Journal* 34, no. 3, Autumn: 322–31.

Cooley, Dana (2009), "Demented Enchantments: Guy Maddin's Dis-eased Heart," in David Church (ed.), *Playing with Memories: Essays on Guy Maddin*, Winnipeg: University of Manitoba Press, pp. 171–89.

Crumbaugh, Justin (2010), *Destination Dictatorship: The Spectacle of Spain's Tourist Boom and the Reinvention of Difference*, Albany, NY: SUNY Press.

D'Lugo, Marvin (1991), *The Films of Carlos Saura: The Practice of Seeing*, Princeton, NJ: Princeton University Press.

D'Lugo, Marvin (2012), "The Producer-Author as Transnational Auteur," in Jo Labanyi and Tatjana Pavlović (eds), *A Companion to Spanish Cinema*, Malden, MA: Wiley-Blackwell, pp. 52–60.

de Montero, Arnaud Duprat (2014), "Les voix des heroïnes de Geraldin Chaplin dans le cinéma de Carlos Saura ou la mise en lumière d'une collaboration artistique," *Entrelacs* 11: 1–12.

de Montero, Arnaud Duprat (2015), "Carlos Saura's *Stress es tres, tres* (1968): A New Spanish Cinema with French and American Influences?", in Elena Ollete-Aldea, Beatriz Oria, and Juan A. Tarancón (eds), *Global Genres, Local Films: The Transnational Dimension of Spanish Cinema*, London: Bloomsbury, pp. 89–102.

Deardorff, Robert (1965), "Charlie Chaplin's Daughter," *Redbook*, March: 58–9, 145–6, 152–3.

del Río, Elena (2008), *Deleuze and the Cinemas of Performance*, Edinburgh: Edinburgh University Press.

Deleuze, Gilles (1989), *Cinema 2: The Time-Image*, trans. Hugh Tomlinson and Robert Galeta, Minneapolis: University of Minnesota Press.

Donald (1966), "Geraldine Chaplin ha elegido España," *Blanco y Negro*, June 18: 100–4.

Dumas, Alexandre ([1844] 2001), *The Three Musketeers*, trans. Jacques Le Clercq, New York: Modern Library.

Durgnat, Raymond (1972), *The Crazy Mirror: Hollywood Comedy and the American Image*, New York: Dell.

Ebert, Roger (1975), "*The Four Musketeers* (Film Review)", *Chicago Sun-Times*, January 1, <https://www.rogerebert.com/reviews/the-four-musketeers-1975> (last accessed March 15, 2020).

Eisenstein, Sergei (1996), "Charlie: The Kid", in *Selected Works*, vol. 3, *Writings, 1934–47*, trans. William Powell, London: British Film Institute, pp. 243–67.

Fallaci, Oriana (1967), *Limelighters*, London: Joseph.

Felski, Rita (2009), *Gender of Modernity*, Cambridge: Harvard University Press.

Flam, Jack (2012), "The Eternal Feminine," in Rebecca A. Rainbow and Dorthe Aagesen (eds), *Matisse: In Search of True Painting*, New York: Metropolitan Museum of Art, pp. 135–41.

Frank, Gerold (1965), "The Tragedy of Charlie Chaplin and his Children," *Journal*, May: 70–1, 128–31.
Gehring, Wes D. (2017), *Movie Comedians of the 1950s: Defining a New Era of Big Screen Comedy*, Jefferson, NC: McFarland.
Gelley, Ora (2012), *Stardom and the Aesthetics of Neorealism: Ingrid Bergman in Rossellini's Italy*, New York: Routledge.
"Geraldine: la Chaplin española" (1969), *Nuevo fotogramas* no. 1073, 9 May: 10–11.
"Géraldine Chaplin" (1965), *Jeunesse Cinema* 91, July: 2–7.
Girard, René (1965), *Deceit, Desire, and the Novel: Self and Other in Literary Structure*, trans. Yvonne Freccero, Baltimore: Johns Hopkins Press.
Goldman, Jonathan L. (2012), *Modernism is the Literature of Celebrity*, Austin: University of Texas Press.
Harris, Radie, "Writings 1944–1953," draft of article on Geraldine Chaplin, Radie Harris Papers, HER.
"Interview with Geraldine Chaplin" (2006), bonus materials, *Cría cuervos*, Criterion Collection, DVD.
Jameson, Joy (1965), "Jameson Communication with Hal Wallis," April 15, Hal Wallis Collection, HER.
Kamin, Dan (2011), *The Comedy of Charlie Chaplin: Artistry in Motion*, Lanham, MD: Scarecrow Press.
Keyssar, Helene (1992), *Robert Altman's America*, New York: Oxford University Press.
Klevan, Andrew (2004), *Film Performance: From Achievement to Appreciation*, London: Wallflower Press.
Kornhaber, Donna (2014), *Charlie Chaplin, Director*, Evanston, IL: Northwestern University Press.
Kouvaros, George (2010), *Famous Faces Not Yet Themselves: The Misfits and Icons of Postwar America*, Minneapolis: University of Minnesota Press.
Leggott, James (2010), "ZPG: Zero Population Growth (review)," *Science Fiction Film and Television* 3, no. 2, Autumn: 335–8.
Long, Robert Emmet (2006), *James Ivory in Conversation: How Merchant Ivory Makes its Movies*, Berkeley: University of California Press.
McCabe, John (1978), *Charlie Chaplin*, New York: Doubleday.
McGilligan, Patrick (1991), *Robert Altman: Jumping Off the Cliff*, New York: St. Martin's Press.
Machado, Antonio (2004), "Proverbs and Songs," *Border of a Dream: Selected Poems*, trans. Willis Barnstone, Port Townsend, WA: Copper Canyon Press, pp. 345–77.
Mailer, Norman and Milton H. Greene (1980), *Of Women and Their Elegance*, New York: Simon and Schuster.
Maland, Charles J. (1991), *Chaplin and American Culture: The Evolution of a Star Image*, Princeton, NJ: Princeton University Press.
Marcus, Millicent (2007), *Italian Film in the Shadow of Auschwitz*, Toronto: University of Toronto Press.
Marshall, P. David (1998), *Celebrity and Power: Fame in Contemporary Culture*, Minneapolis: University of Minnesota Press.
Martin, Harold H. (1966), "Julie Christie and Geraldine Chaplin: The Two Loves of Doctor Zhivago," *Saturday Evening Post*, January 15: 26–31.

Mast, Gerald (1992), *The Comic Mind: Comedy and the Movies*, Chicago: University of Chicago Press.

Morrey, Douglas and Alison Smith (2015), *Jacques Rivette*, Manchester: Manchester University Press.

Neupert, Richard (2002), *A History of the French New Wave Cinema*. Madison: University of Wisconsin Press.

"New Chaplin in Limelight" (1964), *Life Magazine*, January 31: 75–7.

O'Connor, John J. (1981), "The New York of Edith Wharton," *New York Times*, November 2.

Olszynko-Gryn, Jesse and Patrick Ellis (2018), "Malthus at the Movies: Science, Cinema, and Activism around Z.P.G. and *Soylent Green*," *JCMS: Journal of Cinema and Media Studies* 58, no. 1, Fall: 47–69.

Pasternak, Boris ([1957] 2010), *Doctor Zhivago*, trans. Richard Pevear and Larissa Volokhonsky, New York: Vintage.

Reed, Rex (1969), *Do You Sleep in the Nude?*, New York: Signet. [The piece on Geraldine Chaplin in this book was first published in 1965.]

Rivette, Jacques (1963), "On *Monsieur Verdoux*," *Cahiers du cinéma* 146, August: 42–3. [Author's translation.]

Rivette, Jacques (1977), "For the Shooting of *Les Filles du Feu*," trans. Amy Gateff and Tom Milne, in *Rivette: Texts and Interviews*, ed. Jonathan Rosenbaum, London: British Film Institute.

Robinson, David (1985), *Chaplin: His Life and Art*, New York: Da Capo Press.

Rohdie, Sam (2006), *Montage*, Manchester: Manchester University Press.

Rohdie, Sam (2016), *Intersections: Writings on Cinema*, Manchester: Manchester University Press.

Rohmer, Éric (1985), "A Countess from Hong Kong," in André Bazin, *Essays on Chaplin*, ed. and trans. Jean Bodon, West Haven, CT: University of New Haven Press (1985): 73-89.

Rosenbaum, Jonathan (1979), "Remember My Name," *Film Quarterly* 32, no. 3: 55–8.

Rosenbaum, Jonathan and Gilbert Adair (1975), "Les filles du feu, Part Two," *Jonathan Rosenbaum* [website] <https://www.jonathanrosenbaum.net/1975/10/les-filles-du-feu-rivette-x-4-with-gilbert-adair-and-michael-graham-part-two/> (last accessed May 11, 2019).

Ross, Kristin (1998), *Fast Cars, Clean Bodies: Decolonization and the Reordering of French Culture*, Cambridge, MA: MIT Press.

Rothman, William (1988), *The 'I' of the Camera: Essays in Film Criticism, History, and Aesthetics*, New York: Cambridge University Press.

Rowland, Mark (1979), "An Unusually Sympathetic Approach to a Genre Noted for Endemic Pulpiness [Review of *Remember My Name*]," *Take One*, January: 10–11.

Rudolph, Alan (1977), *Remember My Name*, shooting script, RAA.

Rudolph, Alan (2017), email correspondence with author, June 13.

Salgues, Yves (1964), "Géraldine," *Jours de France*, July 11: 34–7.

Schoonover, Karl (2012), *Brutal Vision: The Neorealist Body in Postwar Italian Cinema*, Minneapolis: University of Minnesota Press.

Scovell, Jane (2009), *Oona: Living in the Shadows: A Biography of Oona O'Neill Chaplin*, New York: Warner Books.

Sinyard, Neil (2010), *Richard Lester*, Manchester: Manchester University Press.

Solomon, William (2016), *Slapstick Modernism: Chaplin to Kerouac to Iggy Pop*, Urbana: University of Illinois Press.

"Son père ne s'est pas fâché" (c. 1964), undated French magazine clipping, author's collection.

Straayer, Chris (1990), "*Voyage en douce. Entre Nous.* The Hypothetical Lesbian Heroine," *Jump Cut* 35, April: 50–7.

Stuart, Jan (2000), *The Nashville Chronicles: The Making of Robert Altman's Masterpiece*, New York: Simon and Schuster.

Suchenski, Richard I. (2016), *Projections of Memory: Romanticism, Modernism, and the Aesthetics of Film*, Corby: Oxford University Press.

Toles, George (2011), "Writing About Performance: The Film Critic as Actor," in Alex Clayton and Andrew Klevan (eds), *The Language and Style of Film Criticism*, London: Routledge, pp. 87–106.

Tourneur, Cyril ([1607] 1966) *The Revenger's Tragedy*, Cambridge: Harvard University Press.

Tyler, Parker (1948), *Chaplin: Last of the Clowns*, New York: Garland.

Vance, Jeffrey (2003), *Charlie Chaplin: Genius of the Cinema*, New York: Harry N. Abrams.

Ventura, Michael (1979), "You'll Remember *My Name*," *L.A. Weekly*, January 4: 18–19, RAA.

Warshow, Robert (2001), *The Immediate Experience: Movies, Comics, Theatre, and Other Aspects of Popular Culture*, Cambridge, MA: Harvard University Press.

Wexman, Virginia Wright (2015), "*Nashville*: Second City Performance Comes to Hollywood," in Adrian Danks (ed.), *A Companion to Robert Altman*, Malden, MA: Wiley-Blackwell, pp. 369–89.

Wharton, Edith ([1905] 1999), *The House of Mirth*, New York: Random House.

Whittaker, Tom (2011), *The Films of Elías Querejeta: A Producer of Landscapes*, Cardiff: University of Wales Press.

Wild, Jennifer (2015), *The Parisian Avant-Garde in the Age of Cinema, 1900–1923*, Berkeley: University of California Press.

Wiles, Mary M. (2012), *Jacques Rivette*, Urbana: University of Illinois Press.

Wilson, Emma (2009), *Alain Resnais*, Manchester: Manchester University Press.

Woodward, Ian and Zlatko Skrbis (2018), "Performing Cosmopolitanism: The Context and Object-Dependency of Cosmopolitan Openness," in Gerard Delanty (ed.), *Routledge International Handbook of Cosmopolitanism Studies*, 2nd edn, London: Routledge, pp. 127–37.

Ziarek, Krzysztof (2008), "Carlos Saura: Cinematic Poesis," in James Phillips (ed.), *Cinematic Thinking: Philosophical Approaches to the New Cinema*, Stanford, CA: Stanford University Press, pp. 68–89.

Zuckoff, Mitchell (2010), *Robert Altman: The Oral Biography*, New York: Vintage Books.

# Index

acousmêtre, 72–4
allegory (in relation to performance), 78–80, 83, 89, 92, 96, 98, 106–7, 109, 113–14
Almodóvar, Pedro, 16, 62, 66, 208, 217, 218–22, 231
Alterio, Héctor, 89
Altman, Robert, 4, 15, 16, 29, 30, 43, 45, 115–24, 125, 139, 144, 148, 149, 150, 156, 158, 198, 207, 208
Amalric, Mathieu, 237
*Anne of the Thousand Days* (1969), 43–4
Antonioni, Michelangelo, 190
Aparicio, Rafaela, 78, 113
Arbuckle, Roscoe "Fatty," 8
Arditi, Pierre, 198
Atherton, William, 150
Attenborough, Richard, 204–5
Azéma, Sabine, 198, 200–1

Balsan, Humbert, 187
Bara, Theda, 67
Bardot, Brigitte, 70
Barthes, Roland, 91–2
Baudelaire, Charles, 144–5, 149
Bazin, André, 2–3
Belmondo, Jean-Paul, 24, 32

*Benny and Joon* (1993), 8
Berenson, Berry, 132, 234, 138, 140–1
Bergman, Ingrid, 34–5, 59
Bertoya, Paul, 31
Birkin, Jane, 156–7, 189–91, 193–4, 222–7, 231
Bloom, Claire, 1, 5, 43
*Blowup* (1966), 190
Bo, Facundo, 190
Bolt, Robert, 37, 40
*Bonnie and Clyde* (1967), 43
Bradford, Thomas, 205
Brando, Marlon, 10–11, 14
Brasó, Enrique, 60, 98, 221
Brisky, Norman, 113
Brownlow, Kevin, 19, 21, 40
Bruck, Edith, 30
Bujold, Geneviève, 43
Burton, Richard, 43
Buszek, Maria Elena, 70

Cabrera Infante, Guillermo, 5
Cámara, Javier, 219
*Camille* (1936), 128–30
Carradine, Keith, 121–3, 128–31, 144–6, 148
Carson, Carolyn, 177

Index 247

Castelnuovo, Nino, 34
Cebrián, Fernando, 74
Cézanne, Paul, 144, 147
Chanel, Gabrielle "Coco," 232–5
Chaplin, Charlie, 12–14, 17, 21–3, 26–30
 autobiographical elements of his cinema, 5
 *The Circus* (1928), 5
 *City Lights* (1931), 5, 10, 202–8, 216, 227–8, 237
 *The Count* (1916), 8
 *A Countess from Hong Kong* (1967), 10–14, 15, 16–17, 30, 117, 174–5, 239
 dancing, 3, 8–9, 10–11, 14, 65, 142, 217
 as father figure to Geraldine, 2, 4–6, 10, 12, 14–17, 21–4, 25, 26, 30, 33, 41, 45, 46, 47–9, 56, 58, 63–4, 91, 111, 117, 142–3, 155, 156, 159–61, 174, 190, 204–7, 213, 214–17, 222–4, 227–8, 237, 239
 film style, 9, 10, 12, 14–16, 26–30, 65–6, 117, 136, 142, 174–5, 202
 "Foot Lights" (novel), 8–9
 *The Gold Rush* (1925), 8, 142
 *The Great Dictator* (1940), 10, 65–6, 117, 217, 237
 iconicity of, 44–6, 48, 56–8, 207
 *The Kid* (1920), 5, 26–30
 *A King in New York* (1957), 159–60
 *Limelight* (1952), 1–6, 8–9, 10, 16–17, 22, 43, 91
 Little Tramp character, 1, 2, 3, 8, 23, 26–30, 45, 46, 48, 49, 58, 65, 68, 142–3, 174–6, 202–6, 216, 227–8
 *Modern Times* (1936), 8, 176, 223, 237
 *Monsieur Verdoux* (1947), 1, 2, 174–7
 *My Autobiography* (1964 book), 5

 *One A.M.* (1916), 136–7
 performance style, 8, 12–13, 136, 142–3
 reception in French New Wave film criticism, 173–8
 *Shanghaied* (1915), 8
Chaplin, Felicity, 158
Chaplin, Geraldine
 autobiographical elements in her performances, 90–1, 109, 118, 223
 ballet career, 6–9
 birth (July 31, 1944), 4–5
 and caricature, 145–6
 as child actor, 1–3
 childhood, as theme in films, 20, 25, 28, 41, 59–60, 82–5, 88, 90, 98–102, 147, 169
 *Cinderella* (ballet), 6, 7, 9
 comic performance, 12, 15, 66, 116, 118, 120, 124, 139, 143, 156, 160, 166–8, 195, 197
 cosmopolitanism in performance, 4, 16, 41, 60, 64, 66–7, 73 75–6, 158–9, 160–1, 163, 173, 182, 197, 201, 229, 230
 costumes and fashion in performance, 41, 48, 76–7, 80–1, 85–6, 118, 123, 130–1, 135, 188
 dancing (in films), 9–10, 11, 14, 66, 74, 165, 180, 182, 185, 187, 199, 217, 219, 220, 223, 228
 emergence as star, 11–12, 21–4, 34–6, 37, 43, 57
 embodiment of *La Parisienne* character type, 157–63, 165–6, 169, 173, 200–1
 ethereality in performance, 81, 92–6, 208, 221–2, 224
 as fashion model, 32, 56, 158–9, 162–3

Chaplin, Geraldine (*cont.*)
  and feminine modernity, 69–72, 158–63
  gestures of, 8, 15, 33, 36, 46, 57, 79, 81–2, 87–9, 92, 94, 97–100, 102–4, 106, 108–9, 111, 114, 132–4, 136–8, 140, 142, 144–5, 147, 150–2, 156, 158, 162, 165, 167, 170–3, 175, 177–80, 183–8, 191, 194–7, 199, 202, 204, 205, 207–8, 215, 217, 219–22, 224, 226, 228, 233, 236–9
  improvised performance, 29–30, 78, 116–18, 123–4, 126
  irony in performance and persona, 10, 30, 67, 80, 117, 176, 201, 225, 227
  journalistic and industry discourse about, 11–12, 23, 24, 37, 44, 63–4, 158–63, 173–8
  multilingual abilities, 72–4, 83, 178–80, 181–2, 183–4
  as painted subject by Antonio Saura, 71–2
  photographs of, 6, 12, 14, 17, 32, 46–58; see also Greene, Milton H.
  photography (as theme in relation to performance), 69, 75, 84, 90–2, 100, 141, 172, 222, 225–6
  presence and legacy in Spanish cinema, 9, 16, 59–114, 127, 160, 218–19, 221, 230, 239
  screen test for *Doctor Zhivago*, 18–19
  sexuality (as theme in performance), 32, 78, 81, 132, 198, 230
  tourist characters, 59, 61, 63, 68–9, 71–2, 75–9, 83, 111, 157, 227–30
  transnational aspects of career, 4, 16, 30, 43, 43, 64, 67–8, 161, 198, 219
  use of fabric in performance, 77, 81, 84–5, 86–7, 88–9, 146–7, 155, 169, 171, 220, 232–3

  use of objects in performance, 31–2, 36, 58, 79, 82–3, 84, 90, 104, 137–8, 140–1, 166
  voice in performance, 72–4, 76–8, 83, 90, 92–5, 97–100, 126, 141, 173, 224, 239

Chaplin, Geraldine, films
  ¿… Y el prójimo? (1974), 62
  *L'Amour par terre* (1984), 156, 157, 166, 174, 177, 189–96, 199, 212, 215, 222–3
  *Ana y los lobos* (*Ana and the Wolves*, 1973), 58, 66, 73, 78–83, 89, 96, 109–12, 229
  *Andremo in città* (1966), 30, 33–6
  *Boxes* (2007), 157, 222–7, 231
  *Buffalo Bill and the Indians, or Sitting Bull's History Lesson* (1976), 15, 116, 123–5, 132
  *Casino Royale* (1967), 30
  *Chaplin* (1992), 4, 16, 204–6
  *Cop-Out* (1967) see *Stranger in the House*
  *A Countess from Hong Kong* (1967) see Chaplin, Charlie
  *Cría cuervos* (1976), 59, 83, 84, 89–96, 110, 128, 221, 230, 239n
  *Crime on a Summer Morning* (1965), 23–5, 30, 32, 61, 157
  *Doctor Zhivago* (1965), 4, 9, 10, 16, 18–21, 23, 25, 30, 31, 36–42, 43, 44, 47, 48, 61, 62, 63, 67, 117, 119, 201, 217
  *Elisa, vida mía* (1977), 59, 96–104, 110, 130
  *En la ciudad sin límites* (2002), 221
  *The Forbidden Room* (2015), 232–9
  *The Four Musketeers* (1974), 212
  *The House of Mirth* (PBS telefilm, 1981), 117–18, 150–5

*I Killed Rasputin* (1967), 30, 157
*I Want to Go Home* (1989), 156–7, 196
*In Memoriam* (1977), 60, 221
*La madriguera* (a.k.a. *Honeycomb*, 1969), 59, 73, 83–9, 96, 171
*La vie est un roman* (1983), 156, 196–201
*Le Voyage en douce* (1980), 157, 169–73
*Les uns et les autres* (aka *Bolero*, 1981), 157
*Limelight* (1952), see Chaplin, Charlie
*Los ojos vendados* (a.k.a. *Blindfolded Eyes*, 1978), 59, 66, 96, 104–10, 217
*Mais où donc Ornicar* (1979), 157, 166–9
*Mamá cumple 100 años* (a.k.a. *Mama Turns 100*, 1979), 59, 66, 109–13, 221, 234
*Mariage à la mode* (1973), 157
*The Moderns* (1988), 116, 125, 126, 144–50
*Nashville* (1975), 15, 115–23, 125, 132, 156
*Noroît (Une vengeance)* (1976), 133, 156, 166, 174, 177–89
*Oculto* (2005), 221
"Once and Forever" (2015), 233–5
*The Orphanage* (2007), 221
*Peppermint Frappé* (1967), 9, 59–63, 66, 68, 69–75, 76, 79, 83, 84, 89, 110, 217, 229, 230
*Remember My Name* (1978), 116, 117, 125, 126, 130, 132–44
"The Return" (2013, short film), 233
*Return of the Musketeers* (1989), 212
*Roseland* (1977), 10, 214–18

*Sand Dollars (Dólares de arena)* (2014), 15, 62, 127, 173, 227–31
*Stranger in the House* (a.k.a. *Cop-Out*, 1967), 24–5, 30–3, 35–6
*Stress-es tres-tres* (*Stress is Three, Three*, 1968), 59, 66, 68, 72–7, 83, 84, 89
*Sur un arbre perché* (*Perched on a Tree*, 1971), 157, 163–6
*Talk to Her* (*Hable con ella*) (2002), 16, 62, 217–22, 231
*The Three Musketeers* (1973), 211–14
*Une page d'amour* (1978), 157
*A Wedding* (1978), 15, 115–17, 125, 198
*Welcome to L.A.* (1976), 116, 125–32, 144
*Z.P.G. (Zero Population Growth)* (1972), 208–11

Chaplin, Hannah, 204–6
Chaplin, Josephine, 1–2
Chaplin, Michael, 1–2
Chaplin, Shane, 118
Chaplin, Sydney, 6, 239n
Cherrill, Virginia, 202, 216
Chico, Florinda, 93, 94
Chion, Michel, 73
Christie, Julie, 18–19, 36–7, 40–2, 43–4
Clowes, Edith W., 37
Cocteau, Jean, 177
Considine, John, 124
Coogan, Jackie, 27–9
Cooley, Dana, 236
Copeland, Joan, 215
Crumbaugh, Justin, 68

Darin, Bobby, 31
*The Daughters of Fire* (1854), 177
de Kooning, Willem, 70
Deardorff, Robert, 22, 23, 26
Debraine, Yves, 160

Debussy, Claude, 177
del Pozo, Ángel, 62
Deleuze, Gilles, 196
Depp, Johnny, 8
Deray, Jacques, 23, 157
Deville, Michel, 127, 232, 157, 169, 173
D'Lugo, Marvin, 67, 79–80, 88, 104
Dombasle, Arielle, 233
Downey, Robert, Jr., 8
Dumas, Alexandre, 211–12, 213
Dunaway, Faye, 43, 44
Dussollier, André, 191
Duvall, Shelley, 122

Ebert, Roger, 213
Eisenstein, Sergei, 29
Elorriaga, Xabier, 105

Faithfull, Marianne, 43, 44
Fallaci, Oriana, 118–19, 214
Felski, Rita, 158
Fiorentino, Linda, 147
Fonda, Jane, 43, 44
Franco, Francisco, 59, 60, 63–4, 66–8, 83, 86, 89–90, 92, 96, 102, 177
Frank, Gerold, 22
Funès, Louis de, 157, 158, 164
Funès, Olivier de, 164

Gaines, Charles, 150
Galiardo, Juan Luis, 74
Gallagher, Helen, 215
Garbo, Greta, 126, 128–31
Gassman, Vittorio, 198
Geeson, Judy, 43
Gibson, Henry, 116
Girard, René, 37
Godard, Jean-Luc, 24, 59, 89
Goddard, Paulette, 65, 216

Goldblum, Jeff, 132
Goldman, Jonathan, 44–6
Gómez, Fernando Fernán, 79, 81, 108
Gómez, José Luis, 104, 108
Gottlin, Bradford, 150
Gould, Elliott, 120
Greene, Milton H., 43–58
Gunn, Moses, 132, 139

Hall, Adrian, 150
Harris, Radie, 44
Hepburn, Audrey, 19, 43, 44
Hepburn, Katharine, 44
Heston, Charlton, 212
Hitchcock, Alfred, 60
Hossein, Robert, 157
Hunter, Alberta, 133
Hussey, Olivia, 43
Hutton, Lauren, 127

Italian neorealism, 30, 34–6
Ivory, James, 214–17

Jameson, Joy, 43
Jeanette (British-Spanish pop singer), 95

Kalfon, Jean-Pierre, 190
Kamin, Dan, 136
Karina, Anna, 59
Keitel, Harvey, 127, 130
Kelly, Martine, 199
Keyssar, Helene, 121
Korber, Serge, 164
Kornhaber, Donna, 10, 14, 27, 66, 202
Kouvaros, George, 57

*La viuda de Montiel* (1979), 60
Lafont, Bernadette, 179, 182, 184
Lagerfeld, Karl, 231–5

Lang, Fritz, 177
Lapidus, Ted, 32
Lawson, Steve, 150
Lean, David, 4, 11, 18–20, 22–3, 25–6, 37, 40, 207
Lelouch, Claude, 157
Lester, Richard, 212–13
*Life Magazine*, 6
Loren, Sophia, 161
Los Canarios (rock band), 66, 73

McCormick, Pat, 124
Machado, Antonio, 59, 61–2
McKenna, Siobhan, 35
McKenzie, Edith ("Kay-Kay"), 4
Maddin, Guy, 208, 221, 231–2, 235–8
Maeterlinck, Maurice, 177
Magnani, Anna, 35
Mailer, Norman, 47
*Mandrake the Magician* (comic strip), 156–7
Marcus, Millicent, 34–5
Mardore, Michel, 157
Markham, Kika, 182, 184–6
Márquez, Gabriel García, 60
Martin, Harold H., 23
Mason, James, 24, 31, 33
Matisse, Henri, 130, 144, 148–9
Mayo, Alfredo, 59
Mestres, Isabel, 97
Middleton, Thomas, 156
Modigliani, Amedeo, 144, 148
Mojica, Yanet, 227–8, 231
Monroe, Marilyn, 46–7
*Moonfleet* (1955), 177
Morrey, Douglas, 178, 180, 181, 191
*Mrs. Lloyd* (1775–6, Joshua Reynolds painting), 153
Muñoz, Amparo, 113

Nerval, Gérard de, 177
Neupert, Richard, 160

offscreen space, 2, 18, 26–8, 35, 36, 73, 77, 87–8, 100, 108, 120, 140–1, 153, 165, 168–9, 176, 178, 180, 185, 189, 220, 224, 227–8
Olea, Pedro, 60
O'Neill, Oona, 1, 4, 5, 21, 22, 25, 98, 155, 214, 216, 223
Oscarsson, Per, 73, 84, 87–8

pantomime, 2, 5, 61, 145, 171, 173, 183
Pasternak, Boris, 18, 20, 25, 31, 37, 40
*Pelléas et Mélisande* (1893), 177
Perkins, Anthony, 132, 132, 138, 143
Piccoli, Michel, 22–5
Ponti, Carolo, 19
Power, Romina, 43
Prada, José María, 79, 111
Purviance, Edna, 216
*Pygmalion* (myth), 63–4, 101–2, 104

Quant, Mary, 32

Raines, Cristina, 122
Reed, Oliver, 208, 209
Reed, Rex, 6, 11
Resnais, Alain, 4, 16, 156, 158, 174, 196–8, 200–1, 207
*The Revenger's Tragedy* (1607), 156, 177, 181–2, 184–5, 186
Rey, Fernando, 97, 100
Reynolds, Joshua, 153
Richardson, Ralph, 18, 19, 37
Risi, Nelo, 33–6

Rivette, Jacques, 4, 16, 29, 43, 113, 133, 150, 156, 157, 158, 161, 166, 173–5, 177–91, 193, 195–6, 199, 207–8, 222
Robbe-Grillet, Alain, 190
Robinson, David, 4–5, 8
Roel, Gabriela, 104, 107
Rogers, Ginger, 113
Rohdie, Sam, 183
Rohmer, Éric, 174–5
Rosenbaum, Jonathan, 132–3, 186–7
Ross, Kristin, 165
Rossellini, Roberto, 34–5, 59
Rothman, William, 202, 204
*The Rough House* (1917), 8
Rowland, Mark, 139
Rudolph, Alan, 4, 16, 29, 30, 45, 116–17, 125–50, 158, 207–8

Salgues, Yves, 160
Sanda, Dominique, 169–70, 172–3, 230
Saura, Antonio, 70–1
Saura, Carlos, 9, 16, 29, 30, 34, 43, 45, 59–64, 66–81, 83–6, 89–90, 92–104, 106–11, 113, 116, 118, 128, 150, 157, 158, 171, 177, 178, 181, 207, 221, 230, 234
Schoonover, Karl, 34
Scrobogna, Federico, 34
*Shane* (1953), 177, 178, 181
Sharif, Omar, 9, 36, 37, 41
silent cinema, 14, 27, 67, 183, 232, 236–7
Simenon, Georges, 24, 32
Skrbis, Zlatko, 64
*Slogan* (1969), 190
Smith, Alison, 178, 180, 181, 191
Solomon, William, 29

Spacek, Sissy, 131–2
Steiger, Rod, 35
Stévenin, Jean-François, 167
Stewart, Kristen, 234–5
Straayer, Chris, 170
Stryker, Amy, 198

Tewkesbury, Joan, 118
Toles, George, 204
Tomlin, Lily, 122
Toribio, Ricardo Ariel, 228
Torrent, Ana, 89–95, 100–2, 239n
Torres, Ángeles, 113
Tyler, Parker, 22

Van Effenterre, Bertrand, 157, 166
vaudeville, 1, 2, 205
Vázquez, José Luis López, 59
Ventura, Michael, 132, 139
Verlaine, Paul, 177, 190
*Vertigo* (1958), 60

Walken, Christopher, 9–10, 215, 217
Wallis, Hal, 43, 44
Warshow, Robert, 1, 22
Watling, Leonor, 218
Welch, Raquel, 213
Wexman, Virginia Wright, 120
Wharton, Edith, 117, 150–5
Wiles, Mary, 177, 190
Willis, Jack, 150
Woodard, Alfre, 132
Woodward, Ian, 64
*Wuthering Heights* (1847), 187

Zavattini, Cesare, 30
Ziarek, Krzystof, 96

EU representative:
Easy Access System Europe
Mustamäe tee 50, 10621 Tallinn, Estonia
Gpsr.requests@easproject.com